South Africa's Insurgent Citizens

More praise for *South Africa's Insurgent Citizens*

'A fascinating account of protest based on an unshrinking belief in the importance of an organised, strong, powerful, and vibrant civil society, particularly of poor people. Its controversial thesis is that the early abandonment of protest and settling with the state can retard the strengthening of civil society.'

Justice Zak Yacoob, former judge of the
Constitutional Court of South Africa

'A timely and important book. Julian Brown's persuasive analysis highlights the contradictions and dilemmas confronting the "insurgent citizens" who refuse to accept the current status quo, and who continue their struggle for a more radical vision of the new South Africa.'

Alexander Beresford, University of Leeds

'Whereas conventional readings of South African politics worry about a crisis of post-Apartheid democracy, Brown offers a provocative argument that makes a welcome contribution to how we understand political agency among poor communities in South Africa today.'

Thiven Reddy, University of Cape Town

About the author

Julian Brown is lecturer in political studies at the University of the Witwatersrand. He was educated at the University of Natal and Oxford University. He is a member of the Wits History Workshop, and lives in Johannesburg with his husband.

South Africa's Insurgent Citizens

ON DISSENT AND THE POSSIBILITY OF POLITICS

Julian Brown

Zed Books

LONDON

South Africa's Insurgent Citizens: On Dissent and the Possibility of Politics was
first published in 2015 by Zed Books Ltd, The Foundry,
17 Oval Way, London SE11 5RR, UK

www.zedbooks.co.uk

Typeset in Joanna MT Std
by Swales & Willis Ltd, Exeter, Devon, UK
Index: Kerry Taylor
Cover designed by www.rogue-four.co.uk.
Printed and bound in Great Britain by
CPI Group (UK) Ltd, Croydon, CR0 4YY

A catalogue record for this book is available from the British Library

ISBN 978-1-78360-298-8 hb
ISBN 978-1-78360-297-1 pb
ISBN 978-1-78360-299-5 pdf
ISBN 978-1-78360-300-8 epub
ISBN 978-1-78360-301-5 mobi

MIX
Paper from
responsible sources
FSC www.fsc.org FSC® C013604

For Stuart

Contents

Acknowledgements

The majority of this book was written in Johannesburg between January and September 2014, with some additions made at the end of the year.

The roots of these ideas lie much further back, however, in discussions with friends in Durban in the early 2000s. Any project that has gestated for so long accrues more debts than I can hope to acknowledge in this brief note, but it would be wrong for me not to remember the dinners, drinks, and impassioned midnight debates with Vashna Jagarnath, Richard Pithouse, Raj Patel, Mandisa Mbali, Kerry Chance, and other friends. I was younger then, and many of my ideas have changed over the years – but the friendships forged then have remained, and so too has the influence of our arguments.

In the five years between 2004 and 2009, I studied at Oxford. In those years, I was removed from the heat of local politics, and chose to follow events from a distance. Once again, a host of friends and colleagues helped me think about South Africa's history and contemporary politics – and while many of them will undoubtedly disagree with the arguments I've made in this book, those arguments are stronger for their support, encouragement, and challenges. In particular, among the South Africans and Africanists, I must thank my supervisor, William Beinart. This book is not based upon my thesis, but its arguments were first incubated under his gaze, and with his questions in mind. I am also grateful to the cohort of students who shared these years with me, in particular, among the South Africanists, Marcelle Dawson, Kelly Rosenthal, Tim Gibbs, Simonne Horwitz, and Genevieve Klein. The support, friendship, encouragement, and entertainment I received – and still receive – from Daniel Russell and Dalia Majumder-Russell, Miriam Prys, Naysan Rafati, Graham Harvey, and Elena Schak, among many others, still gladdens my life.

I returned to South Africa at the start of 2009, and joined the University of the Witwatersrand in Johannesburg later that year. Since I have arrived here, Phil Bonner and Noor Nieftagodien have provided me support, encouragement, and critical engagement; Arianna Lissoni, Shireen Ally, Franziska Rueedi, Tshepo Moloi, Zahn Gowar, and the many students at the National Research Foundation Chair in Local Histories and Present Realities at the University of the Witwatersrand have offered me friendship and companionship. In the past two years, I have joined the Department of Political Studies. Shireen Hassim, Joel Quirk, and Gillian Renshaw have been friends and colleagues, and made the adjustment from one discipline to another exciting. Further down the corridor, Prinisha Badassy and Stacey Sommerdyk have offered coffee, gossip, ideas, and encouragement – and have made Wits a home for me.

At the same time, I have benefitted enormously from a continuing engagement with the staff of the Socio-Economic Rights Institute (SERI). My husband is the executive director of the organisation, and his colleagues are our friends and peers. I am not an activist, and am only rarely on the ground among the communities I've written about in this book. I am extremely grateful for the critical engagement I've received from all those associated with SERI, in particular Jackie Dugard, Kate Tissington, Michael Clark, and Naadira Munshi. I have also benefited from conversations with members of the Centre for Applied Legal Studies (CALS) at the University of the Witwatersrand, especially Bonita Meyersfeld and Kathleen Hardy. As part of this engagement, I have participated in a number of workshops organised by the Bertha Justice Network. At these workshops I have met young activists and legal practitioners from across the world, and have learned from them about the apparently universal ambiguities and difficulties that accompany pro-poor mobilisation globally. These young men and women have become a central part of the audience I envisaged when I was writing this book – a group of committed activists with some knowledge about South Africa, great commitment to social justice, and many doubts about contemporary practices of human rights advocacy. It should go without saying that my ideas are not theirs, and that my politics are my own: their engagement should not be construed as agreement.

I am also grateful to those activists who have shared their thoughts with me, and allowed me to share my ideas – however wrong-headed they might have been at the time. These conversations were all informal, and took place in the back seats of cars and over meals over many years. In particular, Sb'u Zikode and Bandile Mdalose – for all their current disagreements, they have both been complementary presences in my life and my mind throughout the writing of this book, and I am grateful for the examples they give of lives dedicated to struggle.

My parents and my sister have been at my side throughout every stage of this process, from long before these ideas and these arguments were part of my everyday life. I would not have written anything without them.

But more than anything else, it is the support, encouragement, challenge, provocations, and love I receive from my husband, Stuart Wilson, that has made this book possible. This book has been planned out in walks around the city's parks, argued over drinks and dinner, with friends and alone. I've not always carried the day – and every argument I make here has been sharpened and refined in response to his sometimes sceptical and always engaged counter-arguments. That's the intellectual part of a marriage. Writing can be a lonely occupation. I would not have survived writing this book without Stuart's excitement for the work, his forbearance for my occasional moods of dejection, and his ability to share every breakthrough, and every moment of excitement and joy with me. Every day, he makes me believe that a society of equals is in fact possible.

INTRODUCTION

There is one story that everybody knows about South Africa: the story of how the violent struggle against apartheid gave way to concessions, discussions, and negotiations at the end of the twentieth century, and of how the leadership of Nelson Mandela and others brought about the 'miracle' of a peaceful post-colonial transition. It is a story of how a civil war was averted, and of how a social consensus was built around a political project – the making of a 'New South Africa'.

It is an unsurprisingly popular story. It has been told and retold in one medium after another. It can be found in textbooks and at least some scholarly books; in the memoirs and autobiographies of South Africa's leaders; and in the movies – in biopics of politicians, or famous sportsmen.[1]

It is also a dated story.

Apartheid ended in 1994: its political institutions were dismantled, and politics changed. And yet, two decades later, South Africa is once again in flux – caught in a moment in which the boundaries of politics and society are unstable, and liable to change without notice. Once again, popular protest has emerged across the country as citizens assert their ability to act outside the confines of the formal political order of elections, representation, and 'service delivery'. In the heart of this moment, South Africans have begun to tell new stories. Few of these stories carry the optimism of the immediate post-apartheid era. And in the past decade, a fierce debate has taken place both inside and outside the country over the present state of South African politics, and its society.

What are these stories?

On the one hand, many South Africans tell stories of complacency and decline: of a new government squandering its promise, of economic policies benefitting a few at the expense of the majority of the population, and of new social tensions – stories of a citizenry disconnecting from political engagement and sliding into apathy. Corrupt officials feature heavily in these stories, as well as the nepotistic allocation of state resources. Where malice cannot be proven, incompetence assumes its place – budgets are left unspent, policies undeveloped, and crisis management has replaced all other efforts at planning.[2] These are the stories told in the hangover that follows the celebration: stories of the restoration of political banality after the dazzling flash of a miracle.

And yet, on the other hand, these stories are fiercely contested. Other commentators defend the actions of the government, and tell a story of the significant strides made towards redressing the political, social, and economic inequities inherited from the apartheid period. There is a lot of evidence to support this: formal citizenship has been extended to all adults, regardless of race. Houses have been built. Water and electricity provision has been extended to hundreds of thousands of households, and millions of people. Five elections have been held – and in each, the majority of the adult population has voted, and Mandela's party has won comfortably. Our government is legitimate, and continues to seek to improve the lives of all South Africans.

Of course, both stories are true, and neither excludes the other: it is possible for a government to be legitimate, and yet uninspiring; to strive towards reducing inequality, but not achieve it.

However, the intensity of the dispute between proponents of these two perspectives – and the volume of their debates – has obscured the fact that, as stories, they face the same shortcoming: they focus on the powerful, and locate politics and political activity in the state and its institutions. When ordinary men and women appear, they are cast either as a chorus, as a crowd carping on the sidelines, or as claimants on the state, as recipients of its largesse. The majority of South African citizens appear as a poorly distinguished mass – and only rarely as actors with real power.

And so yet other commentators – including academics and activists – have tried to tell another story about contemporary South Africa, a story that places citizens at its centre. This is a story about a rising tide of protest in the country, and about how practices of disruptive politics are being driven by South Africa's insurgent and activist citizens. It is a story about how citizens have become frustrated by the limits of the state's actions, and have sought to engage with it in ways that are innovative, challenging, sometimes violent, and only rarely recognised as legitimate by elites. This story does not see apathy in citizens, but anger. It does not presume their impotence, but insists upon their potential power. And, in it the state is cast in an ambivalent role, at once interlocutor and villain – empowered both to respond to public demands, and to silence them.[3]

In this book, I start by aligning myself with those who tell this last story – a story of protest and insurgent citizenship, of disruptive politics and intermittent repression. In the first chapters, I show how South African citizens are asserting their political agency and insisting upon a radical equality within the social order. I argue that these assertions and insistences disrupt and disturb the ordinary workings of established order, drawing attention to habitual practices, and opening up possibilities for new kinds of politics to emerge. These politics might be 'progressive' or they might be 'revanchist' or they might be – and most likely are – some ambiguous mix of the two. Regardless, in the process of struggle over the terrain of political possibility, new ideas, new identities, and unpredictable forms of politics are currently emerging in sites across South Africa.

But it is not enough to assert that these new forms of politics have emerged: it is necessary to show them in action. In the book's later chapters, I turn to examining the ways in which South Africa's newly insurgent citizens enact politics: through protest, through compromises and alliances with non-governmental organisations, with parts of the local state, and with the formal political arena, and through using courts and the legal system to challenge the unspoken logics of contemporary governance. By doing this, I am seeking to show how these new expressions of politics alter the existing order, and are themselves inevitably altered in turn.

The effect of this is to challenge the categories we use to describe contemporary politics. In the final pages of this book, I suggest that we need to adopt a new mode of thinking, a new perspective on politics – one that recognises the real ambiguity and impurity of our political acts. By adopting such a mode of thinking, we can unsettle the assumptions that underpin the contemporary order and begin to work our way towards a new, different kind of political action. This is an open-ended process, and unlikely to bring any sense of security through the institution of stability. It is unlikely to end, as political possibilities will continue to mutate: but it is also an exciting process, and it is one in which politics can be made new again and again, in the present.

It is this vision that I suggest is the future of emancipatory, egalitarian politics in South Africa.

The argument of this book

I am making this argument against the backdrop of what I see as a standard account of politics in the social sciences, focussed on the creation and maintenance of orders of rule and governance in society. This account emphasises the necessity of structures to shape and discipline political energies, and the need to work within the boundaries of the possible to effect material change.[4]

There is, however, an alternative account of politics – one that I adopt in this book, and that places the disruption of order and structures at the heart of politics. Our contemporary world is one in which democratic societies struggle between constructing consensus and order, on the one hand, and on the other, allowing dissent to reshape and reinvigorate – and yet maybe distort – politics. In this account, the establishment of order marks the beginning of the end of politics – the point at which debate and dissent begin to be stifled in favour of constructing compromise and consensus.

There are many ways of locating the history of this dissenting account. The most influential modern source most probably lies in the work and provocations of Friedrich Nietzsche, as interpreted by a series of francophone writers and theorists in the mid twentieth century. These mid-century interpretations took several forms – some that veered close to political nihilism, others that emphasised the importance of contest and dissent to the maintenance and renewal of existing democratic orders. After the disruptions of the 1960s – and, in particular, the student protests of 1968 – these ideas entered into the work of a generation of Marxist scholars and activists, themselves disenchanted with the apparent mechanical predictability of dialectical materialism. Many of these scholars have been aligned with the idea of a 'post-Marxist' politics, including – perhaps most importantly – the work of Ernesto Laclau and Chantal Mouffe on the importance of challenging social and political hegemony through contentious political action.[5]

Some of the scholars of this generation are harder to categorise, however – including the writer whose work has most influenced my arguments in this book, Jacques Rancière. Rancière's work doesn't quite fit with that of the post-Marxists, although it bears some similarities to it. Beginning with his dissatisfaction with Althusserian Marxism, and its implicit disdain for popular political impulses, Rancière argues that politics begin when an established order is disrupted by a claim premised on a strong conception of equality. Politics occur when a group that has not been recognised as belonging to the social order acts as if it nonetheless has a place, acting as if it were equal to those already empowered, challenging the naturalness of the order, and exposing its contingency. In a brief analogy with classic Greek democracies, this may seem as though a barbarian – a being that makes sounds that are not recognised as words, noise without meaning – insisted on being recognised as a citizen of the polis, as someone who had both the ability and right to speak politically. In this moment, the possibilities for action expand, and become uncertain.[6]

This, at least, is how I understand and interpret Rancière's ideas.[7] In the first chapter I develop these themes further. For now, though, it is sufficient to understand that his ideas offer me a model of politics that is premised on the disruption of established order on the basis of a claim to an already-existing (if not previously recognised) equality. This model gives us a set of tools which might help us understand what is happening in South Africa's disruptive politics of protest today.

In this book, I argue that politics occur in sites and moments of disruption. The most obvious of these sites are the sites of public protests: of street gatherings, marches, pickets, and performances. But protests are not the only sites in which politics can occur. Claims to equality – claims that disrupt the ordinary operations of social and political norms – can occur in a diversity of sites, including those on the fringes of formal politics and even, sometimes, those provided by a courtroom. None of those sites provides a perfect context, and each brings with it a set of ambiguities and constraints that may continue to shape the aftermath of a moment of disruption.

These disruptions are made by ordinary men and women, asserting themselves as equal citizens. This assertion of agency brings politics into being whenever a group of people acts out of character, refusing the expectations placed upon them. The most powerful version of this occurs when a group of people constitute themselves as a class of equal agents, and act as such. In South Africa today, that class is made up of the poor – who have often been treated as the subjects of the state's authority, and only rarely recognised as political agents. Even today, political actions taken by poor communities are treated with suspicion, and assumed to be the result of elite manipulation. The political content of their actions goes unrecognised, and their protests are seen as no more than claims on the state's resources. But these assumptions can no longer go unquestioned. By acting, and by asserting that they are capable of political action, South Africa's citizens expose the ordinary operations of a disempowering order – and may begin to change it.

In an ideal world – a world that operates purely according to theory – perhaps it would be enough to assert that disruptive action leads to the recognition of agency, and that this model is sufficient to describe the operation of politics. But the relationship between insurgent citizens and the state, in South Africa, is necessarily more complicated. The ways in which the state responds to these assertions of equality shape the ways in which these moments of politics may develop. When the state embraces an insurgent community, their politics may be assimilated into the public order. When the state seeks to direct these energies into alternative channels, the resulting politics develop unevenly and unpredictably, evolving in response to shifting contextual pressures. And when the state seeks to suppress these protests – too often, through police brutality – the tensions between the official political order and the disruptive politics of insurgency can explode violently.

Accordingly, I argue that contemporary South African politics are being driven by the practices of equality embarked upon by insurgent citizens. The most significant of these acts – those that most disturb the ordinary operations of the existing order – are those made by communities of the poor, asserting their agency as political actors. These actions expand the possibilities of politics. The disruption they create is met by the representatives of the existing order – notably, the state and its police forces – with responses ranging from engagement to repression. These responses, even those which amount to a form of engagement, threaten to contract political possibilities. This interplay between popular disruption and official response shapes the terrain of political opportunity in South Africa, and expands and contracts its possibilities. And it is this dynamic tension between political expression and repression that is the focus of this book.

The structure of this book

In the six chapters that follow, I explore this tension through a series of interconnected chapters. Each chapter contributes to the creation of a whole by focussing on one key set of ideas and examples. Taken together, they provide a kaleidoscopic view of the terrain of political opportunity.

In Chapter One, I consider the rising tide of protest in contemporary South Africa through the lens of politics as disruption. I explore the relationship between ideas of disruption linked to protest, as related to the work of Frances Fox Piven and Richard Cloward on poor people's movements, and the work of Jacques Rancière. I then use the events of the strike, followed by the mass killing of miners by the police, at the Marikana platinum mine in 2012 as a tool to examine the development of the tension between expression and repression in practice.

In Chapter Two, I look at how other scholars have characterised the political order that is being disrupted through claims to equality. This is an order that is internally fractured, riven by fractious struggles between elites. But it is also an order that is fiercely protective of its structures – and that acts rapidly to contain challenges from outside, including implicit and unexpressed challenges by groups of poor citizens. These acts of containment include both attempts to assimilate potential challenges into the existing institutions of the state, and attempts to forcibly suppress them.

Chapter Three returns to this theme, considering the attempts to assimilate challenges. It opens by telling the story of a protest by the Makause Community Development Forum, a small community organisation on the outskirts of Johannesburg. The attempts of this organisation to express itself politically were frustrated by the state, in part because it was not making use of local participatory institutions. I argue that this experience illustrates the development of two models of citizenship in contemporary South Africa – one respectable, and founded on the willingness of citizens to participate, and the other disreputable, uncontainable, and insurgent.

This bifurcated idea of citizenship justifies the often violent suppression of unlicensed public protests. In Chapter Four, I examine the policing of disruptive politics through a close examination of the Regulation of Gatherings Act – the key piece of legislation that has been deployed to justify the suppression of protest, and forcible dispersion of large crowds. This Act was intended to provide a framework within which citizens could be empowered to express themselves in public, but has been turned into a tool of repression. Looking at a series of protests and public gatherings in Thembelihle, an informal settlement in Gauteng, over the past decade, and in Durban during 2013, this chapter shows how the police have deployed extra-legal powers to criminalise political expression.

Chapter Five considers the ambiguous compromises that citizens, communities, and movements are forced into, in the face of this repression. When treated as criminals, insurgent citizens are often forced to rely on non-governmental organisations to provide legal representation; this reliance may bring with it a set of potential expectations and constraints. So too might attempts to engage with the state, through its participatory mechanisms, act to constrain political expression. One potential strategy, adopted by some community groups, has been to engage in parliamentary and electoral politics; but this strategy also necessitates political compromises, while risking the co-option of the original movements into larger, less grounded structures.

In Chapter Six, I look at several attempts by communities to use the constraining structures of South Africa's courtrooms to make political claims, and to contest the structures of the existing order. These take at least two forms: first, by using the courts to prosecute claims in the public interests, insurgent communities can insist on their equal ability to contest the state's reasoning on its own terms. A second, and perhaps rarer, form occurs when communities insist on forcing the state to account for its action on the community's own terms – when, in other words, they insist that their forms of knowledge and understanding are equal in status to those of state officials.

Together, these chapters flesh out the bare armature of my argument with details, illustrations, complexities, and occasional caveats. They present an interpretation of contemporary South African politics that emphasises the agency of ordinary citizens, and their ability to disrupt the everyday operations of power and authority. The results of these disruptions, though, are unpredictable, particularly when considered in light of attempts to assimilate or suppress them. In the final pages of this book, I consider how we might begin to imagine a political future in the light of this argument. I suggest that we adopt a prosaic form of heterotopian thinking to guide us in judging amongst different political possibilities, each emerging from different acts of disruption.

But before we can judge, we need to understand the possibilities of politics in the present.

ONE

Country of Protest

On the sixteenth of August 2012, armed units of the South African police confronted several hundred striking mineworkers on a hill near a mine in Marikana, about forty kilometres outside Rustenberg, the nearest city. That afternoon, the police opened fire and killed thirty-four of the mineworkers.

At first, South Africa's political elite – politicians, administrators, academics, and commentators – struggled to know how to talk about the massacre. In the days immediately afterwards, facts were hard to come by and few outside of the circle of those affected quite knew what had happened. South Africa's President, Jacob Zuma, and the national Commissioner of Police, Riah Phiyega, appeared on television to minimise the effect of the 'tragic event': they told the country and the world that the event was regrettable, that no one should point any fingers or apportion any blame, but that – nonetheless – the police had merely been defending themselves from a mob.

For a few weeks, their version of events seemed plausible. Newspapers reported on the statement, and avoided investigating its substance. Newsreaders followed suit. And around these silences, an official story continued to develop: the strikers had sought to bypass official channels and to negotiate outside collective bargaining structures. They had held the mine to ransom. They were probably encouraged to do so by a rogue union, or by agitators, or by political troublemakers. On the day itself the strikers had charged down from their hilltop – violent and confrontational, armed and aggressive – and the police were forced to act in self-defence.

This was the official story.

In the last week of August, academics, activists, and journalists sought to draw public attention to gaps in the official story, and to evidence that seemed to contradict it.[1] Greg Marinovich was the most prominent and most effective of the journalists; in a series of pieces, he revealed that there were two different sites in which the police had killed mineworkers.[2] The first had been seen in television footage, but the second had not. This second site – a smaller outcrop, several hundred metres away from the main hill – was so crowded by rocks, and so lacking in clear sight lines, that the police's story could not be true. The workers who had been killed there could not have been charging the police, and the police could not have killed them in self-defence: the only plausible story was that the workers had been hiding among the rocks. The police followed them in, in the hour after the first shootings, and chose to kill them – intentionally, in cold blood.

These articles ignited public interest in the shootings – and inaugurated a wave of investigations and re-interpretations. Once scrutinised, the official story fell apart. Over the course of two years, a Commission of Inquiry provided the site for a detailed examination of these early allegations – and, although not without its own controversies, clearly disproved these first reactions. The miners had not been exceptionally violent on the sixteenth, and the police did not act in self-defence. In place of the first story, a new one developed, as it became clear that the miners had been protesting on their own account, without any encouragement of support from any union, political party, or agitator; that the gathering on the hill had been orderly; and that the miners had begun to descend calmly, peacefully, and without violence. As they came down, the police – for whatever reason, following whatever instruction, and ignoring the miners' apparent peacefulness – opened fire on them. Many of the miners were shot in their backs, killed as they turned to run. Others were injured, crippled, and then shot again where they fell. Others made it to the second site, were pursued by the police, and there shot and killed. This was a brutal massacre – and not merely a 'tragic event'.

A country of protest

Nor was Marikana an isolated event – although the violence at Marikana was exceptional, it is also an example of the increasingly frequent clashes between police and protesters in South Africa. The country's political sphere is fractious, fractured, and combative. Protest is a common occurrence in our politics, with some scholars describing the country as 'the protest capital of the world.'[3] Some basic statistics seem to confirm the scale of this activity: in the year of the massacre, the public-order policing branches of the South African Police Services (SAPS) claimed to have 'managed to stabilise 12,399 public incidents, an average of 34 incidents a day'. About 15% of these incidents – 1,882 – were said to be 'violent'.[4]

In the same year – 2012 – two different private surveying organisations used press reporting to identify the scale of highly contentious urban protests. One, Municipal IQ, suggested that the 2012 calendar year was marked by 173 'major service delivery' protests; the other, the Multi-Level Government Initiative (MLGI), based at the University of the Western Cape, suggested that the first eight months of the year had seen between 225 and 250 such protests taking place. Both organisations suggested that these figures represented significant increases on previous years: Municipal IQ had only recorded eighty-two protests in 2011, and, similarly, the MLGI suggested that their figures for 2012 represented 'more than twice as many protests as 2011, and more protests than 2010 and 2011 combined.'[5] These suggest that large-scale public protests were increasing well before Marikana.

This seems to be confirmed by the surveys conducted by Afrobarometer, a research unit based in Cape Town. These surveys of public opinion in South Africa and several other African countries have been conducted since 1999, and the five phases of this survey to date represent the richest source of comparative data on political identification and action on the continent.[6] In each phase of the survey, about 2,400 South Africans have been asked to respond to a range of questions, including questions about their willingness to participate in protests. The survey asks whether, if given the chance, respondents would 'attend a protest demonstration or march' – and, if their response is positive, have they done so 'during the past year'? If so, how many times?[7] Over the past decade, the responses to these questions have fluctuated within a loose band. The single largest figure, in all rounds, is that which represents people who are reluctant to participate in demonstrations – that is, the respondents who say they would (currently) be unwilling to attend a protest. In the first round, conducted in 2000, about 45% of respondents suggested that they wouldn't participate; a similar figure (44%) was recorded in 2006. In the other rounds, that figure rose to 54% (2002), 53% (2008) and, most recently, 58% (2011). Approximately half of the surveyed sample would either resist, or could not imagine themselves participating in protests.

Which implies, strongly, that the other half of the sample could imagine themselves participating in a protest demonstration or march, or, indeed, had already done so in the past year. In the most recent round – conducted a year before Marikana – approximately 42% could imagine protesting.[8]

This is despite the belief that these protests – according not only to the police, but also to these private organisations – are becoming increasingly violent. According to the MLGI, nearly 80% of the major service delivery protests that had taken place in 2012 had 'turned violent'; this was a 27% increase on the average from the previous five years. The events at Marikana had a regional impact – increasing the number of protests noticed in the North West province, and increasing reports of their violence. But this was only an intensification of an existing trend: over the past five years, violent protests had increased exponentially.

It is important to recognise that 'violence' is broadly defined in these surveys. The MLGI's definition is typical: these are protests in which 'some or all of the participants have engaged in actions that create a clear and imminent threat of, or actually result in, harm to persons or damage to property. This includes instances where police disperse protestors with tear gas, rubber bullets or water cannons, rocks are thrown at passing motorists, or tyres are burned to blockade roads'. The actual and possible actions of protestors are thus taken into account, as are the actions of the police. All of these are – once again – lumped together, obscuring the distinction between stones thrown at cars by a handful of protestors and the use of deadly ammunition by police officers. These distinctions – between different kinds of public activities, protests, and marches, as well as between the potential violence of protestors and that of the police – are obviously important. They are also missing from almost all of the statistical data we have on protest politics in South Africa. So too are any detailed accounts of the motives for protest: 'service delivery protest' is a catch-all term, invented to describe a wide range of possible political motivations.

And yet the idea of increasing violence has also been used by the analysts at Afrobarometer to explain an oddity in levels of potential participation recorded in their 2011 survey. The largest decline in their figures was, in fact, for actual participation in protest in the past year: while willingness to imagine participating in protest increased from 25% of the sample in 2008 to 29% in 2011, the size of the group actually protesting in the past year declined from 19% of the sample in 2008 to only 11% in 2011. Afrobarometer's briefing paper explained this by reference to the 'violent and destructive nature of many protests along with increasingly aggressive police and security responses. It is reasonable to assume that many South Africans feared becoming victims of violence at demonstrations and consequently chose not to attend protests in 2011'.[9] Of course, this does not explain the increase in people imagining themselves participating in one of these violent protests over the same time period. Something is clearly missing from these analyses.

Protest and political expression

Recently, Jane Duncan has embarked upon an attempt to capture a more fine-grained statistical portrait of public political activity in

South Africa – and even this has its flaws, being based on formal notifications for public gatherings filed with the police in line with the official Regulation of Gatherings Act. These statistics demonstrate the existence of a wide spread of political actors, including official parties, church groups, trade unions, community groups, and student movements; as well as of political causes – in addition to complaints about 'service delivery', protestors were complaining about crime and the ineptitude of the justice system, about political and bureaucratic corruption, and about education and access to land.[10] This survey suggests a picture of contemporary South African public politics, albeit one painted in broad strokes: protests are a frequent occurrence, organised by many different groups in society and in a given community. Most public gatherings take place without incident, but a significant minority involve violence – whether against property or persons. And an uncertain proportion of these so-called 'violent' incidents involve the use of deadly force by armed police officers against protestors.

If these impressions are right, then South Africa is a country of protest – and its people are protestors. They present a snapshot of a dynamic in the country's politics: of a relationship between political expression and repression that is not resolved – and is, possibly, unresolvable.

How should we understand this? And what does it mean to say that protest pervades our politics? In the course of attempts to disaggregate the thousands of 'public incidents' reported by the police, Jane Duncan defines protests as part of a particular sub-set of public gatherings: they are 'gatherings that are directed towards state institutions or other power holders, and that seek to influence or contest decisions made by them'.[11] Duncan's definition locates protest firmly within discourses of a politics of public engagement: disputes with policies adopted and decisions taken by the state, and its allies. In this, protest is formal politics conducted by informal means.

This definition is well suited to the sources that Duncan's study covers: notifications of public gatherings filed with the police by organisers in advance of their planned gathering. These notifications are required

by the Regulation of Gatherings Act – a piece of legislation drafted in
the transition period to reduce the possibility of violence erupting in
the course of large-scale protests. The Act is often interpreted – arguably
erroneously – as requiring activists to apply for permission before holding a gathering; and that the police are able to permit or prohibit their
gatherings.[12] This means that these notifications are more likely to be
filed by activists embracing a traditional notion of politics as directed at
engaging with the state and its policies; and they are also more likely to
be filed by groups who accept the state as legitimate. It thus places protest
firmly within the framework of political society, and situates it as a form
of political expression.

Duncan's positioning of protest as part of a broader repertoire of political expression is important, because it directly addresses widespread
concerns about South Africans' practices of political participation, often
raised by representatives of the state. These have often been framed as
critiques of South Africans' apparent inability to act legitimately: according to Robert Mattes, the African National Congress – South Africa's
ruling party since 1994 – has defined legitimate political expression as
something which would 'ultimately manifest itself negatively', that is,
'in citizens refraining from emigration, insurrection, protest, boycotts,
or stay-aways, and positively, through regular political participation, tax
payment, and law abidance.'[13] Participation, in this perspective, means
participation in state-directed channels of consultation and debate; disruptive protest – in any form – is excluded from participatory (and thus
legitimate) politics. A similar set of ideas can be found in a body of literature that links protest to the failure of either 'participatory democracy'
or 'developmental local government'. For example, Doreen Atkinson's
otherwise complex and nuanced account of the problems of local governance assumes an unsustained connection between the failures of
public figures to respond to participatory forms of engagement and
the increasing occurrence of public protests: protests are what happens
when engagement fails.[14] Taking this a step further, recent statements
by the Gauteng provincial government suggest that protesting citizens
are either wilfully irresponsible or, more relevantly, ignorant of alternative methods: the solution to protest proposed in these statements is for

citizens to petition the state and participate in its institutions.[15] In these approaches, formal political expression is differentiated from protest action, and preferred to it.

By locating protests firmly within a far broader discourse of political expression, Duncan implicitly challenges this distinction between protest and legitimate political expression. In this, her approach chimes with the work of a number of other scholars. Faranak Miraftab, for example, has argued that grassroots political organisations seek to use both formal (what she calls, following Andrea Cornwall, 'invited') spaces of participation and informal ('invented') spaces to pursue their political claims.[16] The purpose of her terms is to defamiliarise the ordinary distinction between a 'legitimate civil society' and an 'outcast civil society' – and thus between groups whose political expression is accepted and groups whose expression is criminalised. Miraftab suggests that scholars and professional politicians should recognise that the movements of poor people in South Africa often shift from one mode to the other, depending on which is more likely to serve their immediate interests. Recognising the malleability of actual political practice on the ground reveals something of the complexity of people's agency, the range of political practices open to them, and the breadth of their concerns.

If fully adopted, Miraftab's approach would displace insurrectionary and public protest from both its vilified position in state discourse and, simultaneously, its privileged position in the radical imagination: not only would protest no longer be an outcast activity, only embarked upon by those who reject the legitimacy of the political and who thus refuse to participate in it, but it would also no longer be the site of authentic political expression, untainted by compromise. Instead, protest becomes part of a broader repertoire of political expression – one among many different forms of politics that may be made use of by a wide range of groups at any given time. This idea seems implicit in Duncan's work – and indeed in comparative discussions of protest.[17]

To an extent, these ideas have been adopted by South African scholars, with Miraftab's work in particular being widely cited. This adoption reflects the apparent reality of political action: the Afrobarometer suggests that South Africans who participate in protest are far more likely to engage with formal politics. One figure stands out: 56% of those who protested also contacted a government department to raise an issue, while only 11% of those who indicated that they didn't protest had done so.[18] This suggests that the most politically active South Africans are likely to be those who use protest as part of a broad repertoire of political expression and public action.

But the adoption of this broader definition, within which protest is only one tool among many, poses a question: why should we privilege protest, or suggest that its prevalence is significant?

One answer is provided by the work of Frances Fox Piven and Richard Cloward, who suggest that the significance of protest lies in its disruptive potential – a disruption that is perhaps not necessarily alien to more participatory forms of politics, but that is nonetheless far more likely to be expressed outside these official spaces. They suggest that disruption is a strategy that 'rests on withdrawing cooperation in social relations'. Given this, 'the activation of disruptive power ordinarily requires that people break rules'. Classically, such disruptive political rule breaking 'takes the form of the mob, of the physical threat of the defiant crowd'.[19] Disruptive rule breaking, they go on to argue, forces the institutions of power to reconsider their approaches to the dissenting and disruptive communities – most commonly in contemporary orders, the poor.

In Piven and Cloward's approach, protests are part of a broader repertoire of political expression – as they are for Miraftab and for Duncan, in South Africa – but protests can be differentiated from other forms of political expression because they are always contentious and conflictual. As Piven suggests: 'conflict is at the very heartbeat of . . . [protest] movements.' And thus, unlike participation in official institutions, for example, 'the urgency, solidarity, and militancy that conflict generates lends movements distinctive capacities as political communicators. At least for a brief time, marches and rallies, strikes and shutdowns, can break the monopoly on political discourse otherwise held by politicians and the mass media'.[20] This is protest's significance: it is the form of political activity that is most likely to open up new possibilities for action on the part of the state.

If Piven and Cloward's suggestions can be developed in this way, then protest can indeed be distinguished from other forms of political expression – and, importantly, the choice to protest rather than participate is not simply instrumental: it poses a broad challenge to the distribution of authority and material goods within an unequal political society. Given this, the prevalence of protest in contemporary South Africa suggests the significance of this historical moment: if post-apartheid South Africa is a country of conflict and protest, then it is also a country of possibilities.

A disruption of the sensible

But what kind of possibilities? The disruptive potential of protest is not at the centre of most definitions of protest as political expression – as a gathering directed against the state and contesting its policies and particular decisions. Nor is it central to the discourse that emerges around Miraftab's work, which emphasises the potential instrumentalism of protest. The limits of this approach – which identifies protest with disputes within the political system – are exposed by the difficulty of applying it to many of the more prominent protests of our time. The strike at Marikana is undeniably one of these – and although this approach could be stretched to include the gathering of striking mineworkers, it would have to be stretched to near breaking point to do so. At different moments, the miners articulated their protest in different ways: on the one hand, it was a clear protest against the unsatisfactory results of a wage negotiation and – in classic terms – a demand for a fair wage.[21] At other moments, however, a different discourse emerged: the protest took place because the official structures of union representation were no longer working. The majority union was concerned with national politics, and not with issues in the mine shafts themselves; the minority union was powerless, and joining it would resolve nothing. In this discourse, the miners did not contest the decisions made by their unions, or seek to influence them; instead, they rejected the political system of labour representation and sought to bypass it entirely – to use their gathering as an act of protest intended to open new political possibilities, whether these be new and direct channels to the management of the mining company, or perhaps new forms of organisation based around shaft committees and a direct form of decision making.[22]

If the first demands made by the strikers fit neatly into a definition of protest aimed at the decisions made by the powerful, their second set of complaints implies a more far radical vision of political action and protest – one that does not fit Duncan's pragmatic definition. It may also even exceed the description of disruption given by Piven and Cloward's account of protest. Instead, in this vision, politics is about challenging the legitimacy of the political order: of challenging not simply the right of a particular organisation to represent their interests, or the particular distribution of institutional power and authority within the system, but the principle of delegated representation itself. In the week leading up to the massacre, the miners at Marikana insisted on their ability to speak for themselves – using their words, their grammar, and not anyone else's.

In this, their actions resemble the definition of political activity given by Jacques Rancière – a definition that goes beyond concepts of 'protest' to incorporate a wider vision of political acts. Rancière's approach is central to the arguments made throughout this book – and so it is important to take a few pages, here, to understand how he has conceptualised disruptive politics.

Rancière's account of 'politics' divides the concept into two: on the one hand, there are the visible and invisible institutions of power and authority that structure the social order, and, on the other, there are acts that disrupt that structure. The first, he terms 'the police' – drawing upon the expansive connotations of the term in French, as famously described by Michel Foucault. Sometimes, he also calls this 'the distribution of the sensible' – that is, the ways in which all political actors, roles, and scenes are imagined and parcelled out within a social order. Only an act that disrupts this order can be called 'politics': 'political activity is always a mode of expression that undoes the perceptible divisions of the police order by implementing a basically heterogeneous assumption . . . [which is] the equality of any speaking being with any other speaking being.'[23]

A definition of protest that emphasises its engagement with existing structures of the political order is a definition that diminishes the disruptive possibilities of protests – that positions them within the distribution of the sensible; that asserts that they have a proper place – a proper form, and a proper time – within the existing order of politics. This is a definition that assumes not only the legitimacy of that order, but also the potential completeness of its account of political actors. This is as true for Piven and Cloward's radical ideas as it is for accounts of politics as participation.

For Rancière, the police order is an order in which all potential interests and groups are said to have been accounted for. In an order founded on an idea of democracy, for example, it may be asserted that all potential citizens have been identified; that they are seen by the state; and that they are all empowered to participate in the democratic processes of election, representation, and decision making. But any such account is likely to be incomplete: there are likely to be interests unaccounted for, identities unrecognised, and groups of actors entirely uncounted. There are also likely to be groups that do not accept their assigned roles, and who chose to act inappropriately – literally acting 'out of order'. In the classic example of Greek democracy, the count of citizens excluded women, slaves, and foreigners; in nineteenth-century democracies, the proletariat were expected to accept a passive role in politics and allow reformers to represent them and improve their lot.[24] Claims that disrupt this distribution of actors and roles – whether these be Antigone's insistence on her right to mourn excessively, or workers' insistence on their ability to speak for themselves – expose the contingency underpinning this count, this distribution of the sensible.

These disruptive claims are founded on a presumption of equality – that is, on the belief that all speaking beings are already equal and that, therefore, any division of roles and responsibilities between different groups in society is contingent, not necessary. Rancière describes this claim to equality as a claim to mutual understanding: as 'the power to make oneself understood through another's verification . . . only an equal understands an equal'.[25] Any speaking being is equally capable of understanding any other: of recognising any other speaking being as such, and of being recognised in turn. These moments of mutual recognition are rare, and often fleeting. But in these moments, the equality of all actors reveals the inability of the police order to account for all potential interests, all potential groups, and all potential political claims or political demands.

At the same time, the disruption of the sensible can give rise to what Rancière calls 'subjectification' – 'a dis-identification, removal of the naturalness of a place, the opening up of a subject space where anyone can be counted since it is the space where those of no account are counted, where a connection is made between having a part and having no part'. In this disordered moment, actors can become aware of the 'multiple fracture lines' that undermine the official order. This changes the possibilities of politics: instead of the creation of a new order, founded on a new consensus, subjectification asserts 'a multiplicity of speech events – that is, one-off experiences of conflict over speech and voice, over the distribution of the sensible'.[26]

The essential elements of Rancière's theory of politics are therefore the existence of a police order in which all actors are believed to be accounted for; a fundamental miscount in that order – a group, or an interest, or a set of people unaccounted for; and a assertion by those who have been miscounted, or misplaced, of their own equality – and thus of their own actual political agency. Their acts must make visible the miscount at the heart of that order, revealing its contingency.

This is a stringent standard, and on Rancière's own account genuine political acts are rare events. They are also unpredictable: 'nothing is political in itself. But anything may become political if it gives rise to a meeting of these two logics' – of a police logic and an egalitarian logic. This means that: 'the same thing – an election, a strike, a demonstration – can give rise to politics or not give rise to politics. A strike is not political when it calls for reforms rather than a better deal or when it attacks the relationships of authority rather than the inadequacy of wages. It is political when it reconfigures the relationships that determine the workplace in relation to the community.'[27]

From a Rancièrean perspective, the strike at Marikana was political only insofar as the actions of the workers were founded on a presumption of equality that disrupted the ordinary relationships of authority and responsibility that structured their working environment. Neither claims for a better wage nor claims for better representation would rise to this standard; both are demands for a better distribution of resources and fall within the existing – and unchallenged – broader order. But if the miners were indeed insisting on their ability to speak for themselves without expert representation, and to reimagine their relationships with each other and with their employers as relationships between intellectual equals, then – perhaps – their acts were political. They exposed the contingency at the heart of distribution of authority and responsibility in the mining sector – the artifice shaping the hierarchy of mineworkers, unions, and management.

As Peter Hallward has pointed out, in a critique of Rancière's approach, these ideas can seem to converge with those proposed by Piven and Cloward – but then, almost immediately, they diverge again.[28] Like Piven and Cloward, Rancière recognises the role of power in maintaining an ordered political society, and like them focusses on the disruptive potential of political acts and the opening up of new political possibilities that this disruption creates. However, where Piven and Cloward focus on the processes that constitute a movement, Rancière focusses on individual acts of protest; Piven and Cloward focus on the ways in which groups and organisations form around dissenting and disruptive politics, while Rancière's approach is suspicious of institutionalisation.

And, of course, Piven and Cloward measure the success of poor people's movements through the impact they have on the material lives of their constituents: on the ways in which protest forces states and power holders to revise or develop their policies and create a more inclusive society. Rancière, on the other hand, does not do this: his approach to politics locates the success of a claim to equality in the fact and the moment of its occurrence. The consequences and effects of this claim on power holders and state policy is – if not entirely immaterial – secondary; politics works by making the contingency of

an order visible, not by repairing or improving it. Disruption is a good
in itself, and not because of any particular effects that it might provoke.

Political repression and the restoration of order

This may be a difficult position to hold in South Africa's contemporary
political order, however. After all, the most obvious and immediate
effect provoked by the disruption of the police order at Marikana was
a violent assault on the gathered protestors. Despite the efforts of the
country's President, and the highest officials of the police, to ascribe
the massacre to an unexpected confrontation between threatening
protestors and threatened police officers, it has become clear that it
was part of a broad strategy to suppress the disruptive effects of the
protest. How can an approach that locates politics in an unrepeatable
moment of disruption respond to this?

The apparent idealism of Rancière's conception of political activity
has given rise to the two principal criticisms laid against his theory:
first, that it under-emphasises the processes through which the police
order is maintained and defended, and second, that it ignores the processes by which moments of politics – in his stringent terms – either
transform the police order or are folded back into it.[29] In essence, the
fundamental complaint is that Rancière's focus on the aesthetic and
imaginative dimensions of political disruption may blind him to the
practical realities of power.

I want to suggest, however, that thinking about repression in the
terms of Rancière's overall political approach – founded on the disruptive potential of a claim to already-existing equality – can reveal
complexities that are otherwise hidden in accounts that emphasise
clashes of power. In particular, it can reveal how the processes through
which the police order is maintained are connected to those which follow moments of political expression. In this light, the suppression of
the disruptive politics at Marikana took at least three forms, of which
only one was the violent dispersal of the gathering. The second was a
denial of the independence of the strikers, linked to an assertion that
their actions were taking place at the behest of a rival union. And the

third was the incorporation of the dissenting workers into the union sector after the strike's end.

The violence of the sixteenth of August was undoubtedly the product of a desire to end the protest before the disruption affected either the mining sector beyond Marikana or the country's economic reputation. For days, communications flowed between executive board members at the affected mining company – Lonmin plc – and the state; most notably, between Cyril Ramaphosa – then a member of the Lonmin board of directors, and now South Africa's Deputy President – and the then-Minister of Mineral and Energy Affairs, Susan Shabangu.[30] Many commentators have noted the cosiness of the exchange: the brevity and informality of the emails, and the ability of the correspondents to speak to each other casually, without spelling out the details of their concerns and requests.[31] Other messages – printed and adduced before the Farlam Commission of Inquiry into Marikana – were passed between ministries, preparing the police to expand their containment exercise. There are indications in these messages that the police were instructed to bring the protest to an end on the sixteenth – and that the means by which they were to do so were to be left up to the discretion of the police. But the protest would have to be ended soon.[32]

Although some have found evidence of conspiracy in these exchanges, there is no need to assume that any individual or institution was planning a massacre to still draw the conclusion that the suppression of this protest – by any means necessary – was in the interests of the state and mining capital. Nor does one need to presume conspiracy to recognise the interconnection of state and capital in the structures of post-apartheid politics and society: the relationship between them is unquestionably a central axis in contemporary political orders – whether in South Africa, or almost anywhere else. It is enough to recognise the existence of this relationship to understand the necessity of protecting mining capital from disruption, and the state from the knock-on effects of this disruption. In these circumstances, an expeditious end to the protest was desirable. For the state, the risks of acting with excessive violence were outweighed by the risk of not acting at all.

On its own, the use of the coercive apparatus of the state at Marikana was clearly part of a classic attempt to preserve the integrity of the existing political and economic order, and to contain an unpredictable disturbance, and can be immediately understood in this light.[33] However, a focus on the workers' claim to an existing equality – and their concomitant rejection of the principle of indirect representation embodied in the union movement – draws our attention away from the state's act of violence, and highlights that this coercive action took place against the background of a public attempt to reposition the gathering in the hierarchical framework of union activism.

In the course of the seven days of the strike, this took the form of repeated attempts to locate the miners' actions within the context of an inter-union rivalry. Their rejection of the official majority union – the National Union of Mineworkers (NUM) – was described as an embrace of the rival minority union, the Association of Mineworkers and Construction Union (AMCU). Some commentators assumed that the striking workers were, in fact, AMCU members; others, that AMCU and its leadership was manipulating the striking workers from behind a metaphorical stage curtain. This is certainly how the NUM perceived the strike – and how some scholars have chosen to interpret it.[34] Although existing disputes undoubtedly contributed to creating the context of these workers' rejection of the union movements, it is a significant stretch to insist that their protest is reducible to the choice of one union over the other. The accounts of the protest that have emerged in the Farlam Commission make it clear that this was not the case: the gathering included members of both unions, and of neither; they had organised themselves around shaft committees, and not around shop stewards or union structures; their complaints transcended sectional union loyalties.

This is despite the fact that the presumption that the workers must have belonged to the dissenting union was replicated in the terms of reference developed for the Commission: these terms identified the major players in the events, and mandated the Commission to investigate their roles. These players were (in the order listed in the terms) the mining company, the police services, AMCU, the NUM, relevant government departments, and any 'individuals or loose groupings' who might have been involved in 'fermenting or otherwise promoting a situation of conflict and confrontation'. The Commission was directed to examine the relationship between the two unions: whether AMCU or the NUM 'had exercised its best endeavours to resolve any dispute/s which may have arisen' between them, and between them and the mining company.[35] The assumption that the strike was the result of an inter-union rivalry that distorted ordinary bargaining procedures was thus built into the structure of the Commission, and its discourse.

If this was true – and the strike managed by AMCU or some other recognised organisation – then the disruptive potential of the protest would be lessened: instead of a rejection of the principle of representation, and a claim to equal intelligence and understanding, the strike would represent nothing more than an intensified version of an ordinary labour dispute. It could be resolved by the mine's management sitting down with the new union's leaders, and negotiating a new settlement, thus ensuring that the implicit hierarchies of labour were preserved, and political order restored. This would preserve the social order, prevent violence, and be in the overall 'public interest'.[36]

The plausibility of this presumption was enhanced by the attempts of both unions to establish relationships with the striking workers. On the morning of the fifteenth of August – the day before the massacre – representatives of the NUM and AMCU confronted each other on a radio talk show, and dared each other to address the workers. That afternoon and the next morning, AMCU's leader – Joseph Mathunjwa – made several attempts to intercede with the striking workers, and to convince them to leave their gathering and allow his union to negotiate on their behalf. The image of him on his knees, speaking through a megaphone to a crowd of silent workers, was broadcast across the country; and – in the days afterwards – cemented the impression that there was a firm link between AMCU and the striking workers gathered on the hill.

In the aftermath of the massacre, this imagined link became an actual one. As over 200 of the striking miners were arrested by the police, and charged with murder of their colleagues, and as the state seemed likely to white-wash the massacre, the miners searched for political allies. In this context, the sympathy shown by Mathunjwa carried the day – and most of the striking workers aligned themselves with AMCU, making use of the union's legal and media contacts to defend themselves. The proclamation of the Farlam Commission placed AMCU centrally in the narrative; and it was through AMCU that most of the miners, as well as the widows and family members of those who died on the sixteenth, obtained legal representation at the Commission. All of this served to bind the union to the emergent community of mineworkers.

In the months following the massacre, AMCU's membership swelled at the expense of the NUM. As its numbers grew, AMCU abandoned its earlier resistance to the principle of majority representation – that is, to the principle that the company only negotiate with the majority union and exclude smaller unions from the bargaining table. Shortly before the first anniversary of the killing, AMCU was acknowledged as the majority union at Lonmin's mines – representing approximately 60% of the workforce, to the NUM's 20%.[37] This acknowledgement was a major victory for the union – and also represented a restoration of normality to the mining sector. Although AMCU may be more aggressive in its negotiating strategies than the NUM, its position as the sole official representative of the mine's workers restores labour relations to a bargaining framework – in which disputes must be resolved around a table, or through recourse to court.

Indeed, in an irony that is sometimes difficult to appreciate, Lonmin and other platinum companies have since found themselves in the position of seeking to bypass the ordered structure of negotiation, while AMCU asserts its necessity. In the course of a lengthy strike in the first half of 2014, these companies sent text messages to the cell-phones of striking workers, spelling out their wage offers seemingly in the hope of weakening AMCU's bargaining position. In response, the union sought an urgent interdict against companies, preventing them from communicating with its members.[38] It is hard to imagine a neater illustration of the restoration of a police order than this: a new union emerging from the disruption of the formal order now insisting on its sanctity.

The dynamic of expression and repression

In this book, I want to develop the insights offered by this approach to the interpretation of protest and disruptive politics in the context of post-apartheid South Africa's contemporary order.

This approach does have its limits. By directing our attention towards the 'one-off experiences of conflict' it can lead us to understate the importance of the development of social movements and organisations, and may even suggest that these can – under certain circumstances – operate as agent of the existing order, smothering the emancipatory potential of disruptive and dissenting energies. It can make us suspicious of claims to represent the poor or any other social grouping, and can lead us to embrace a broad scepticism towards the politics of civil society representation. Most importantly, it seems to deny the possibility of a radical resolution: it locates emancipation in moments of conflict, and identifies the creation of consensus with the maintenance of order.

But a Rancièrean approach can help us understand and interpret the fundamental claim to equality that is at the base of dissenting and disruptive politics in this country: it moves us away from strict ideological interpretations and away from circular debates about the authenticity and legitimacy of a particular spokesperson, group, organisation, or event. It focusses our attention on emancipatory acts of political expression, and alerts us to the unpredictability of these acts – the unbounded range of sites within which they can occur, and the elastic effects that they can have, both on the consciousnesses of the individuals involved and on public awareness of the contingency and malleability of the distribution of the sensible. It can also help us to identify points of tension between political expression and its suppression – a process that goes beyond coercive repression, and includes the ways in which disruptive energies are defused, and the political possibilities they create may be folded back into the ordinary working of the police order.

As a consequence, this approach directs us towards a study not simply of emancipatory moments or coercive responses but of the ever-developing dynamic between them – the dynamic between 'politics' and 'the police' or between political expression and political repression. This dynamic can develop in many different sites: one of the key insights of Rancière's approach is that there is no exclusive site of politics – neither parliament, nor protest – and that, therefore, any site can provide the context within which a political act can be made and responded to. In South Africa, these sites include public protests and the street; direct engagements with the police, in their stations and in holding cells; between citizens and non-governmental and civil society organisations, as well as organised social movements; and even in the country's higher courts.

These sites provide examples of both assertions of equality on the part of individuals, groups, and communities and – sometimes simultaneously – attempts to reassert the governing logic of the existing political order. None of these assertions, though, needs take the same form in each site. Indeed, the forms taken by assertions of equality are likely to mutate, in response to the particular ways in which inequality and hierarchies are asserted not only across a given distribution of the sensible, but also more locally in a given site of power and authority. Likewise, the ways in which that hierarchy is re-established – or, perhaps, repaired – are also likely to mutate, in response.

This is in part why Rancière himself emphasises that his approach is one linked to possibility, rather than assertion: he suggests that 'it might be' is the central phrase in his work, consistent with his claim to provide a method rather than a theory. He suggests that his 'books are always forms of intervention in specific contexts' and 'never intended to produce a theory of politics, aesthetics, literature, cinema or anything else'. These interventions are polemical and directed towards addressing at least two questions: 'how can we characterise the situation in which we live, think and act today?' and 'how does the perception of this situation oblige us to reconsider the framework we use to "see" things and map situations, to move within this framework or get away from it?' – or, as he reformulates it, 'how does it urge us to change our very way of determining the coordinates of the "here and now"?'[39] His work is a series of responses to the provocations of his time, and his political and aesthetic experiences; it is a series that is united, however, both by its continuing questioning of the normalised arrangement of perception and social position and, simultaneously, by its repeated assertion of the equality of each speaking being to each other.

In the chapters that follow, I use these ideas to shape a free-flowing investigation of the dynamic of political expression and repression – of the dynamic interaction of the logics of emancipation and policing – in key sites in South Africa. I hope that this study will shed light on both the ways in which we can characterise the South African situation, and ways in which it might be changed. For if South Africa is a country of protest, then it is also a country in which its citizens are repeatedly and regularly asserting their own equality, and thus the equality of all – even if these assertions are often short-lived, sometimes compromised, and regularly suppressed. Regardless, they destabilise the existing order – and give rise to new political possibilities, and thus new forms of public action.

TWO

Politics after Apartheid

Disruption does not occur in a vacuum. In South Africa, the contemporary political order has been shaped by the country's history of colonialism, segregation, and apartheid. The long struggle against these racist regimes provides the legitimating myth of the contemporary state: our fathers and our mothers fought to eliminate the racial injustices at the heart of our society, and – in doing so – they laid the foundation for a renewed post-segregation and post-apartheid order. It is this order that is disrupted by protest and other claims to politics; it is an order that is believed to be legitimate, and yet it is repeatedly being contested, disputed, and challenged – and, perhaps, expanded – through these disruptions.

In this chapter, I outline the principal themes that recur in attempts to understand the political order that has emerged after apartheid – and the places assigned to the agency of South African citizens within it. This is the order that is threatened by protest, and by political acts; it is the order that is defended against those acts of disruption – sometimes peacefully, sometimes violently.

Before we can understand it, we must know the myth that founds it.

This myth sometimes traces the roots of this struggle back to the colonial era, but most commonly locates them in the emergence of new political movements in the early twentieth century. The most significant of these, the South African Natives National Congress – which would soon rename itself the African National Congress (ANC) – was formed in 1912; in the same decade new unions emerged to organise black workers, and the Communist Party of South Africa insisted on remaining open to a multi-racial membership. These movements became yet more important in the second half of the 1940s, as the National Party emerged as the leading voice of Afrikaner nationalism and racially stratified 'separate development' – or *apartheid*. The differences between the Congress, unions, and the Communist Party were all subsumed into a shared opposition to apartheid; the alliance between them gave rise to the Defiance Campaign, the Congress of the People, and the Freedom Charter – two events and a document that provide a roadmap for a future South African nation and nationalism based on a shared vision and a shared struggle.

The struggle for the new nation was neither uninterrupted nor unchallenged. The Sharpeville Massacre – at which over sixty people were killed, many, if not most, of whom were shot in the back by the police as they fled – shocked the country and the world, and galvanised the forces of reaction. In 1960, membership in the ANC and its allied organisations was made illegal; its leaders were arrested *en masse*; a state of emergency was declared and the government's discretionary powers extended. With a year, the movements were scattered and their leaders imprisoned, or in exile. In the decades that followed, the ANC sought to reconstruct a broad opposition on the basis of the alliance and the Freedom Charter. Meanwhile, inside the country, a new generation of activists was coming of age – a generation with no direct experience of the organised opposition. In 1976, young students rose up in protest against the imposition of Afrikaans-medium teaching in their schools; the state and its police forces once again resorted to violence, killing dozens of youths in Soweto in June – and scores more in the months afterward. The Soweto uprising inspired a range of protests across the country, and sparked a resistance that would not die down: for the next decade, South Africa's townships became battlegrounds for a war between state and people.

In the 1980s, the ANC sought to coordinate these protests and direct this revolution – and, to a surprising extent, succeeded. Many of the new movements that emerged in the course of this disruption were identified – by the state, by the media, and by many of their members – as proxy organisations, representing the ANC within the country. The conflation of these local struggles with the broad struggle inaugurated by earlier movements helped to unify the opposition to apartheid; and, at the end of the decade, as the state began to weaken, this unity allowed the government to enter into a series of negotiations – first in secret, and then in public – with the ANC and its leaders. These negotiations represented a vital success for the movement: it had forced the state to recognise it as a legitimate player in the political arena. From this position, they were able to force the government to recognise that the apartheid order could not continue, and that a negotiated and orderly transition to a full electoral franchise was preferable to a further collapse into sectarian violence. In these negotiations, the ANC represented the country's previously unacknowledged majority and cemented its central position in the new political order.

In April 1994, South Africa held its first post-apartheid elections. This moment represented the culmination of a struggle that was not only against racism, but simultaneously for a new social and political order. The franchise was universal, participation was widespread, and the new government of national unity – led by the ANC, and incorporating all other major parties, movements, and perspectives – was recognised as the rightful inheritor of the institutions of governance, the state, the army, the police, and the bureaucracy. It was also – and perhaps more importantly – the inheritor of the tradition of political struggle against the pervasive injustices of the apartheid order. In holding these inheritances in balance, the new government was able to begin the task of forging a newly free, consensual, egalitarian, and universal political order.

This myth glosses over both the complexities of political practice, and the violence of the period. It is a myth of coordinated struggle and planned transition – and, as such, it serves to obscure the role of disruptive politics in the late apartheid years. These disruptions took many different forms. Elsewhere, I have written about the importance of student assertions of political agency in the 1970s. Clive Glaser has written about the role of youth gangs in disrupting panoptic township orders. Colin Bundy has written about the emergence of new forms of political expression and ideology through 'pavement politics' – through the everyday experiences of oppression in the 1980s. Others have emphasised the importance of violence in the shaping of contentious local politics – through challenges to the police, assaults on informers, and the movement of crowds through their familiar neighbourhoods. At the height of these protests, large areas of South Africa were rendered 'ungovernable' – which is to say, not only beyond the ability of the apartheid state to control, but also beyond the ability of the exiled liberation movements to constrain or harness.[1]

Perspectives on a fractured politics

But the myth clears the ground for the assertion of South Africa's post-apartheid return to normality: for some, this meant the establishment of regular elections and a party-political system; the extension of the bureaucratic state to cover the whole of the population; and the entrenchment of representation and institutions of governance. Social and economic policy would be adopted by consensus and the state should work for all the people.

In the months and years immediately following the transition, this myth may have seemed plausible. The institutions of the apartheid state were dismantled, and South African citizenship was extended to all those who lived in the country, regardless of race. The instrument of this was the adoption of an interim Constitution in 1993 – and then, after the election, the development of a final Constitution, adopted in 1996. This document set out the foundational principles of the post-apartheid order: in a Bill of Rights that guaranteed social, economic, civil, and political rights to all citizens and that forbade discrimination, and in a set of institutional arrangements that sought to secure these rights by remaking the relationship between the South African state and its citizens.

The result of these changes was to remake parliament: populated by a wide range of representatives – members of the old parties, active under apartheid, the liberation movements, and a few new parties – it became a more democratic institution, one that sought to reflect the country's reality.[2] This institutional shift was not only enabled by the constitutional framework, but also by the adoption of a new electoral system – one which replaced the first-past-the-post, constituency-based system used in the apartheid era with a system of proportional representation (PR). The primary reason for introducing this new system was to secure the legitimacy of the new order by ensuring that all votes counted equally, no matter where one lived. This was not the only consideration, however. Another reason for the adoption of a PR system was to ensure the representation of minority parties and minority interests in parliament: both to ensure the continuing security of the old guard, and also to guarantee that politics would remain open in the new order. In theory, too, PR systems guard against the possibility of one-party dominance – and, indeed, in most states where used, they tend to result in the formation of coalition governments. The adoption of this system was thus meant to secure the legitimacy of the post-apartheid parliament, and thus the official political arena, both by ensuring a diversity of representation at the highest level of the state and a set of constraints upon the power of any one political party.

In South Africa, however, it did not work out this way.[3] The ANC won the first post-apartheid election with a clear majority of the country's votes – and although it formed a Government of National Unity, it did not need its partners to govern. In the course of its first term in office, the ANC slowly shed most of its coalition partners. By the late 1990s, the Government of National Unity was no more. In each election since, the ANC has won significant majorities and formed the government. Twenty years after the end of apartheid, no commentator asks who will win an election – the answer is self-evident. The only questions likely to be asked are: by how much will the ANC win? Will they lose a slice of their vote? And what might this mean?

The consequences of the ANC's electoral dominance have been the subject of much discussion. It is this feature of the post-apartheid political system that has animated the dispute between those who tell stories of post-apartheid complacency and those who defend South Africa's new order.

This dispute is one of the most powerful motors of narrative production in South Africa: for critics of the party, it is the background to an argument that the successes of the ANC suggest the potential failures of democratic institutions. Unchallenged power soon becomes untrammelled power – and that power, once held, is a corrupting force. In their eyes, the dominance of the ANC in legitimate elections threatens to be a precursor to the dissolution of meaningful democracy – and, ultimately, to the creation of a one-party state. For others, also unsympathetic to the ANC, the consequences are less dire – but still disheartening. In these accounts, power leads to complacency: as the threat of electoral challenge recedes, so too does the pressure upon a government to fulfil its political promises. What follows is a slow collapse of political will, energies dissipating like air from a leaking balloon. Infrastructure decays, or is only intermittently maintained – and high-profile prestige projects drain resources from everyday maintenance. The connection between the party and the electorate erodes, and leaders become an isolated elite.[4]

In response, supporters of the current government emphasise the legitimacy of the electoral process, and the undoubted validity of the outcome: the ANC has won all post-apartheid elections because it has remained the most popular party in the country. Although the active portion of the overall electorate may have shrunk in this period, nonetheless the ANC has been able to command a steady share of the votes of those South Africans who do participate in elections.[5] Its governance is legitimate – and sufficiently successful to justify the continued re-election of the ANC's members to political office. Given this – and given the scale of the party's repeated victories – suggestions that the state is in decline are inappropriate, and unfounded. The ANC will continue to be elected to office, as long as it continues to respond to citizens' needs.

In recent years, this debate has framed public discussions around the rise of an aggressive parliamentary opposition: first in the context of the official opposition party, the Democratic Alliance (DA), and, since the most recent national elections, held in 2014, a new party, the Economic Freedom Fighters (EFF). For some commentators, the increasingly confrontational nature of formal politics signifies a healthy development, and a resurgence of democratic energies; for many representatives of the government – including, seemingly, the Speaker of Parliament – it is a sign of disrespect for the government, and disdain for democratic processes.[6]

It has also framed, to a lesser extent, many discussions of popular politics and civil society. Insurgent politics are often studied in the context of civil society organisation and mobilisation. Too often, this can mean that these politics are taken to have been effective only when they give rise to some form of organisation. These forms can include those associated with 'new social movements' or those associated with mass movements. In 2014, the efforts of the trade union NUMSA (National Union of Metalworkers, South Africa) to launch a 'United Front' of left-wing social movements, civic organisations, and other groups have taken centre stage in progressive political thinking. The aim of this front appears to be to provide a counter-hegemonic voice within formal political spaces – and, ultimately, to lay the ground for the launch of an electoral challenge.

These discussions are blinkered by their acceptance of a stratification in South African politics, with formal politics the preserve of a set of governing elites. Even then, elite politics themselves are fractured and fractious as individuals and groups fight on ideological and personal grounds for control over the state. The relationship between economic and political elites has fluctuated between cooperation and contempt. Both groups continue, however, to influence state policy.

Ordinary citizens appear as the subjects of efforts to reach out and include the majority of South Africans in participatory and decentral-ised forms of governance through the creation of new structures of engagement. However, these structures have succeeded only in repro-ducing hierarchies at local level, construing citizens as subjects to be empowered by existing elites. These efforts at empowerment through participatory institutions have also created disputes over the legitimacy of post-apartheid protest – that is, of political activity that takes place outside of these structures.

These problems emerge from a set of questions associated with the classic 'structure–agency' debate: what is the relationship between structures of authority and the exercise of agency? What kinds of institutions can best nurture individual agency in a democratic society?[7] In South Africa, though, this debate is largely unacknowledged, and rarely engaged with: few scholars explicitly set out to build their arguments on the framework of structure vs agency. This is not to say that it is irrelevant to discussions of post-apartheid politics. In practice, the apparent consensus of standard approaches to this debate – that agency occurs within social structures, and that some structures are better equipped to promote that agency – guides much political thought.

Given this, the fractured politics of post-apartheid South Africa have been analysed from at least three perspectives – one that sees the disputatious nature of party and parliamentary politics as determining the country's future, another that locates the country's position within a globalised economic order, and a third that looks at the emergence of a new civil society and perceives in it new political possibilities. These are simplifications, no doubt, but they are useful ones. They help map out a terrain of political analysis – of its clichés, as well as its insights – and situate our vision. They also each allow insights into significant aspects of the development of protest in the country.

These three perspectives all start from the image of an immediately post-apartheid consensus, itself founded on a burst of social optimism in the wake of the first election. The language of a 'Rainbow Nation' and a rainbow nationalism was in the air.[8] This was the period of the Truth and Reconciliation Commission, established in 1995 to resolve the conflicts of the past and create the conditions for 'the pursuit of national unity, the well-being of all South African citizens, and peace'.[9] This pursuit was founded on the sense – as stated in the interim Constitution – that in a renewed South Africa there was the 'need for understanding but not for vengeance, a need for reparation but not for retaliation, a need for ubuntu but not for victimization'.[10]

This heady optimism fuelled a surging nationalism, and a public discourse of political and social inclusion.[11]

And then, at some point, this optimism soured.

If you identify politics with the performance of parliamentary and executive authority, then perhaps it soured in the second half of the first ANC government. After the adoption of the final Constitution in 1996, the government of national unity splintered; political leaders of all stripes resisted the Truth and Reconciliation Commission's attempts to investigate apartheid-era violence; and both parliamentary and public discourse became more acrimonious. The government appeared to turn away from the idealism of its first years, and towards a pragmatic embrace of international *realpolitik*. The transition from the presidency of Nelson Mandela to that of his successor, Thabo Mbeki, became emblematic of the abandonment of 'rainbowism'; the election that accompanied this transition – the second in the post-apartheid era – was also marked by the abandonment of political civility.[12]

A series of elite disputes descend from this moment. Mbeki's refusal to allow anti-retroviral medication to be widely distributed by the national health services in the face of the massive crisis caused by the spread of HIV and AIDS caused a rift to open between the executive and civil society; his refusal to alter his position in the face of overwhelming opposition created a public perception of Mbeki as an embattled, paranoid, and vengeful personality.[13] Whether fair or not, this perception then influenced reports of elite in-fighting throughout the two terms of his presidency. Several high-level members of the executive resigned: some after having been investigated by the National Intelligence services, apparently at Mbeki's instruction. Mbeki also distanced himself from Jacob Zuma, his Deputy President, when Zuma was facing criminal charges of corruption, racketeering, and sexual assault. This gave rise to a bruising conflict between the two for leadership of the party – a conflict that stretched over Mbeki's second term and brought it to an early end. Zuma's victory within the party led to his election to the presidency, in 2009. This presidency – recently reaffirmed in the 2014 elections – has brought with it a settling of old scores, including the apparent expulsion of Mbeki's supporters from the executive, and their sidelining in the party. This in turn has led to a series of splits within the party, as Zuma's opponents have launched their own rival parties – the Congress of the People in 2008 and the EFF in 2013. The fracturing of the elite in this period, then, has led to the opening up of political space, and new contestation in electoral and parliamentary politics.

The attractions of this analytical approach are obvious: it is immediately comprehensible and clear, structured around big men and their personalities.[14] The narratives it produces develop as these leaders shift ideologically and intellectually, as they gather and lose supporters, and as they move up and down party lists, in and out of the executives, and in and out of favour. In its reductive variants, this approach is limited to a study of the personality clashes between Mandela, Mbeki, and Zuma; in its more nuanced versions, however, this approach can identify key power-brokers within the South African political order – sometimes civil society actors, sometimes other representatives of the state, organised labour, and so on – and trace their interactions.[15] The disputes and alliances between these representatives thus shape the formation of real politics.

The chronology of this approach – locating the instigating break in elite politics to the second half of Mandela's presidency – coincides with that adopted by proponents of the second major approach to explaining South Africa's post-apartheid politics. The bulk of this body of scholarship revolves around the transition from the ANC's initial commitment to the Reconstruction and Development Programme – an ambitious economic policy, aimed at state-directed redistribution – to its adoption of the Growth, Employment, and Redistribution (GEAR) strategy, which recommitted the state to international economic norms and development through macro-economic growth.[16] Although a handful of scholars suggest that this transition could have been anticipated,[17] the adoption of GEAR symbolised an important ideological shift in policy, as the government retreated from a rhetoric of redistribution to one of economic responsibility and global influence.

An emphasis on the relationship between the country's economic policy and global economic trends serves to emphasise the constraints within which national political elites function. The key brokers identified by the proponents of the first perspective are all beholden to the powers and dominions of contemporary capitalism: labour elites act within spaces shaped by global labour markets and trade policies; businesses can only extend their reach as far as international laws, agreements, and institutions permit. The possibilities of politics within South Africa – or any other similarly situated country – are constrained by the interactions of states, governments, international organisations, the disciplining ideologies of the World Bank, the International Monetary Fund, and major credit-rating agencies.[18] Given this perspective, a national state is best understood as a funnel through which the international order asserts itself – or is moderated.

This approach, too, has its attractions: it combines the broad economism of older left-aligned analyses of racial capitalism in apartheid South Africa with the diffuse radicalism of a contemporary, post-communist anti-capitalism. It provides a code through which political choices can be interpreted, understood, and judged. It allows for a review of South Africa's political order that does not personalise political choices, but instead highlights the ways in which fundamental economic and ideological forces structure the range of political possibility. Its internationalism also enables a politics of solidarity that overflows territorial boundaries, and links struggles in Johannesburg with struggles in London. However, this approach runs the risk of minimising local agency – and, when attempting to transfer its critique into a call for action, runs the risk of adopting a shallow form of vanguardism that seeks to cultivate an international mass movement out of a series of diverse and distinct local struggles, commitments, causes, and protests.

These approaches to explaining South Africa's post-apartheid politics are supplemented by a third, focussing on the emergence of civil society organisations and social movements. Scholars who work in this tradition tend to start their narratives in the early 2000s. Although civil society bodies clearly existed in the preceding decade, a new wave of organisations emerged in response to the United Nations-sponsored World Conference Against Racism, in 2001, and the World

Summit on Sustainable Development, a year later. These high-profile events saw protestors gathering on city streets and in public spaces to articulate their political beliefs in a moment during which the world's cameras seemed to be trained on South Africa; their ideologies differed, but they soon came to share a singular experience – that of being harassed, assaulted, and dispersed by the police.[19] The movements that participated in these protests, and those that emerged in their wake, shared an awareness of the state's coercive powers and strove to define the territory of civil society as both the site of social engagement and of political contestation.

A number of different organisations gained public prominence in these years. The Treatment Action Campaign (TAC) sought to challenge the state's blinkered approach to the provision of anti-retroviral medication to HIV-positive South Africans.[20] The Soweto Electricity Crisis Committee began to protest electricity and water cut-offs in the densely populated ex-townships of Johannesburg.[21] The Anti-Privatisation Forum emerged at about the same time, bringing together a number of localised and community-based organisations to present a broad front against the adoption of neoliberal economic and social policies by the government.[22] A number of scholars were involved in these organisations, and others wrote about them. This body of writing sought both to establish a set of precedents for these new protests, and to present an interpretative framework within which these organisations could be placed. Ashwin Desai's *We Are the Poors* was the most significant early text in this vein, describing the birth and growth of a community-based organisation in Durban.[23] His work was joined by a series of works by Patrick Bond, who – along with a community of activist scholars, many based in Durban – helped popularise the term 'new social movements' to describe these protesting organisations.[24] This literature linked South African civil society with an earlier tradition of dissenting activism in the country and, simultaneously, with a large international wave of public activism and protest.[25]

These movements are defined not so much by a shared political programme – although there are significant similarities between many of them – but rather by a shared approach to civil society activism. The new social movements combine community organising, public protests, and carefully orchestrated social activism; these activities all take place in the territory of civil society, adjacent to that of the state – or, to borrow Gramsci's term, 'political society'. Some movements experiment with legal activism; others have considered entering directly into the realm of electoral politics. Most, however, remain outside the state and seek – from this position – to reshape formal institutions by organising social groups, placing pressure on elites, and altering state priorities.

These three approaches all presume a particular set of relationships between political actors and the poor: in each, the poor is a constituency whose consent to be governed is either presumed or sought. The governing elite presume the poor's acquiescence, and seek to deploy them in support of one or another factional claim; the financial elite seek only their quiescence, bought through the provision of basic services and economic opportunities; while civil society activists seek to empower and uplift the poor, in service of their own best interests – too often, as determined for them. Only the last of these approaches acknowledges the potential agency of the poor, but even it may easily slip into an assumption of existing powerlessness and lack of interest – as it does when social movements presume the need to educate the poor in political agency.

In each of these approaches, too, there is an assumption that South Africa's poor are best served by the creation of structures of organisation – either within the state, or in civil society – that can develop, nurture, and direct the political impulses of individuals and communities into action.

These presumptions have been challenged by a handful of scholars who assert that South Africa's poor are already political agents – that they are already equal to all other citizens in understanding and capacity for action. Richard Pithouse and Nigel Gibson, for example, have both drawn extensively on the works of Frantz Fanon to argue that political consciousness is present and flourishing in the context of South Africa's poor communities, and that this consciousness could form the basis of an alternative politics – one of radical equality and emancipation in the present.[26] Both Pithouse and Gibson have focussed on the emergence of Abahlali baseMjondolo, an organisation of South Africa's shack-dwellers that emerged in Durban in the mid-2000s. This movement works to organise local communities in informal settlements and other sites of insecure tenure; they articulate claims to the agency of the poor, and argue that the governing discourses of the South African state deny them their existing agency. Importantly, Abahlali has a history of resisting civil society representation, and of insisting on its ability to speak on its own behalf.

An explosion of protest

These perspectives map out the terrain within which disruptive politics might occur. In the face of the eruption of protests, described in the last chapter, these attempts to understand and explain the post-apartheid political order are also supplemented by a new history of political protest – which takes these three perspectives into account and uses them to illuminate the development of spontaneous and uncoordinated local uprisings.[27] In this light, it might be suggested that if the fractures of elite politics have opened up spaces for public contest, and the acceptance of global economic policies provided a cause for contest, then the emergence of social movements and civil society organisations has given a shape and a form to these contests. There is some truth to this approach. But it is insufficient to describe all of these uprisings, many of which have emerged out of local tensions, unconnected to any ideology or social movement.

These uprisings are shaped by the relationships between different groups within a community, between members of that community and their local political authorities, and between the community and the local institutions of the state. The final shape – and potential political significance – of these uprisings, though, was formed by the local state's response to them. A typical example is provided by a land occupation in Bredell, a derelict plot of ground outside Johannesburg, in the middle of 2001. Here, a group reportedly associated with an opposition party, the Pan Africanist Congress, sold plots to men and women who had no other formal access to land. They believed this sale to be legal and valid; the state, however, disagreed and – perhaps concerned that this occupation would connect South Africa to the ongoing conflict over land in neighbouring Zimbabwe – decided to evict the settlers. To do so, they used the legal excuse granted by the Trespass Act (an apartheid-era law that remains on the statute books, and is still used to control access to public spaces). On this authority, the state sent in armed police forces, accompanied by dog units and armoured cars, to evict the settlers from their newly built homes and to remove them from the land.[28] If you were watching the television news that evening, you would have seen images of the police demolishing shacks and brutally mishandling men and women. The community resisted the assault: some sought to escape the police, others organised pickets, a building was hurriedly consecrated in an attempt to prevent its destruction, and – in a protest that drew the prurient interest of the media – a group of women stood in front of an group of police officers and bared their breasts, literally and symbolically exposing themselves.

At Bredell, the armoured might of the state met the naked vulnerability of South Africa's poor: government ministers dismissed the possible rights of the settlers, whether to land or to dignity, and instead explicitly preferred the interests of international capital. The settlers 'should go back where they came from', the Minister of Land Affairs said. And, if they would not, it was in the interests of the state to intervene forcefully and forcibly, because 'when the foreign investors see a decisive government acting in the way we are acting, it sends the message that the government won't tolerate such acts from whomever'.[29] The destruction of an emerging community at Bredell, as well as the nakedness of the state's avowal of an explicitly market-orientated approach, broke an unstated trust. Afterwards, it was impossible to accept the state's assurances; afterwards, it was possible to imagine it acting in any way, even with brutal disregard for the law and its citizens.

In the years that followed, the examples set at Bredell have been repeated across the country. Gillian Hart has suggested that this event inaugurated a new phase of crisis in post-apartheid politics.[30] Communities located at the periphery of South Africa's social and political order – whether living in shacks, informal settlements, or 'bad buildings' in the inner city; whether working as informal traders, or as casual labourers; or, often, both – regularly erupt into protest.[31] Many of these protests are defensive in nature: erupting in response to private or state-backed attempts to evict communities from their homes; or in response to attempts to displace them from sites of trade or remove them from their ability to secure a livelihood.[32] Those protests provide a space for the articulation of other concerns – including dissatisfactions with local councillors and other political representatives. They are the site not only of the public articulation of a dynamic of political expression and repression, but also of confrontations between protestors and police.

The state and its citizens

This suggests that a survey of the political order in South Africa – the order that is disrupted by protest – must begin to unpick the relationship between the state and its citizens. This relationship exists in both the undisturbed order, and – of course – in its disruptions. As the rest of this book will deal with the disruptions of this order, it is important to spend a few pages on understanding how the relationship is meant to work in the ordinary course of events, before protests may erupt.

The state is a large and complex beast, and ordinary citizens rarely encounter many of its institutions: both the presidency and the national parliament, for example, are largely removed from the everyday realities of most South Africans. It is only in the regular rituals of elections that we seem likely to engage with these offices of the state; in between, they are the subject of headlines and news stories, gossip, and investigations – but they are neither transparent in their workings nor ordinarily accessible. Likewise, the country's large bureaucracies seem designed to insulate aspiring technocrats from individual complaints.[33] Many bureaucrats seem to imagine the citizenry in statistical and abstract terms – as demographics to be addressed, numbers to be allocated, and problems to be resolved. This can exacerbate the alienation of citizens from certain parts of the state – particularly those that seem to be distant in both space and internal logic.[34]

It is the local state that is – in official terms – 'the sphere of government that interacts closest with communities, is responsible for the services and infrastructure so essential to our people's well being, and is tasked with ensuring growth and development of communities in a manner that enhances community participation and accountability'. The local state is thus primarily to be seen as 'a system . . . which is centrally concerned with working with local citizens and communities to find sustainable ways to meet their needs and improve the qualities of their lives'.[35] In some ways, this is the grand and empty speech of government statements – but it is none-theless a reality that most South Africans encounter the state through its local institutions. The relationships we develop with local councillors and service providers, bureaucracies and school boards, urban planning offices and the local police station all shape our experiences of the state. These are the institutions that most citizens encounter; for a large minority, this group of institutions can be expanded to include those of law – small claims courts, magistrates' courts, labour courts, the High Court, and the higher courts of appeal. All of these are sites of engagements that shape citizenship, and the relationship between citizens and the institutions that make up the state.

These local institutions, therefore, were the focus of the post-apart-heid government's attempts to reform the state. These took the form of suggesting that principles of 'participatory democracy' and 'partici-patory governance' be integrated into the workings of the local state. In the words of a government policy, these 'forums for deliberative democracy' would 'promote self-management, awareness building and ownership of local development'; they would also 'enable faster access to information from government . . . provide clarification to communities about programmes . . . [and] enhance transparency in administration'. The purpose of this approach was to encourage com-munities 'to be active and involved in managing their development, claiming their rights and exercising their responsibilities' through the 'legitimate structures of community participation'.[36]

The White Paper on Local Government, published in 1998, instructed municipalities to 'promote the involvement of citizens and community groups in the design and delivery of municipal programmes'. It did not, however, provide specific instructions on how this could be done; and so, for the next several years, participatory mechanisms were developed in an uncoordinated manner. This led to the proliferation of potential spaces of participation – bargaining councils, school governing bodies, community health committees, and community policing forums, for example – each of which was empowered in terms of different pieces of legislation and policy, and each of which was developed at the discretion of a local municipality, councillor, or community body.[37] In the mid-2000s, the state embarked on an effort to coordinate its ambitious plans for participatory governance at the local level. In 2005, the Department of Provincial and Local Government published a draft version of a proposed national policy framework for public participation in which the already-existing institutions of 'ward committees' were placed at the centre of the state's plans. These committees were intended to be independent advisory bodies, in which members of the community could discuss local matters with their elected ward councillors, who would then pass on the substance of these discussions to other representatives of municipal government.

The timing of this development seems unlikely to have been coincidental. Steven Friedman remarked, at the time, that it appeared to be a response to the growing wave of protests across South Africa's cities. Several other scholars have suggested, in the years since, that the further development of this participatory framework might address many of the complaints of protesting citizens, and might even serve to prevent protests from developing in the near future.[38]

There are a number of assumptions about the nature of the citizenry and its communities embedded in the language of this policy framework. First, that local communities in South Africa are relatively unorganised: that the state needs to promote self-management and awareness building amongst them. Second, that these communities are largely ignorant of formal political processes, and that they need to be provided with information and clarification to be active and involved in politics. Third, that these communities are effectively disempowered: that they need the institutions of local governance not merely to organise and educate themselves, but also to allow themselves to become empowered citizens. Those three assumptions suggest strongly that the purpose of installing participatory mechanisms of governance at the local level is not simply to ensure that the state receives better information about the needs and desires of its citizens and is thus better able to address them (although, no doubt, it is this too), but also that these mechanisms are meant to produce politically mature, able, and responsible democratic citizens.

And there is thus, of course, one further set of assumptions to be noted: that the power to organise, educate, and involve is vested in the state – and not in ordinary members of 'the community'. This presumption of inequality runs like a seam through the logic of empowerment, which itself animates the state's approach to the participation of citizens in governance.

South Africa's political order

These perspectives on the country's post-apartheid politics – presented in different manners, by academics, popular commentators, and representatives of the state – map out the terrain of South Africa's contemporary political order. This order is grounded in the state, but spirals outwards, into the disputes within the ruling party, between potential leaders and followers, cliques and combatants. Or, perhaps, into the crannies of the world system, where economic priorities and norms are established. Or, even, into the realm of civil society, adjacent to the state, where communities and organisations can gather themselves and resist the imposition of clumsy power.

This order may be disturbed by protests and by the political expressions of its citizens; but it has means of containing these disturbances. Unexpected disruptions – like the land occupation at Bredell, or the protests that accompanied the World Summit in 2002 – could be suppressed: coercively if necessary, but, more importantly, suppressed rapidly and visibly, before that localised disruption could impact on the delicate network of relationships that characterised the general order. Other sources of potential disruption – the demands of an unruly citizenry – could be channelled, directed into the benign disciplines of participation, deliberation, and consultation.

Although the most common approaches to understanding this order each seek to identify different contested elements in it – the fractures of the elite, the structures of the global economy, or the ambiguous autonomy of civil society – all of these circle back to the state, in its many forms. Despite the tendency of much of this writing to allow the state to sink into the background, nonetheless it is its institutions that do the work of maintaining and restoring the political order.

There is an elegance to this order, and to the systems through which it is maintained. It seems almost designed, capable of withstanding the ordinary tempests of discontent; but it is of course not designed, no more than an emergent property of the workings of the state, of power, and of the processes that Rancière calls 'the police'. And while it may be capable of withstanding occasional protests, it is also unsteady in the face of the continuing eruption of discontent.

THREE

Citizenship and Insurgency

In October 2012, a flyer was distributed in the Makause informal settlement in Germiston, calling upon residents, 'churches, employed
and the unemployed students, youth, women & children' to attend
a gathering at the nearby sports ground and – from there – to march
to the local police station to demand: 'an end to police brutality,
[the] end of forced bribery/corruption, [a] proper investigation of
un-attended cases of crimes, an end to police politics and the support
of mob groups, an arrest of the mob group that attacked Macodefo
[Makause Community Development Forum] leadership and destroyed
the community office, [and] an urgent response to crime'.[1]

One day before the march was scheduled to take place, the organisers
were called to a meeting at the Primrose Police Station – ostensibly, to
discuss security arrangements for the march.[2] This meeting took place in
terms of the Regulation of Gatherings Act (1993), following a notification
by the leaders of the Community Development Forum of their intention
to march. There, three representatives of the Community Development
Forum were met by three senior members of the police, including the
station commander, and three members of the local ward committee.

The leader of the Community Development Forum, General Moyo ('General' is his given name, and not an official title) objected to the presence of the ward committee. The committee members, in response, told the police that they worked with the local Community Policing Forum, and with the local ward councillor, and – as far as they were concerned – Moyo 'was not the leader and they don't know who he represents'. The ward councillor, they added, 'had no idea of the above mentioned march'. Their interventions, according to police statements, enraged Moyo and he once again insisted that the meeting could only continue in the absence of these men.

They were ushered out of the room, and asked to wait in the corridor outside. After they left, the meeting continued to degenerate. According to the officer responsible for running the meeting: 'I asked Mr Moyo again what was the reason for the march and his complaints. Mr Moyo refused to answer me and shouted at me and told me that he submitted his application. I asked Mr Moyo if he stayed in Makause, and who he's representing. Mr Moyo again started shouting at me and accused me of taking sides.' Tensions rose. The other two officers – both based at this particular police station, and thus both targets of the march – intervened, telling Moyo that 'these are normal questions . . . We told him to calm down and respect the meeting and officials'.[3]

The events of the following minutes are the subject of ongoing litigation and thus the account of the meeting provided should be treated with some caution. The station commander and her colleague allege that Moyo acted and spoke in such a way as to 'intimidate' them – with intimidation here understood as a criminal act defined by the Internal Security and Intimidation Amendment Act of 1991, which updated and amended several of the apartheid state's signature laws, including the Internal Security Act, the Internal Security Act, and the Intimidation Act.[4]

According to the charge sheet, Moyo acted to intimidate the station commander and her fellow senior officer in several ways. First, by saying 'that he will make sure that they are removed' and then – alternatively and cumulatively – by 'threaten[ing] to repeat what happened at Marikana, and/or [that] there will be bloodshed, and/or by pointing [his] finger(s) at Lt-Colonel Nkhwashu, and/or charging at her, and/or said Lt-Colonel

Shiburu will not last at Primrose [police station]'. This confrontation made the two Lieutenant-Colonels fear for the safety not just of 'themselves' but also of 'the Primrose Police Station and/or its officials and/or its property.'[5] In several of the affidavits, much is made of the fact that Moyo and his companions were wearing t-shirts with slogans referencing the very recent massacre of workers at Marikana blazoned on them.

The confrontation ended with Moyo and his companions leaving the police station. According to the affidavit of one of the members of the ward committee – who describes himself as the 'Chairman of Makause Informal Settlement' – the group passed him as they left, but said nothing. He did record though that once he entered the station again 'I was told that General was threatening the Station Commander, that there will be bloodshed in Primrose'. This seemed plausible to him: 'From the look of General Moyo and his group [they] want to unsettle the peace within the Community to create a situation that people will fight for nothing'. He concluded that Moyo 'is provoking the situation to create doubts in people's minds and to cause violence in our area'.[6]

The next day, Moyo was arrested.

One of the many striking features of the affidavits prepared by the police officers who attended this meeting, and which were submitted as part of the case against Moyo, is the way they refer to the members of the ward committee: they are described, unproblematically and unquestioningly, as 'the community leaders of Makause informal settlement' and 'the leaders of Makause'. They are treated as the only legitimate representatives of the community, and their legitimacy is confirmed in these affidavits by their connection to the Community Policing Forum and the ward councillor: in other words, through their connections to official institutions of participation.

At the same time, the authority of the Makause Community Development Forum was persistently undermined. The ward committee members refused to recognise them as leaders and were recorded as saying that they had no constituency – although, as a later affidavit made clear, Moyo and the Forum had been the subject of several community meetings over the past fortnight. They backed up their claim by insisting that the elected ward councillor knew nothing about the march, or the protest. The police officers asked Moyo if he lived in Makause – with the implication that he might not; they asked him to identify his constituency and justify his reasons for marching.

There are a number of reasons for believing these questions to have been intentionally provocative: the Community Development Forum had been founded in 2007, five years earlier, and had organised many high-profile protests over that period.[7] Moyo had been a leader of the Forum since its inception, and had lived in Makause for years beforehand. The purpose of the march – as the flyer and, presumably, the notice given to the police made clear – was to protest against the perceived corruption of the local police station: that is, the police station where the meeting was being held, headed by the officers questioning him. In these circumstances, the claims that these were just 'normal questions' appear to be more than a little disingenuous.

More importantly, though, the approach of the police to Moyo and the Development Forum, in this meeting, was obviously aimed at delegitimating their political challenge by questioning Moyo's ability to represent anyone. The Makause Community Development Forum was dismissed in favour of the official ward committee; and its right to organise, demonstrate, and challenge the police was similarly dismissed. It was subject to an aggressive cross-examination, designed to undermine its authority and to emphasise the police's ability to suppress its public activity.

It is clear, in this case, that the police were operating with an unspoken set of assumptions: first, that politics within certain spaces of citizenship – ward councils and community policing forums – are legitimate forms of politics and, second, that politics that arise outside of those spaces – in the alternate spaces of citizenship represented by the Development Forum – were thus illegitimate. This places the legitimacy of certain forms of political acts at the centre of post-apartheid disputes, and – with this – the legitimacy of certain kinds of political actors: in other words, citizens.

Disruptive citizenship

Citizenship is a central term in contemporary South African politics. The struggle against apartheid could be conceived of as a simultaneous struggle for citizenship, at least in the way the idea was articulated by T.H. Marshall six decades ago: 'a status bestowed on all those who are full members of the community . . . [and] equal with respect to the rights and duties with which the status is endowed'[8]. The struggle against a racist order that did not accept all South Africans as full members of a national community sought to overthrow it, and replace it with one that did.

In the small communities of the classical Greek *polis*, citizenship was not recognised by the state but, rather, by a citizen's peers. Citizenship was defined as the ability to be both ruler and ruled – to participate in the governance of oneself and one's peers – and was guaranteed by one's intrinsic ability to act. In other words, citizenship attached to agency: to the ability to act politically. This was not a universal status: most inhabitants of the Greek polis were excluded from citizenship, and the ability to act as self-governing agents. Nonetheless, those who were recognised as citizens were recognised as equals. In his account of the classical idea of citizenship, Pocock directs our attention to the central role of political agency in Aristotle's philosophy – to be able to act politically is to be able to be human. 'Citizenship is not just a means of being free; it is the way of being free itself.'[9] The classical idea of citizenship thus emphasised the absolute equality of citizens and located that equality in their inherent political agency. The equality was guaranteed by these inherent attributes, and established publicly through the mutual recognition afforded to citizens by the small community of the *polis*. In the space of the *agora*, all citizens could see and recognise each other – and, in so doing, affirm their shared identity.[10]

However, 'citizenship' can mean many different things. In the anti-apartheid struggle, and for the post-apartheid order that followed, it could simply mean formal recognition, on the part of the state and the community as a whole, of an individual's political and civil rights – the rights to vote and stand for office in regular elections.

For many political struggles throughout the past two centuries, this is – of course – what citizenship has meant: for working-class men in the nineteenth century, for suffragettes in the early twentieth, and for colonised peoples later that century. At several points in the struggle against apartheid, then, the primary meaning of citizenship was a formal claim to belong to, and act within, a national community: to be a political actor. In the last decades of the twentieth century, though, many feminists argued that this was insufficient: that the granting of formal equality did not guarantee that women and other structurally disempowered groups would be able to exercise their political rights.[11] Any account of citizenship should include a consideration of the social and economic prerequisites necessary to allow women to exercise their formal political rights; in a standard liberal democracy, these might include – but would not be limited to – the rights to health care and housing, to education, to employment, and to a fair wage.[12] This approach – sometimes called 'social citizenship' – has often aligned with human rights-based politics to produce a thick account of effective citizenship.

In South Africa, this approach gained prominence among feminist scholars and activists during the negotiated transition of the early 1990s, in the wake of the collapse of the apartheid order. Shireen Hassim has suggested that – for these activists – 'the transition facilitated a shift away from nationalism as the overarching framework within and against which women's identities were conceived . . . to a discourse of citizenship that has subsequently shaped women's movements struggles'. Within this discourse, 'new ways of thinking about women's political participation' opened up: formal participation in the institutions of the state could be linked to the exercise of political agency in alternate spaces – 'through participation in social movements outside the state that seek to articulate interests of different groups of citizens autonomously from party politics.'[13]

The start of the post-apartheid era was thus marked by an expansion of the political possibilities connected to citizenship: the end of the struggle to achieve formal recognition brought about – for many activists – the birth of a new wave of struggles, this time to give effective substance to the formal rights of citizenship. The sites of these struggles were multiform: they could take place within the formal structures of the state, or they could take place in social movements outside the state, or in grassroots and community-based organisations, or elsewhere. In these sites, women (and other groups) could express their political agency and express their demands for social citizenship and effective democracy – meaning, at least, a responsive and accountable state. The scope of these movements is clear: articulating claims for proper health care, for access to education, for housing, and for basic services such as electricity, water, and sewage removal. These claims for the social and economic prerequisites for effective citizenship are entangled with claims to political agency – to be exercised both through formal structures and outside of them. Taken together, these movements can be said to articulate a critique of universalist and formalist ideas of citizenship and to argue aggressively for a thicker and more substantive practice of citizenship.

These thicker and more substantive practices need not remain outside the state: participatory forms of governance – and the discourse of empowerment that underpins them – seek to develop expanded notions of citizenship through engagement with institutions of the state.[14] This form of citizenship has been described by Engin Isin as 'active citizenship' – that is, as a form of citizenship that attempts to enmesh notions of status into ongoing practices of empowerment and self-realisation. This creates a kind of 'habitus' of citizenship, a set of 'routines, rituals, customs, norms and habits of the everyday through which subjects become citizens' – which can be channelled through the institutions of the state, or arise in civil society, everyday life, or other sites outside the formal political sphere.[15] This normalises existing relationships: between institutions of empowerment and citizens, between groups of citizens and the state, and amongst the range of ideas, habits, and practices that constitute common-sense notions of citizenship.

Isin's account shows how both notions of citizenship founded on status – as T.H. Marshall's was – and notions of citizenship founded on practice and substantive rights-claims – as many of the notions that emerged in the post-apartheid era were – can be incorporated into what Rancière calls a 'police order'. In the modern world, this order is characterised by the identification of citizenship with the legal status granted by territorial nation-states, and the minimising of the potential political agency implied by classical ideas of citizenship. Only men and women recognised as citizens by a nation-state can claim most social and political rights; and the substance of those rights is determined by each state's particular constitutional framework. This order can be disrupted by the assertion of different kinds of claims to citizenship – what Isin then calls, in his account, 'acts of citizenship' or more generally a form of 'activist citizenship'.

Two things distinguish these disruptive acts of citizenship. The first is that they are undertaken by those who do not ordinarily have a place within the order of citizenship: these may be groups within the nation that have been excluded from a notion of political agency, such as black communities in apartheid South Africa or segregationist America, or women in pre-suffrage democracies, or they may be groups left out of contemporary notions of political status, such as unlicensed immigrants, refugees, or the stateless.[16] The claims made by these groups disrupt the habitual exercise of citizenship practices, and force the state and other citizens to recognise the potential agency of otherwise unaccounted-for groups. There is an obvious affinity between this account of the disruptive potential of citizenship claims – based on the classical notion of citizenship representing political agency – and Jacques Rancière's account of the disruptive potential of similar acts of equal agency by those who have not been counted in the political order's distribution of parts.

This is not the only such affinity. The second element in Isin's scheme is that acts of citizenship actually must be – in philosophical terms – 'acts'. That is, they must occur in a single, irreducible moment (which distinguishes their temporality from ongoing practices and habits); they must rupture the given order; and they must create a situation of answerability, in which actors are forced to recognise each other as such. Isin draws this concept from Mikhail Bakhtin's early work on 'the philosophy of the act', in which he suggested that an act serves to constitute both an actor and an audience simultaneously, the one required for the other

to recognise itself.[17] In some aspects of Bakhtin's work, the audience of
the act is the world itself – or, perhaps, the order within which an actor
comes to realise that he or she is embedded – and not necessarily a particular group within society.[18] In later work, Bakhtin developed these
insights into a theory of utterances, containing both linguistic and extra-
linguistic elements, that sought to establish relationships of signification
between speaker and listener, or text and reader.[19] These relationships –
whether defined in terms of 'act' or 'utterance' – form the basis of an
ethical engagement with the world, and with other beings. This ethics of
engagement and answerability is – in Isin's account – at the core of how
acts become political, by constituting an actor and his or her audience
in social and political terms, as a series of potential agents possessing
political will.

In this account, political acts are only one type of act. They are
political when they constitute their actors as social beings: 'through
orientations (intentions, motives, purposes), strategies (reasons,
manoeuvres, programmes) and technologies (tactics, techniques,
methods) as forms of being political, beings enact solidaristic, agonistic and alienating modes of being with each other'. In engaging
with each other in these ways, 'we enact ourselves as citizens, stran-
gers, outsiders and aliens rather than identities or differences'. Existing
practices may guide the ways in which these enactments occur, but
they do not determine them. Political acts are creative: they enable
new forms of identification to emerge. In the context provided by
practices of citizenship as the basis of political agency, they enable
new kinds of citizens to emerge. As Isin puts it: 'we contrast "activist
citizens" with "active citizens" who act out already written scripts.
While activist citizens engage in writing scripts and creating the scene,
active citizens follow scripts and participate in scenes that are already
created. While activist citizens are creative, active citizens are not.'[20]

These acts can take many forms, of which protest is only one. James
Holston, in his study of 'insurgent citizenship' in Brazil, points to the
complex array of repertoires of disruption available to urban citizens.[21]
These include actions at the boundaries of legality – unlawful occupation of housing, house building, and land usage; communal and

gang organisation, and the establishment of localised public spheres. These acts test the boundaries between a respectable notion of citizenship and often-disreputable processes of social formation and practice. They develop in response to the different arrays of power and resistance available at any given time. Holston's approach – which has had some impact on scholars of South Africa[22] – emphasises the development of citizenship in the cracks of the social order and shares Isin's concern with creativity.

The theatricality of Isin's language – a repertoire of 'scripts' and 'scenes' – is reminiscent of Rancière's aesthetic disruptions, as well of Bakhtin's later work on the idea of carnivalesque.[23] In each of these cases, the disruptive effects of acts – of citizenship, or equality, of disorder – are expressed in terms of a visible alteration in the fabric of the world. In Rancière's account, actors seem to speak to the world – there is no part of society or the political order that is abstracted from the whole, and then addressed; in Bakhtin's work, the entirety of a small community is involved, its order overthrown, and an ambiguous performance enacted by all in front of all. In Isin's account, however, the focus on the specificity of political acts – as both ethical and social acts – seems to impose a more formally theatrical structure, in which actors address an audience. This audience seems to be composed of the powerful, whose solipsism is disrupted by these acts.

If this last characterisation is correct, then there is at least a family resemblance between the political approach suggested by Isin – the disruption of relations of power, the assertion of agency, and the recognition of new social groups and actors as potential bearers of power – and the 'radical incrementalism' of Piven and Cloward. In these approaches, the disruptions of the political order serve to provoke incremental and instrumental changes that open up spaces for new developments, for the potential redistribution of goods, power, and authority, and for an increasingly just social distribution. These are achievements that are not to be dismissed lightly.

But the response of the powerful to these political acts – whether of equality, in Rancière's terms, or citizenship and political agency, in Isin's – cannot be guaranteed. The state and various elites might seek to ameliorate social conditions; they might seek to co-opt the surging energies of protesting citizens, and direct these energies to different ends; or they might choose violent means of suppressing the disruption, and suturing the wound made in the social fabric.

The experiences of the Makause Community Development Forum speak to this ambiguity: their attempts to act as citizens and political agents – by organising, planning marches, and notifying the police of their intentions – were frustrated by the resistance of the police, acting as an arm of the local state. Their credentials were challenged, and their authority to speak for their constituents denied – in this case, by reference to the existence of an official ward committee. Beyond this, though, their attempt to protest was restricted: the police refused permission for the Forum to march on the police station, thus restricting the protest to a single site in the settlement. And their spokesman – General Moyo – was arrested at this gathering, and charged with having intimidated the commander of the local police station in the course of the previous day's meeting. The effect of these actions was to stifle a protest, and pre-empt attempts to develop it.

The discourses of legitimacy and empowerment

In the context of an account of the Anti-Eviction Campaign (AEC) in Cape Town in the early 2000s, Faranak Miraftab describes political citizenship as being formed in two different – but mutually constituted – types of space: 'invited' and 'invented' spaces of citizenship. The first of these are 'created from above by local and international donors and government interventions', and political action within these spaces is legitimated by these external structures of power. The second – 'invented' – set of spaces are those 'carved out from below, demanded and seized by collective action'.[24] The actions of the AEC sought to move between these two types of space, allowing Miraftab to argue that politics in these spaces reflect different strategic choices – and are thus not mutually exclusive. Indeed, it is unlikely that either would be imaginable without the other, and – as discussed in the first chapter – many activists make use of both kinds of political space.

The state, however, has demonstrated a clear preference for political actions in 'invited' spaces – and an equally clear distaste for political actions in 'invented' spaces of citizenship. Thus, although the practice of the AEC should demonstrate that bifurcated notions of political action – that is, notions that describe one set of actions as legitimate and another as illegitimate – can be discarded, the practices adopted by the state suggest that this bifurcation remains alive and powerful. As Miraftab points out: 'in South Africa the state and the media are promoting such stratification of civil society by classifying people invidiously as "authentic" or "inauthentic" citizens'. Community action that fits into established stereotypes (such as working in a soup kitchen, in Miraftab's example, or participating in 'invited' spaces of politics) 'is sanctioned and legitimised as [the] heroic acts of the poor' while actions that do not fit into these spaces (such as resisting eviction, reconnecting services, or protesting) 'are derided . . . as acts of extremism'.

When activists articulate their political claims in invited spaces, their rights to speak and to act politically are recognised. They face little resistance, and potentially much encouragement. But when AEC activists acted outside invited spaces, through public protests and other actions they have, as Miraftab reveals, 'often suffered brutal repression by the state's police, facing rubber bullets, house arrests and prison terms. As recently as February 2005, for example, an AEC activist was shot in the leg'.[25]

The Makause Community Development Forum represents an example of an 'invented' political space, one that is outside of formal institutions; the local ward committee is, of course, an 'invited' space – in which political claims are legitimated by the state's involvement. In the context of the Forum's attempts to organise a public gathering and march to make visible a shared complaint about the nature of policing in their community, their status as 'outsiders' counted heavily against them. The police may have been reluctant to encourage a direct challenge to their own authority, even if it came from an establishment source; but it was easy for them to frustrate the efforts of the Forum and to prevent the march from happening because they had no institutional support. Without the legitimacy conferred by the state, the Forum's efforts could be treated as illegitimate.

Miraftab's account of invited and invented spaces of citizenship points us towards the processes by which the state has come – over the past two decades – to regard some forms of political action as legitimate and others as not. This is linked to the use of institutions of participatory democracy, and 'empowerment'. And it is this project that Barbara Cruikshank emphasises when she argues that 'the making of citizens is a permanent political project for democracy'. There is no one model of what democratic citizenship should look like, she suggests: 'citizens must be made . . . [and] can be remade'.[26] In other words, notions of citizenship are altered, developed, and reinvented to reflect different constellations of political power in different societies. Cruikshank suggests that a division between citizens and subjects has been fundamental to most discourses of citizenship: citizens are those who have the power to act, and subjects are those who are acted upon.[27] In the modern democratic state, however, the discourse of empowerment that drives both government and civil society projects has changed this: communities and classes of people are identified as disempowered subjects, and are then made the targets of efforts to empower them and thus convert them into active citizens. Cruikshank argues that these efforts produce a version of citizenship that belongs simultaneously to both of the standard categories: to be able to act, citizens must be acted upon. In democracies, we are simultaneously citizens and subjects.

This, she suggests, must destabilise accounts of political citizenship founded on an absolute distinction between disempowered subjects and empowered citizens. Her argument suggests that these accounts should focus on 'technologies of citizenship' – on the ways in which citizen-subjects are produced. These technologies can include pedagogic programmes, social services, and social movements.[28] This approach assumes that power is diffuse and widely distributed, rather than concentrated – and that traditional challenges to power have often failed for not recognising this.

The state remains, however, the most visible and most effective site of empowerment. Although it may often work in collaboration with civil society institutions, non-governmental organisations, and – potentially – social movements to produce a shared model of effective and empowered citizenship, it can also act on its own. It is therefore the site in which citizenship is most likely to be produced, and most likely to be exercised. Miraftab's account of invited and invented spaces acknowledges this: although citizenship can be formed and enacted in many different spaces, the state is only likely to treat political actions that take place in its invited spaces as being legitimate. This does not mean that the state is the only site in which citizenship is produced, but it does suggest that – in contemporary South Africa, at least – it is the only official site for that production. In later chapters, we will consider the ways in which civil society and the legal system may act to shape particular forms of citizenship. At this point, though, we are concerned primarily with the way that invited spaces of the state shape citizenship and – in this context – the choice of ward committees as the primary vehicle for these processes of production has had a number of implications, some of which undercut their apparently democratic and empowering intentions.

First, the structure of ward committees themselves militates against either broad or direct forms of participation. It also militates against aggressive political expression by the community and its members. The committees themselves are constituted as localised structures of representation, in which the community elects individuals to constitute the committee itself. The processes of this election are unusual: the ward councillor decides when to convene a constituency meeting at which an election of up to ten representatives can take place; this election is then administered by the municipal speaker's office.[29] So far, so ordinary. The councillor is, however, empowered to place certain restrictions on the election – principally, to promote the involvement of under-represented groups in the committee. A standard requirement is that part of each committee should be constituted by women – although this is often ineffective in practice.[30] Other possibilities include prioritising the election of representatives of the youth – often overlooked in practice[31] – or prioritising the election of people involved in specific sectors, such as health care. The capacity to decide how to structure 'sectoral representation' within any given ward is delegated to the councillor and the municipal speaker's office. The effect of these powers should be to shape the representation of the community on the committee so as to ensure that neither the loudest voices nor the most historically privileged parts of the community dominate the committee. They should allow the state to shape the voices of the community – to prevent 'narrow interest groups' from 'being allowed to "capture" the development process.'[32]

These are significant powers – and even if they are only used as they are intended to be, and not actively abused, they still indicate an uneven balance of authority intrinsic to the system. This is underlined by one further requirement: the final national policy framework does not prescribe a set of term limits for ward committee members but, instead, prescribes that 'the term of office for ward committee members and ward councillors are the same'.[33] Although this is not entirely clearly phrased, it suggests that the terms of committee members and ward councillors are directly linked – and that the election of a new councillor should trigger the election of a new ward committee. This may mean that each ward committee is reshaped by each incoming councillor; new councillors may make use of the powers invested in their office to alter the 'sectoral' makeup of a ward committee, and potentially remove established representatives.

Conversely, it may also mean that a particular set of ward committee members can become closely associated with a particular ward councillor. They can become – in fact or in appearance – the clients of a particular councillor: elected and re-elected into office alongside their councillor, and only removed once that councillor retires, resigns, or is voted out of office. (And – given the ambiguous wording of the policy framework – perhaps even spared the ordeal of re-election until the ward councillor finally leaves office.) In these circumstances, the structures of participation – of participatory democracy and governance – are tied to the interests of the state's representatives.[34]

The effect of these processes, therefore, is to restrict effective citizenship to a small number of elected community representatives; to restrict eligibility for this election, so as to shape the representativity of the participants; and then to link the elected committee to the political career of the ward councillor – a professionalised political actor. These processes indicate the foundational role of the state in structuring, developing, and legitimating this space for participation, and the ways in which 'citizenship' can easily be constrained in this space.

These processes produce a stringently limited version of citizenship: one that operates in a cascading pattern of representation, with each elected body engaging with another elected body. In each case, responsibility for effective action shifts upwards – from the masses of the people to their local representatives, to their councillors, to the municipality, to the provincial state, and onwards. The political potential of the vast majority of citizens is reduced to a short list of legitimate actions: electing municipal and parliamentary representatives, and electing community representatives to the committees that advise these representatives; participating in discussions with the committee, or local forums, to develop a shared approach to that advisory function; and petitioning those representatives to address any supervening issues of great personal urgency.

Any other approach – protest, political organisation, or insurgency – is then excluded from those practices of citizenship. Those men and women who act in these manners are viewed with suspicion, and their actions are treated as illegitimate and as dangerous to the social order.

Xenophobia and other illiberal politics

Of course, we should be careful not to romanticise politics outside the participatory framework. Even if we reject the notion that some forms of political expression are legitimate and others not, it is undoubtedly true that some political acts may be dangerous – may corrode the social order.

When justifying the disciplinary forms imposed on political expression by the state and its institutions, their proponents have been able to suggest that they are at least in part intended to restrain dangerous forms of politics, and thus to serve to maintain a social order within which all citizens are able to speak openly. Outside of these structures, they imply, inclusive forms of citizenship may break down, and be replaced by exclusionary, xenophobic, or sexist politics. However, we should be similarly careful not to assume that this argument is necessarily true: indeed, these forms of illiberal politics have emerged within the structures as well as outside of them.

There are certainly vivid examples of this in South Africa. The most notorious outbreak of illiberal politics must be the wave of violence aimed at foreign nationals that shook the country in May 2008. In the month, a series of scattered attacks cohered into mass violence. In Johannesburg's townships, large groups attacked foreign men and women, and destroyed their businesses and homes. Foreign nationals sought refuge in police stations, while crowds gathered outside. Similar outbreaks of xenophobic violence then took place in Cape Town, and other centres. In the last week of the month, the state authorised the military to involve itself in the policing of the public violence. By the end of May, at least 56 people had been killed.[35] Several hundred shops had been looted, and destroyed. A large number – 'tens of thousands' – of people had been displaced: either driven out of the country, or into temporary shelters on the urban periphery.[36]

As this xenophobic action took the form of mass gatherings, some commentators suggested that it was a symptom of urban poverty and social dislocation – thus linking it to the politics driving the country's 'service delivery' protests. Others have suggested that this was a form of local political action, a 'reactionary form of popular . . . policing.'[37] In these approaches, both disruptive politics and xenophobic violence are rooted in social alienation; both represent dangerous and illegitimate ways of asserting political agency in the face of an uninterested state. The implication of these arguments is that xenophobia is a symptom of illiberal popular politics – the kind of politics that thrives outside of the regulated spaces of participatory democracy.

There may be some truth to this, but it is at best only partial. More considered responses have emphasised the pervasive nature of xenophobia in South Africa's national discourse – and argued that it cannot simply be linked to either social or economic exclusion. In 2006, two years before this violent explosion, Michael Neocosmos wrote a striking critique of the xenophobic nature of the official discourses of

citizenship, and the legislation and institutions that underpinned it –
in particular 'the police and home affairs officers'. Neocosmos argued
that 'citizenship and xenophobia are manufactured by the state, both
under apartheid and post-apartheid forms of rule'.[38] In the same year,
a large-scale survey of South Africa's attitudes to foreign nationals
was conducted. It found high levels of xenophobia to be present in
all segments of society, and in all social groups. For the committee
reporting on this survey, this suggested that the state was implicated
in xenophobic attitudes – if only because its policies had done little to
discourage or divert them. The media and other communicators were
at least equally to blame, if only for failing to publicise warnings from
academics and civil society in the years before the 'perfect storm' of
2008.[39] Xenophobia was so widespread that it was nearly invisible.

In 2008, in at least some areas, xenophobia within state structures became more visible: in particular, in participatory governance
structures – such as ward committees – which either directly encouraged attacks or indirectly enabled them, by 'failing to muster the will
to prevent anti-foreigner violence'. The prevalence of these sins of
omission was highlighted by those few wards in which the committee took a clear stand against the violence.[40] In addition, state officials
chose to facilitate the deportation of foreign nationals, in preference
to protecting them on the ground – a decision which has largely pre-
vented prosecutorial responses to the violence, by removing potential
witnesses from the country. In addition, state-backed humanitarian
interventions were reluctantly implemented, and – in the aftermath
of the violence – rapidly terminated, with displaced foreigners being
evicted from emergency shelters.[41] In these cases, the illiberal and
xenophobic elements of (apparently) popular politics were aided and
abetted by state-backed participatory institutions – and even, sometimes, driven by forces within these institutions.

Although some of these participatory institutions sought to restrain
violence, not all did. Indeed, condemnation came at least as much
from social movements and community organisations – such as
Abahlali baseMjondolo, in Durban, the Anti-Privatisation Forum, in

Johannesburg, the Treatment Action Campaign, and others.[42] They asserted that xenophobia had no place in their politics; and some – perhaps more committed to disruptive politics than others – suggested that it was a way of undercutting potential sources of solidarity, and thus a tool of the political elite.[43]

In sum, any claim that political expression is restrained by the participatory structures set up by the state – and that popular illiberal sentiments can be filtered out of legitimate politics by these structures – is unfounded. Instead, these structures can incubate these sentiments as effectively as an apparently disorderly crowd. This suggests that any distinction drawn between politics in invited spaces – to return to Miraftab's repurposing of Cornwall's term – and politics in invented spaces cannot be founded on an assumption that the one is likely to be liberal, and inclusive, and the other illiberal, and exclusive. Elements of inclusivity and exclusivity coexist in both spaces, whether legitimated by the state or not – at least, they did so during 2008's xenophobic attacks.

And much the same argument could be advanced for other forms of illiberal and exclusivist politics. Patriarchal and anti-feminist politics can be found throughout state structures – and expressed by representatives of formal politics, from the President of the country downwards – as well as in popular movements.[44] Patriarchal politics are closely associated with the official structures of traditional authority in South Africa's rural areas; and – despite some exceptions – anti-feminist assumptions shape legal judgments, restricting women's access to public space.[45] Nor are civil society organisations exempt from criticism, as many have seemed willing to accept an informal segregation from, and deprioritisation of, women's issues in their political struggles.[46]

This suggests that, while exclusionary and illiberal sentiments occur in South African politics, they are not restricted to any one space of political expression. They may occur in invented spaces, among grassroots organisations or civil society movements; they may also occur in formal spaces, structured and legitimated by the state. Exclusionary politics do not simply arise in disruption.

The dynamic of disruption and discipline

And yet, the state continues to act as though disruptive acts of expression (that take place in invented rather than invited spaces) are significantly more likely to involve discriminatory politics.

One further vignette may help illustrate this approach: in the first months of 2014, a wave of protests was registered across South Africa – and, in particular, across Gauteng, the country's smallest and most populous province. These protests attracted an unusual degree of attention, as a series of news reports suggested that this wave was unusual – that the number and intensity of protests were unprecedented in recent times. This, however, was an exaggeration: the 'wave' of protest simply reflected a mild intensification of the patterns identified over the past decade.

Still, the situation seemed to call for a political response.

On 10 February, the Gauteng provincial government issued a statement in which it announced the formation of a 'high level task team' – consisting of the Premier, members of the provincial cabinet, and the bureaucratic heads in charge of the departments of Health, Community Safety, Human Settlements, Economic Development and (inexplicably) Sports, Art, Culture and Recreation – to devote 'high level attention and resources to the situation which has claimed human lives and essential public properties'.[47] As a first action, the task team 'appealed [to] and encouraged communities to protest within the confines of the law and refrain from destroying or damaging public property or infrastructure during protest actions'. The task team explained that 'protesting communities' should remember to 'allow ambulances to go through and . . . allow children to go to school' during their protests; in addition, the task team explained – this time in a direct quote, attributed to the team itself, rather than in the apparently neutral text of a press release – that 'the destruction of public property deprives communities of much-needed services and creates the additional burden of resources being diverted to restore and repair the damages . . . the cost of the destruction and long-term damage to the economy runs to millions of rands'.

The remainder of the statement developed into a civics lesson: after having reminded protestors to remain within the bounds of the law, and having warned them of the perhaps-unintended economic consequences of their actions, the task team proceeded to alert the public to the existing institutions already in place to resolve their potential discontent.

> If community members are unhappy with any aspect of service delivery, be it the pace or quality of the services, they should take these up with the ward councillor, if they do not get any assistance, they should escalate the matter to the municipality, then the department of Cooperative Governance. If these do not yield any positive results, they must lodge a complaint with the Premier's Office through the Premier's hotline on 0800600 1 100. . .

All these were the 'proper procedures' to follow.

A second statement followed two days later, in which the roll call of these procedures was amplified to include: 'ward councillors, ward committees, petitions committees in municipalities, public petitions committee in the legislature, Community Development Workers (CDWs), Community Liaison Officers (CLOs), Premier's Hotline, Presidential Hotline, Integrated Development Plan (IDP) forums and izimbizo'. This came in the context, again, of a reminder to 'disgruntled communities to abide by the Regulation of Gatherings Act during the protest action'. It added that: 'the task team further emphasised that it is vital for organisations and individuals to empower themselves with the detailed provisions of the Regulation of Gatherings Act.'[48]

This was not all.

A few days earlier, the provincial commissioner of police had held a press conference in which he announced that recent 'protest actions have stretched our resources to the limits'. He gave figures: 569 protests had taken place in his jurisdiction over the previous three months; 122 of these protests (i.e., approximately one in five, or 20%) became violent, or involved violent clashes between protestors and police. The scale of these protests was such that the official section of the police responsible for public order policing was being forced to call in assistance from under-trained police officers – and this, in turn, was perhaps contributing to the exacerbation of the situation. Indeed, this might have contributed to the increase in deaths in the course of these protests: at least eight people had been killed in January alone, and confrontations between the police and protestors had become increasingly fraught.[49]

The police commissioner told the gathered journalists that: 'the South African public must realise what is confronting members [of the police service] on a daily situation with the issues of protest marches and demonstrations. These are not petty things, these are not issues where you can say "go read a book . . . and it will tell you how to deal with these issues".' The protests themselves were dangerous situations, more dangerous than 'armchair critics' might realise: 'the community actions that we've seen in the last few days are pure criminality in the form of vandalism'.

'In the long term,' he added, 'the people are seeing the police in front of them and may think the police are the enemy. And the situation might build up where the police become the enemy.'

The way in which the state sees its citizens is demonstrated by the government's responses to protests in Gauteng. There is a thread running through these responses: a suspicion of protestors, reinforced by a distinction between them and respectable members of the public. Citizens are divided into those who follow the 'proper procedures' – and thus receive rapid and appropriate support from the state – and those who do not. The public follows procedure. Protestors do not, and are thus assumed, in the first place, to be ignorant of the existence of these proper procedures, and of their ability as citizens to petition the state – through ward councillors, committees, and telephonic help lines – for appropriate aid. In addition to this fundamental ignorance, protestors are also imagined as fundamentally irresponsible: as likely to prevent ambulances from travelling through an area of protest, or forbidding children to go to school. This irresponsibility shades easily into 'pure criminality': from blockading streets to vandalism.

In other words, the existence of a wide range of legitimate ('proper') mechanisms through which citizens can participate in the state's practices of governance validates the rhetorical and actual exclusion and criminalisation of citizens who do not choose to make use of these mechanisms.

For the state, then, the legitimate avenues for political action – as defined in this case by the government in Gauteng – are those associated with 'participatory democracy' or 'participatory governance'. These are intended to provide mechanisms through which citizens can either petition the state for a particular response, or more simply articulate their particular position on an issue or set of issues. These petitions and preferences will then be taken into account by the state and, ideally, shape both the development and implantation of policy at the local level. These processes of participation serve an important legitimating function in South Africa's democracy: they create a space within which the desires and needs of citizens can be incorporated directly into the country's politics, thus emphasising the democratic nature of the post-apartheid order.

They also serve as the primary means through which the state seeks to shape practices of political citizenship – to shape, in other words, the expression of political agency by South Africans, and their communities. As such they are the sites within which certain practices of citizenship are legitimated by the state – and others, by implication, delegitimated. But there is more to this – the effect of following the prescriptions set out by the government of Gauteng would be to limit political action to participation in the election of officials, and to intermittent acts of petition.

In the following chapters we will see that many protesting communities have in fact attempted to make use of these participatory institutions – and have attempted, repeatedly, to petition the state for support and engagement. It is often only in face of the failure of these processes that they have embarked upon protest. In the words of an activist in Thembelihle – the site of several disruptions in the past decade – the community only embarked upon protest once it had 'lost confidence in the petitions committee, the City structures, Region G administration and the Office of the Speaker, amongst others'.[50] This is not the voice of someone who is ignorant of the resources formally available to him;

nor is it the voice of someone who has wilfully chosen to ignore them. Instead, it is the voice of experience – and of disillusion.

This book is concerned with teasing out the dynamic between political expression and repression in contemporary South Africa, and this set of actions by the police and the state – in Makause, in 2012, and across Gauteng, two years later – points to a particular set of relationships within this dynamic: those between disruption and discipline. Not all protests provoke a violent response; nor are all disruptions of order themselves protests. Nor is the police response to potential disruption necessarily repressive – in some circumstances, the state may seek to discipline and direct grassroots political energies into its own project of consensual governance.

But when this fails – and discipline gives way to disruption – the state may turn violent.

FOUR

From Discipline to Repression

The post-apartheid Constitution entrenches a set of political rights at the heart of South Africa's legal order. In addition to the rights to participate in elections and stand for political office (s.19), these include the right to freedom of expression (s.16), the right 'peacefully and unarmed, to assemble, to demonstrate, to picket and present petitions' (s.17), and the right to freedom of association (s.18).[1] Read together, these rights establish a general right not only to form and hold political opinions, but also to express these opinions in public – individually and *en masse*.

This was confirmed, in the early years of the Constitutional Court, in the context of a dispute over the constitutionality of a legal prohibition of the participation of members of the Defence Force in 'public protest action'. The court held that 'these rights taken together protect the rights of individuals not only individually to form and express opinions, of whatever nature, but to establish associations and groups of like-minded people to foster and propagate such opinions'. The Court held that this did not require the state to approve of a view: 'In essence, it requires the acceptance of the public airing of disagreements and the refusal to silence unpopular views.'[2]

At its best, then, the South African order entrenches a right to political expression. It is not, however, an unlimited right: the phrase 'peacefully and unarmed' in section 17 clearly limits the application of the right – although the extent to which it may do so is still subject to debate, in public and through the courts. The right to assemble and demonstrate is also restricted by the provisions of the Regulation of Gatherings Act, passed in 1993 and implemented in 1996.

It is this Act that the Gauteng government referred to, in the statements reproduced in the last pages of the previous chapter, when it called upon citizens to 'abide by the provisions of the Regulation of Gatherings Act during . . . protest action'. If they did so, their protests would be treated as legitimate. Otherwise – if they did not do so – the police would treat their protests as criminal. Statements such as these suggest that the Gatherings Act is central to the dynamic of political expression and repression in South Africa – and that obeying its provisions is one way of demonstrating discipline in the face of an apparent suspicion of disruptive political expression. For dissenting communities and political activists, then, an understanding of and an engagement with this Act is essential to defending their ability to make use of their formal rights to protest.

But the Gatherings Act is one of the most misunderstood and abused pieces of legislation in contemporary South Africa. Its history is often distorted in civil society and media debates; its purposes are misunderstood by both police and activists; and a restrictive interpretation of the provisions of the Act – and, implicitly, the rights to political expression – has been adopted by the country's courts, further constraining unlicensed access to public spaces. In addition, importantly, its provisions are regularly either circumvented or abused – more often than not by the police.

In this chapter, then, we will consider how the dynamic between disruption and discipline structures the possibility of public protest action in contemporary South Africa through a consideration of the Regulation of Gatherings Act itself – its history, the opportunities that it represented, and the ways in which those opportunities have been frustrated. In the following parts, we will turn to consider the implementation of the Act – that is, the ways in which the South African order attempts to regulate and contain protest so as to discipline its disruptive potential. The effect of these efforts has been to transform a system formally committed to disciplining protest into one in which the police act to violently and forcibly repress the expression of dissent.

Protest and political expression after apartheid

Many accounts of the difficulties faced by protestors in the post-apartheid era begin by describing the Regulation of Gatherings Act as a 'repressive . . . apartheid era' law.[3] Others, choosing their language more carefully, emphasise that the Act was part of a package of 'legislation from the apartheid era that impacts on the full enjoyment and practice of what are now constitutionally guaranteed civil-political rights'.[4] These start from the presumption that the passage of the Gatherings Act in 1993 – the year before the start of the democratic era – taints the Act itself. This is wrong: although there are problems with the Act, these are not those of the apartheid era.

Indeed, the roots of the Act lie in attempts, at the very start of the transition era, to recognise the legitimacy of protest action as a form of political expression in the face of often-violent policing tactics. On 14 September 1991, representatives of the majority of South Africa's political organisations signed a National Peace Accord, which sought to establish a framework for political activities in the transition from apartheid.[5] The relationship between police and protestors was at its core, and among its many provisions are a series of instructions to the police on how to respond to 'unlawful gatherings'.[6] These instruct the police to engage with the gathered crowd 'to ascertain the purpose of the Gathering and [if necessary] to negotiate the immediate dispersal of the group'. Further provisions require the police to give 'a reasonable time' for the gathering to disperse, and that – if the protestors should refuse to cooperate – 'the least degree of force should be used' as 'persuasion, advice and warnings should be used to secure co-operation, compliance with the law and the restoration of order'. To assist this, and reduce public risk, the Accord also required protestors to refrain from carrying any 'dangerous weapons' in any public gathering.[7]

These provisions represented the initial achievement of a consensus on the recognition of public protest action as a form of political expression; the Accord represented the minimum agreement necessary for a consensual transition from apartheid to a post-apartheid political order to proceed. Further discussion of these forms of political expression was postponed, and the task of considering how to deal with breaches of this Accord was made the problem of a judicial commission: the Commission of Inquiry Regarding the Prevention of Public Violence and Intimidation, more commonly known as the Goldstone Commission – named for its chairman.

The Goldstone Commission's remit was wide and unwieldy: to investigate all acts of public violence in the transition period, from July 1991 until the first democratic elections. The Commission also interpreted its remit broadly, investigating both individual incidents of violence and the broad social and political context of the times. In April 1992 – approximately six months into its operations – the Commission appointed an 'international panel of experts' to advise its committees on 'the most desirable rules and procedures for the conduct of mass demonstrations, marches and picketing'. This expert panel made a series of recommendations about the nature of these rules and procedures; these recommendations were then taken up by the Commission, amended and discussed, and formed the basis of the Regulation of Gatherings Act.

The Commission – and its panel – was clear on the importance of this Act, and of the role of public protest in a future democratic South Africa. As the panel puts it:

> The right to demonstrate is as fundamental a right of democratic citizenship as the right to take part in political campaigns. Where the purpose of the demonstration is protest, the demonstration is at the core of free expression in a democracy. One of the central responsibilities of the police is to facilitate the right to demonstrate.[8]

The panel's discussion and recommendations were aimed at entrenching the right to protest, and ensuring that this right was respected by the police; the only important limitations placed on this right involved restrictions on the carrying of weapons, and on violence.

The panel called for the establishment of a system 'for co-ordinating the views and resources' of the three principal stakeholders in any planned protest: the organisers, local authorities, and the police. Notice of the planned march would be presented 'no later than six working days before the event' to allow 'local government authorities to arrange and hold meetings with the police, officials responsible for the location, and the organisers of the demonstration'. This system was intended to permit the building of a consensus, with no individual groups being able to dominate the discussion. Indeed, it was designed in such a way that if disagreements over the plans for the protest could not be resolved amicably, then a higher authority – ideally, 'a judge of the Supreme Court' – would be deputed to resolve the dispute in a fair, even-handed, and expeditious manner.

However, the panel recognised that not all protests could be planned. When

> a symbolic event precipitates an almost instantaneous reaction among a group living in close physical proximity with each other and communicating quickly and effectively through informal 'grapevines' . . . the demonstration is likely to lack clearly identifiable organisers and the demonstrators are likely to fail to give the required notice.

In these circumstances, the panel argued, the police should treat 'the absence of compliance with notice as an inconvenience but not as a ground for immediately taking action to prevent the demonstration'. Indeed, 'the response of the authorities in these situations should be to attempt, even at that late date, to facilitate the demonstration'.[9]

In a brief discussion of this process, Durrheim and Foster emphasise the importance not only of liberal ideology in the Commission's recommendations – expressed in its 'wholesale rejection of repression in favour of the ethical principles of liberal democracy' – but also of ideas about 'the crowd as a self-regulating entity . . . founded on recent developments in the scientific understanding of the crowd'.[10] This meant that the responsibilities of the police and the state to facilitate and support public political expression did not end once a protest began – or once an unruly crowd had formed. In the eyes of the Commission's experts, almost all crowds could regulate themselves – and the police should act to enable that. Indeed, the panel recommended that police practice be designed to achieve the rapid restoration of peaceful protest through the least invasive measures possible. In cases of violence, individuals should be identified and arrested and – in so far as it was feasible – the demonstration should be allowed to continue. Even under assault, the police should act with the greatest possible restraint: if threatened by thrown stones and bottles, for example, the police should be protected by shields, and aim to use water cannons and tear gas to keep the protestors at a distance. If someone in the group fired a weapon, the police should target only the shooter – 'the others are not responsible for his actions, which may indeed be those of a provocateur hostile to the aims of most of the demonstrators.'[11]

Throughout the text of their report, the expert panel emphasised that protest was a legitimate and important form of political expression, and argued that it was important to continue to permit a demonstration to continue – whether it was planned or spontaneous, ideally peaceful, or threatening to become violent – because 'even a truly democratic government will have to anticipate more or less violent, organised demonstrations by many South Africans of different persuasions. Demonstrations are particularly the form of protest of the most numerous and uninfluential'.[12] The best way of ensuring peaceful protests would be for the state to act to support, rather than forbid, political expression. 'The capacity of the organisers of demonstrations to speak for their followers must be nourished and made to grow. Everything possible must be done to strengthen these mechanisms of self-control on the part of the demonstrating group.'[13]

In essence, the report of the expert panel set out to establish a political framework which acknowledged and facilitated the intermittent disruptions caused by protest. This was a framework that recognised the limits of formal political institutions, and the real difficulties that poor and marginalised communities face in attempting to conform to their requirements. Although it argued that activists and communities should seek to work with the state and its police forces to contain the disruptive potential of a planned protest, nonetheless the report maintained that this was not always possible – and that a just order would recognise this reality.

The Regulation of Gatherings Act

The expert panel presented its recommendations in July 1992, four months after it was first convened. That month, an interim agreement on the 'conduct of public demonstrations' – 'pending any new legislation which might flow from the recommendations' – was signed by the South African Police and the African National Congress's (ANC's) alliance partners. This agreement followed from the principle that 'members of the public have the right to demonstrate peacefully in public, in order to convey their views effectively, and the South African police have the duty to protect this right'. Protestors should refrain from carrying dangerous weapons, and should give 'reasonable notice of demonstrations'.[14] Afterwards, the Commission again emphasised that these were indeed notices, which would give rise to 'bona fide negotiations', and not 'applications for permission' to gather.[15]

Over the next months, the Commission sponsored the development of legislation to entrench these recommendations. In February 1993, a draft bill was printed in the Government Gazette, and comments were solicited. In April that year, a final version was published by the Commission, as part of its own report; in the introduction to this version, Justice Goldstone emphasised that the proposed bill was not 'designed specifically to cater for the current political climate' but, rather, was 'directed at the rules and procedures which should now apply to public marches and demonstrations now and in the future'.[16] This draft went to parliament that year, was debated, and assented to by the President at the start of 1994. The operation of the Act – formally,

205 of 1993 – was, however, delayed until November 1996, eighteen months into the new order.[17]

The final version of the Act, though, took a more ambiguous line than that of the expert panel.

The text of the Act begins by following the panel's recommendations, before diverging noticeably from them: first, after a flurry of definitions, section 2 of the Act focusses on the appointment of representatives by a protesting organisation, and of a 'responsible officer by the police and the local authority', while section 3 outlines the processes through which notice of a proposed gathering should take place and section 4 addresses the 'consultations, negotiations, amendment of notices, and conditions' undertaken by these different representatives. However, section 5 then sets out conditions under which a gathering can be prohibited by 'a responsible officer', and section 6, the processes by which this prohibition can be appealed to a magistrate and only then – if the magistrate's decision is unsatisfactory – to a judge of the High Court. The next chapter of the Act prohibits gatherings in the vicinity of a courtroom, parliament and the Union Buildings (s.8). The third instructs demonstrators on how to behave in public (s.9); and empowers the police to intervene to either alter the progress of a demonstration or to order the demonstrators to disperse (s.10). The remaining chapter (sections 11 to 16) primarily deals with the liability of organisers for any damage that might arise, and makes the convening of a gathering without the provision of notice an offence penalised by fine or imprisonment – with the sole legal concession that 'it shall be a defence to a charge of convening a gathering in contravention of subsection (1)(a) that the gathering concerned took place spontaneously'.[18]

There are a number of subtler differences between the framework proposed in the expert panel's report and that actually instituted by the legislation. For one, a distinction is drawn between a 'demonstration' – which is defined both in terms of numbers ('no more than 15 persons') and in terms of purpose ('for or against any person, cause, action or failure to take action') – and a 'gathering' – which is of more than 15 people, takes place in public, and 'at which the principles, policy, actions of failures to act of any government, political party or political organisation . . . are discussed, attacked, criticised, promoted or propagated'. Demonstrations require no special notice, and little dedicated policing; actual gatherings, however, are bound by stricter regulations.

The effect of these divergences and differences is to obscure the clear right to protest articulated by the expert panel in Goldstone Commission. This takes many forms. The proposed notification framework assumed the right of the protestors to gather, and assumed that this right could not be abrogated by the police or the local state – but only by a neutral and external judge. In the Act itself, however, the 'responsible officer' – appointed by the state, and party to the negotiations – is empowered to prohibit a gathering, on receipt of 'credible information on oath . . . that there is a threat that will result in serious disruption of vehicular or pedestrian traffic, injury to participants in the gathering or other persons, or extensive damage to property'. This decision is ordinarily appealed to a local magistrate; only after the magistrate's decision is made would a protesting organisation appeal the prohibition to a judge of the High Court. What was intended as a rapid process, overseen by a neutral party, has become complex and bureaucratic, and dependent on the opinion of an officer of the local state, backed up by a statement made by any party.

In addition to the power to prohibit, the police are empowered to disperse a gathering. Although the Act enjoins the police to refrain from exercising this power prematurely, it also grants them a wide discretion: 'if a member of the Police of or above the rank of warrant officer has reasonable grounds to believe that a danger to persons or property' will arise from the gathering, he or she may then call upon the demonstrators to disperse. If they do not do so, the officer may authorise the use of 'proportionate' force to break up the gathering and scatter the massed protestors. Any protestor who challenges, 'hinders, interfere with, obstructs or resists a member of the Police . . . in the exercise of his duties' commits an offence in terms of the Act and is, on conviction, 'liable to a fine not exceeding R20,000 or to imprisonment not exceeding one year or to both such fine or such imprisonment'. Likewise, failing to implement the restrictions set out by the responsible officer

in advance of an otherwise-authorised gathering is made an offence
in these same terms. Most significantly, though, is the criminalisation
of convening a gathering 'in respect of which no notice or inadequate
notice was given'. This offence carries the same penalty as refusing to
disperse, obstructing the police in their duties, or intentionally mislead-
ing the state authorities.

The purpose of the final Act, according to Durrheim and Foster, is
to 'change the nature of the relationship between the crowd and [the]
state. The crowd is incorporated into an apparatus of social administration'. The process of negotiations creates a bond of cooperation
between the protestors and the state; the appointment of marshals and
the apportionment of responsibility aims to inculcate 'commitment'
on the part of the crowd to the consensual resolution of disputes that
might occur in the protest. Overall, they suggest, the Act suggests that
'the economy of crowd regulation has shifted from one of repression
to one of management', with management understood to be coopera-
tive – both imposed by the law, and encouraged within the crowd.[19]

The policing of licensed protest

This legislative framework, however, represents an ideal situation. The
actual practices regularly followed by the police in controlling demonstrations simply do not fit it. In a measured and understated report,
published in 2006, the Freedom of Expression Institute (FXI) suggested
that the practices that have developed around the Gatherings Act have
obscured the possibilities provided by the text of the Act. The report
argues that 'there is a gap between what the role players perceive the
RGA [the Regulation of Gatherings Act] to be providing for in certain
instances and what the legislation actually says. Role players tend to
regard what has generally evolved through practice and implementation over the years to mean that this is what the RGA provides'.[20]

It goes without saying that different role players have had different
experiences of these practices, and thus different understandings of
how the Act operates. Trade unions, for example, have reacted against
attempts to constrain their activities by reference to the Gatherings

Act – and have argued, unusually, that the Act should not apply to these activities at all. Rather, their strikes, pickets, and protests should be regulated under specific pieces of labour legislation.[21] Their experiences of the Act have led some unions to reject the Act. Political parties, by contrast, have shown a degree of faith in its formal processes – no doubt because it is rare for a large political party to experience significant problems with the police. When a party does, it is national news. In 2014, for example, the prohibition of a march by the Democratic Alliance on the Johannesburg headquarters of the ANC provoked a flurry of attention. The party's press release revealed its surprise at the conduct of the police in the run-up to the prohibition: they had 'strung us along by delaying meetings, giving verbal permission several times, but refusing to put it in writing, and by placing every bureaucratic obstacle in our way'.[22]

This experience may have seemed unusual to the party – but it is typical of the experiences related by community organisations and civil society movements. Over and again, they testify to the obstructive attitude of local authorities and the police; to the disingenuous use of coordinating meetings to delay the formal processes; and to the sudden prohibition of gatherings at the end of the process – with this prohibition often coming too late for the organisers to effectively appeal the decision to the courts. (Indeed, this is exactly what happened to the Democratic Alliance: it was able to appeal the decision, but that appeal was heard too late to be effective and a new march, on a different date, had to be organised for a fortnight after it had been planned.[23])

The working of these practices can best be understood in a specific context. Over the next pages, I consider the experiences of the Thembelihle Crisis Committee (TCC), a community-based organisation in the greater Johannesburg region, with the organisation of gatherings since 2001.

Thembelihle is an informal settlement on the southern outskirts of Johannesburg, in the area of Lenasia. Lenasia – which was once designed an 'Indian' area under apartheid – provides the residents with employment, and access to schools. Thembelihle itself is built on peripheral land, of little commercial value and some insecurity:

the ground is dolomitic, which means that it is prone to subterranean erosion which may, in time, lead to the formation of sinkholes. This erosion can be managed technically, through specialised water management measures, the establishment of low-density settlements, and forms of land rehabilitation. According to expert reports, the land on which Thembelihle is built is susceptible to these measures and forms of rehabilitation.[24]

Rather than implement these measures, however, the post-apartheid state decided that Thembelihle was unsafe for occupation – and that all of its residents would have to be removed from their homes and resettled to a location approximately eight kilometres to the southeast of their current location. In 2002, the City of Johannesburg began the process of relocating the residents – sometimes forcibly. The relocation was resisted by the residents, under the aegis of the newly constituted TCC.[25] The TCC had been formed in the year preceding the relocation process, at least in part in response to the activism of the Soweto Electricity Crisis Committee and other community organisations responding to issues around the provision of water and electrical services in the greater Johannesburg region.[26]

In its first months, the TCC sought to engage with the City of Johannesburg to develop a plan to electrify the settlement; the imposition of the relocation process, however, radicalised the Committee. Several different strategies of resistance were adopted, including public protests. The adoption of these strategies created an immediate tension between the Committee and the local police forces: in July 2002, while the protests against the relocation were continuing, the Gauteng police attempted to prohibit a gathering organised by the Anti-Privatisation Forum (APF) on the basis that members of the Thembelihle community would be participating in the planned march. This was thought to be the result of the criminalisation of the ongoing protests, extended to cover the community as whole.[27] As discussed in earlier chapters, the APF march was part of widespread protests against the World Summit on Sustainable Development, and although it was eventually permitted, the actions of the police first in containing the gatherings and then in forcibly dispersing the protestors catalysed a new and more suspicious relationship between civil society organisations and the state. Thembelihle and the TCC were central parts of that process.

The contentious relationship between the TCC and the state was confirmed in the following years. In 2003, the City approached the High Court to obtain an order requiring the relocation of the community; the TCC opposed this, working pro-bono legal representatives to resist the state. In resisting the City's application, the TCC won an immediate postponement of the process and – over the next several years – successfully delayed the implementation of the relocation.[28] By 2005, the City appeared to have abandoned their case – leaving the court process in indefinite abeyance; new research was commissioned, new plans were developed, and the City's strategy for relocating the residents was revised.[29]

In the years of this case, however, the tensions between the TCC and the state were reflected in their attempts to organise authorised protests. In 2003 and 2004, the APF – as an umbrella organisation, with which the TCC was affiliated – submitted at least twenty notifications of plans to hold a gathering. In each case, negotiations, as prescribed by the Act, followed. In ten of the twenty cases, the gathering took place; in the other ten cases, however, the police prohibited the gathering. The reasons given for these prohibitions included 'credible information on oath that your march will result in lawlessness' and, in another case, a history of 'extensive damage to Council property' in earlier marches. Three of these proposed gatherings would have taken place in Thembelihle. All three were prohibited. In November 2004, the TCC twice attempted to organise a picket of 100 people in Lenasia to draw attention to the lack of development in the informal settlement. The processes of engagement around this planned picket reveal something of the ordinary practices through which the Regulation of Gatherings Act is implemented.[30]

The TCC submitted a notice of their intention to gather on 2 November – six days before the planned picket. They were called to a meeting the next day, to discuss 'planning and logistics'; later that day, however, a letter was sent to the TCC by the Johannesburg police informing them that the gathering was to be prohibited. The police letter provided two reasons for the decision: first, 'the proposed times . . . will result in serious vehicular traffic because it is peak hour period' and, second, 'there is also reasonable suspicion that your gathering will result in lawlessness and damage to property'. This was based – again – on 'incidents of the past i.e. blockage of the road and the stoning of vehicles, there is no guarantee that such conduct will not be repeated'. Supporting this – and fulfilling the requirement of the Act that such allegations be based on 'credible information on oath' – a police officer swore an affidavit stating that the TCC had been violent in the past, and that he suspected that the gathering would lead to 'lawlessness'.

The picket did not occur. A fortnight later – on 15 November – the TCC submitted a second notice to the police, again informing them of their intention to picket, this time on 29 November. One week later – and a week before the intended gathering – a second planning meeting took place. Once again, the police wrote to the TCC after the meeting, prohibiting the gathering. Once again, two reasons were given: 'the proposed times . . . will result in serious vehicular traffic because it is peak hour traffic', and 'there is also reasonable suspicion that your gathering will result in lawlessness and damage to property'. These are identical to the reasons given three weeks earlier; a different officer placed his concerns on oath, and – in a substantially different text – suggested that 'these people are planning to cause a problem. In the past I have policed the gatherings of Thembelihle along the same route and we experienced street blockade with rocks, stones were thrown at passing vehicles including police vehicles'. Once again, a history of contentious and confrontational protests was used to pre-emptively prohibit a gathering.[31]

Other gatherings in Thembelihle were approved during the same period: but principally, when applied for on behalf of the Landless People's Movement rather than the TCC. (This should not suggest that the TCC was absent from these gatherings: a split in the leadership led many activists to throw their weight behind the Landless People's Movement in this period.[32]) But few – if any – of the gatherings planned by the trouble-making organisation were permitted. Their experiences reveal the ordinary practices through which the requirements of the Gatherings Act are implemented, and distorted.

First: the meeting between the organisers of the gathering and the local authorities was not used as a means of ventilating concerns, discussing solutions, and building consensus. From the text of the letters, it is clear that these were contentious encounters – and that the initial proposals of the organisers were repurposed as evidence supporting the police's case against the gatherings. Second: the 'credible information on oath' required to justify the prohibition of the gatherings was provided by police officers, rather than neutral members of the public. This made the police interested parties to the dispute, rather than referees of it. And third: rather than investigate any specific threats to the public order presented by a proposed gathering, the police allowed vague and general allegations of the likelihood of disruption to serve as cause to prohibit the gathering.

The effect of these police actions was to strip core provisions of the Act of their meanings. These processes no longer seek to balance the interests of the organisers of a gathering with those of the local community, as mediated and facilitated by the police and local municipal authorities. The notification process is rendered meaningless. The initial meeting is not to be used to develop a consensus on how the proposed gathering should be organised and policed, but is, rather, to be mined for evidence to use against the organisers. A community organisation is unlikely to benefit from providing the mandated notice, or attending the meeting, as it will not receive aid in either organising or securing its proposed public gathering. In addition, neither specific knowledge nor external evidence is required for the police to prohibit a gathering, and the Act no longer provides meaningful protection to organisers. Instead, the police are able to use general suspicions of an organisation, or accounts of past behaviour at earlier gatherings, as a valid reason for prohibiting a gathering, thus stretching the formal requirements of the Gatherings Act thin. This approach empowers the police – improperly – to act as authorising agents: as gatekeepers exerting near-absolute control on the lawful exercise of a fundamental political right.

Spontaneity and violence

These tactics are used on those gatherings that are (theoretically, at least) permissible in terms of the Act. Other tactics are deployed to control gatherings that do not fit into its formal framework.

Durrheim and Foster note that, in the Act, 'categories of protest which are not tolerated still exist, and are explicitly encoded into the law. Elements of despotism are incorporated into ethical liberal governance, as demonstrations which do not comply with the provisions of the Act may be forcibly dispersed'.[33] They suggest that those categories of protest excluded from legal protection are simply those which are violent – thus setting up a conceptual distinction between these and 'peaceful' protests. The concept of peacefulness is not – they suggest – a simple 'descriptive category, but . . . one which actively constructs the socio-political landscape, producing effects of social control'. Peacefulness is defined both as the absence of violence, and as the presence of disciplined self-regulation on behalf of the crowd. It is a malleable concept, rather than an absolute one – and can be, and often is, 'invested with an overt political purpose and meaning'.[34] In this context, I would suggest that these purposes and meanings relate to the need to maintain the country's political order – as suggested by the Gauteng government.

Although they do not explicitly say so, it is clear that they – and the courts at large – consider that the only category of protest that is not tolerated within the framework established by the Gatherings Act is that of protests that are not peaceful, but violent. But, as important as this is, we must recognise that the account of the Act given by these scholars elides one further category of unlicensed protest: spontaneous and unplanned outbursts of mass public protest. These protests vanish under the shadow of violent protests – and all too easily become identified with them.

The text of the Gatherings Act – unlike the expert panel of the Goldstone Commission – is almost silent on spontaneous protests. Instead, its approach to spontaneous protest can be discerned in its implicit presumptions. Its text assumes that gatherings of more than fifteen people, 'at which the principles, policy, actions of failures to act of any government, political party or political organisation . . . are discussed, attacked, criticised, promoted or propagated', are ordinarily planned and coordinated by an institution – whether that be a political party, a trade union, or a civil society movement. This institutional coordination is necessary to ensure that gatherings remain 'peaceful' – and failures in organising the protest are likely to result in avoidable disruption.

This disruption – brought about by the failure of an organisation to plan adequately – would strip the gathering of its legal protection, and enable the police to act to disperse the crowd forcibly. Even if this was not done, and order was restored without a confrontation between the police and protestors, the interests and rights of bystanders and non-participants would be protected by requiring the organising institution to be liable for any damages caused by these disruptive moments. At least, this is the position adopted by the South African courts in recent years: several judgments, each arising out of the events that accompanied strikes by the South African Trade and Allied Workers' Union in Cape Town in 2006, emphasise the importance of these provisions. The Constitutional Court's final judgment in this matter upheld the principle that organisations must predict potential outbreaks of violence, and be held liable if their predictions are incomplete or incompetent. This was required to ensure that an equitable balance was struck between 'the conflicting rights and interests of organisations and members of the public'.[35]

But the Constitutional Court's judgment went further than this, and provided organisations with some advice: 'the fact that every right must be exercised with due regard to the rights of others cannot be overemphasised. The organisation always has a choice between exercising the right to assemble and cancelling the gathering in the light of reasonably foreseeable damage.'

There is little in this judgment – or the judgments of the lower courts that preceded it – that speaks to the real likelihood of unpredictability in mass gatherings. Indeed, the intermediate appeal court could only imagine three types of events which could be unpredictable by an organising body: the unplanned discharge of a police weapon, causing panic; the arrival of 'a gunman unconnected to the trade union, who bore a grudge against society and who started firing indiscriminately', likewise causing panic; and the incursion of a motorist who, having broken through all protective barriers, 'drives into the marching crowd causing panics and a riot'.[36] Only in situations in which violence was caused by acts of absurd and cruel chance could organisers be held innocent of failing to plan for that violence. This approach establishes a connection between planning and peacefulness, and between a lack of planning and predictable violence.

Outside the courts, this process of reasoning gives rise to a syllogism: given that the lack of planning leads to violence, and given that spontaneous protests are by definition unplanned, then we should conclude that spontaneous protests are necessarily violent protests – and thus unlikely to be protected by the Constitution or its subsidiary laws. When laid out like this, the syllogism is evidently flawed. It depends on overly general statements, each of which can be unpicked. Violence is not the necessary consequence of a failure of planning. Spontaneity need not rule out the possibility of coordination or order developing on the ground, in real time. And – obviously – not all spontaneous protests develop into violently disruptive protests. Many simply fizzle out.

Nonetheless, this syllogism guides the actual policing of spontaneous gatherings in contemporary South Africa, regardless of whether these gatherings are violent or, in an ordinary sense, peaceful.

An example of the latter can be found in the events at Cato Crest, in Durban, on Monday 30 September 2013. These events took place against a background of intense contestation between the police and the community: the residents of an informal settlement who had been evicted from their homes seven times in six months. In the months leading up to the end of September, they had approached the local High Court and obtained an order interdicting the municipality, its 'land invasion unit', and the local police from continuing to evict them; in the last weeks of September, though, these orders had been ignored and residents had again been evicted by members of the police.[37]

Over the weekend, the community decided to embark on a public protest to draw local and national attention to the recalcitrance of the police. The protest in Cato Crest would be one of many, coordinated by Abahlali baseMjondolo – a shack-dwellers' movement – across Durban. According to the detailed account provided after the fact by Abahlali, preparations began late on Sunday night as the Cato Crest residents collected materials to form a road blockade. At about 3.30 a.m., the residents gathered on the main road outside the settlement. They brought branches and broken furniture, and rubber tyres – which they laid across the main road and set on fire.[38]

The police were waiting for them, though – and, it seems, were determined not to allow the gathering to proceed. It is vital to realise that, at this point, no violence had occurred – and the disruption was limited to the makeshift blockade. No testimony – whether by the community or the police – suggests otherwise. But at some time between 4.00 and 4.20 a.m., a number of police officers left their vehicles and drew their weapons. The residents panicked, and began to scatter, turning their backs on the police; in these moments, some of the police officers opened fire with their handguns, and shot two women as they tried to flee. One was killed, and the other injured.

The police withdrew from the scene, and the residents regrouped. The injured woman was taken to hospital for treatment. The dead woman – Nqobile Nzuza – was covered with a rough blanket.

All of this took place before dawn. The day's events were barely beginning.

An hour later, the police returned, this time with a video camera. The footage from this camera has been disclosed to the court, and is in the public domain.[39] The existence of this footage allows the events of the reminder of the day to be discerned in detail. It shows the police driving back on to the road at 5.17 a.m.: over branches and around smouldering tyres. The camera focusses on a few dozen men and women, clustered along the road and – in the centre of it – a silver-foil body bag, laid out in front of an ambulance. This is the aftermath of the earlier confrontation. Over the next dozen minutes, the camera films the interactions between the community and the police: there is tension, but no violence. Women gesture with their arms and stamp their feet. Most of the crowd signal that they do not want the police there, that they want them to leave. But there is little to suggest an appetite for confrontation, on either side; instead, the community seems shocked – gathered around Nqobile Nzuza's corpse – while the police seem somewhat chastened.

This part of the footage ends at 5.29 a.m., before resuming four hours later.

In the hours between, representatives of Abahlali – including their General Secretary at the time, Bandile Mdalose – arrived at Cato Crest. After speaking with them, the community decided to continue to protest – now not only against the history of illegal evictions, but also against the callousness and brutality of the police, expressed in the pre-dawn killing of Nqobile Nzuza.

It is with this march that the footage resumes: several dozen men and women are walking down one quarter of a four-lane road; there is debris on the road – scattered bags of garbage. The central groups of marchers seems to be dancing, moving in rough unison with each other, bobbing as they go forward. Behind them, several police vehicles – including the one holding the camera – creep forward. They appear to have been following for some time and, five minutes into the footage, pull in front of the marching crowd. The police appear to negotiate with the protestors; on the soundtrack, you can hear the crowd calling out 'Phansi!' – down with the police, with corruption, with brutality. The chanting continues throughout the negotiations, but the negotiations themselves appear peaceful. By 9.35 a.m., the crowd is moving forward once again.

At about 9.40 a.m., the camera begins to focus on Bandile Mdalose. It follows her progress alongside and within the crowd for ten minutes: the crowd pauses and then progresses; Bandile speaks to the police officers, and addresses the crowd. Again, there is tension – but no confrontation. The footage skips five minutes, and resumes with the crowd stopped – some seated on the ground – while police officers bearing large weapons approach them. Bandile is filmed discussing the events with the police, and seems to be conveying the crowd's refusal to disperse. The next several minutes of footage show a small core of the crowd – perhaps three or four dozen men and women – standing in the road, while the police vehicles reverse and retreat from them.

At 10.04, the camera captures a police vehicle rounding the corner of the road – a water cannon blasting from its roof. The cannon is trained at the crowd, and the force of the water drives them off the road; they run down an embankment, towards the informal settlement, and briefly vanish. Armed police leave their vehicles, and head towards the embankment. A handful of protestors re-emerge on the side of the road, including Bandile. By 10.09, the camera has zoomed in on a discussion between her and the police; she raises her hands, wrists together, indicating that the police can arrest her – and although the sound is not clear, both her frustration and her calm are.

The footage continues to move forward; the march does not resume, but the community refuses to vanish. The police huddle and separate; vehicles move forward, and then stop; and – after about ten minutes – armed police begin to move down the embankment, into the informal settlement. The camera follows them from a distance. According to the time stamps on the footage, the record suddenly fragments: at 10.22 (and 48 seconds) the footage stops, holding an overview of the settlement; it resumes at 10.25 (and 53 seconds) with footage of armed policemen strolling to the embankment, while in the background a worker calmly clears debris.

It is important to consider the lengthy footage of peaceful protest, disrupted primarily by police action, because in these three minutes – conveniently missing from the otherwise detailed footage – the police say that they were assaulted by stones thrown by Bandile Mdalose, the General Secretary of a national movement, in an attempt to cause or incite public violence in the crowd.

Because of this, she posed a threat – and had to be arrested on a charge of 'public violence'.

This, at least, is the police's case as pleaded in the Durban courts.[40] It is wildly implausible: despite having filmed the previous forty minutes, the police camera just happened to be switched off for the nearly three minutes in which the only alleged act of violence took place. Despite the crowd gathering to march to the police station in the immediate aftermath of the death of a young girl at the hands of the police, there had been no noticeable violence for hours – and yet, suddenly, without preparation, uncontainable violence was threatened by one woman.

The actions of the police throughout the morning of 30 September are incomprehensible without recognising that – regardless of the plausibility of the claim in this particular circumstance – the police were acting as if an unplanned gathering was necessarily perpetually on the edge of collapsing into violence. The flawed syllogism that links spontaneity to violence seems to underpin the police's action: whether this was the apparently pre-emptive violence that led to the death of Nqobile Nzuza before dawn; or the use of a water cannon to disperse a small crowd of visibly peaceful protestors; or the arrest of a notable activist on an implausible criminal charge. In the absence of any actual public attacks – and the police's own footage does not disclose any such thing – the sole reason for the use of these aggressive policing measures was the police's own fear that if the gathering was allowed to continue, it would inevitably collapse into violence.

The 'criminal injustice system'

The behaviour of the local police in Cato Crest gains in significance when compared to the behaviour of the local police in Thembelihle, when they have been called upon to address protests there. In two examples – one from 2007, and the other from 2011 – the approach adopted in response to similarly spontaneous protests is so similar as to be almost identical. There is only one significant difference: in Thembelihle, these protests actually did involve some violent acts.

In 2007, the TCC embarked upon a protest without providing notice to the police. The morning after a public meeting, in which 'more than 500 people . . . demanded a report about the housing developments in the area' and took issue with 'the empty promises

of the councillor', the TCC coordinated a march to the local municipality office, to present a memorandum of demands. Although this
march was peaceful, the unwillingness of any functionary to accept
the memorandum inflamed the crowd, who set up a blockade across
a major regional road – 'so that the Mayor of Johannesburg Amos
Masondo can come address their grievances'.[41] There are reports of
clashes between the protestors and the police as the blockade developed and, overnight, the police reportedly fired rubber bullets to
forcibly disperse the gathered crowd.

Despite this, the protest resumed the next day. In the morning,
the community engaged with officials from the housing department.
These officials promised to return in the afternoon but did not do so.
When the community regrouped in the afternoon, the police were
ready for them, and seemed to be unwilling to countenance the continued protest: 'when the community gathered . . . the South African
Police Services together with the Johannesburg Metropolitan Police
Department opened fire to the community as they didn't want to disperse from the road'. Unsurprisingly, once fired upon, the protesters
scattered. The police followed them into the settlement and, over the
next hours, arrested seventeen people – many of whom seem to have
had no relationship with the protest or the TCC as an organising body
at all. They appear – from accounts of their court hearings, a month
later – to have been selected at random, by chance.[42]

In 2011, a similar sequence of events saw the escalation of an
unplanned gathering into a violent confrontation, and – again – the
random arrest of residents. In this case, however, another arrest followed: a local organiser, Bhayi Bhayi ('Bhaiza') Miya, days after the
violence had died down.

Once again, the community's call for the settlement to be properly
electrified came up against the continuing reluctance of the City of
Johannesburg to accept Thembelihle's permanence. This struggle had
spilled over into electoral politics – in which Bhaiza Miya had stood as
a candidate, against the local ANC.[43] He lost, and the ANC carried the
ward comfortably. However relations between the TCC and the representatives of the local state continued to be tense. According to an

activist, quoted after the fact, the community had 'lost confidence in the petitions committee, the City structures, Region G administration and the Office of the Speaker, amongst others'.[44] It was against this backdrop that several weeks of discontent erupted into a protest on 5 September.

The TCC did not apply for permission to gather. Nor was their gathering peaceful. The community blockaded the main roads into the settlement. They threw stones at police vehicles and passing motorists. At least some participants in the crowd were caught up in more destructive activity, vandalising electricity sub-stations in Lenasia.[45] The police arrested and detained several people. According to police statements, up to 1,500 people were involved in the protest on the first day – and a similar number on the second: 'the violence continued over to the 6th of September 2011 with the situation persisting in its previous form', in the words of the police.[46]

On these days, at least some members of the TCC sought to calm the crowd, and to discourage their violence. In at least one case, Bhaiza Miya actively assisted the police in containing the violence: after meeting with police officers on the ground, Miya 'agreed that he will call for the protest action to subside on condition that the police hold back on firing rubber bullets. On [his] command . . . the violence and protest almost ceased to exist.'[47] After this, direct confrontations between the police and community appear to have declined in both frequency and intensity.

Meanwhile, the protests continued. On the second day, the TCC told the police that they intended to march to the local Magistrates' Court, apparently to protest the earlier arrests. According to the police: 'It should be noted that from the onset the leaders of the group had requested an escort in order to enable them to march . . . This request was refused on the basis that prior arrangement for permission had to be obtained.' Despite the police's refusal to countenance the march, about fifty protestors nonetheless gathered on Wednesday. At this point, 'the protesters were informed of the illegality of the gathering' and more of them were arrested.

In the week that followed, an intensified police presence seemed to contain the situation. Although protests continued, the violent clashes of the first two days – in which property was damaged, stones thrown at the police, and rubber bullets fired at the crowd – were not repeated. Protests spread to other parts of the greater Gauteng region, and Thembelihle began to settle.

But as part of this process of policing, on 13 September – a week after the main protests – Bhaiza Miya was arrested on charges of public violence and intimidation. The state opened two cases against members of the community. The first of these was *The State vs Nkosi and thirteen others*, in which a seemingly random assortment of Thembelihle residents (including Miya) were accused of participating in an illegal gathering, acting violently, being in possession of ammunition and/ or dangerous weapons, causing malicious damage to property, and inflicting acts of grievous bodily harm.[48] The second was *The State vs Bhayi Bhayi Miya*, in which Miya himself was accused of public violence and intimidation – acts arising out of an encounter with the ward councillor in late August, in which the councillor's person and home were allegedly threatened with violence.[49]

The most striking element of these accounts lies in their ends: regardless of whether the protest was actually violent, or not, and regardless of whether the accused person or persons were in fact identifiably guilty of any offence, each of these three protests ended with the arrests of either bystanders or activists. In each case, too, the arrested men and women were accused of an assortment of crimes – always including 'public violence'. None of these crimes arises from the Regulation of Gatherings Act: instead, they are either common law offences, developed over centuries of jurisprudence in Europe and South Africa, or they arise from other statutory frames.

In each of these cases, the charges have been proven baseless. Once a lawyer had been obtained for the seventeen residents of Thembelihle in 2007, the state dropped all charges. In 2012, the state consolidated its case against Miya with that against the thirteen other residents – and, after nine postponements, was forced to abandon its case when it could offer the court no evidence that any of the accused had been involved in any identifiable acts of violence. Indeed, of these three examples, only the case against Bandile Mdalose reached trial – and this, too, collapsed at the end of the state's case, after it failed to prove any connection between her and the charges.

But the police have also regularly deployed delaying tactics to ensure that the validity of these charges is not immediately established. For example, in 2007, the seventeen residents of Thembelihle had to wait seven days before bail was determined; the police then applied for a series of week-long postponements, to gather evidence, before lawyers for the residents were able to force a hearing on the merits of the charges.[50] In 2011, Bhaiza Miya was detained for three days before his bail hearing; the case was then postponed three times, each time because the state sought to gather evidence to support its case. It took almost a month before the Magistrates' Court finally decided to refuse him bail – and then another three weeks before the High Court overturned this decision, and ordered his release. All told, Miya spent seven weeks in detention.[51] And in 2013, Bandile Mdalose was detained in prison before she, too, was finally granted bail – at a hearing a week after her arrest.[52] Regardless of the validity or plausibility of the charges, simply by arresting these activists the police succeeded in removing them from society. Their attempts at political expression earned them the stigma of criminality, and time in prison.

And this practice is not confined to arresting activists in the heat of the moment. Nor is it confined to a handful of police stations. The practice is widespread, and accepted throughout the state.

In Makause, in the aftermath of the confrontation between General Moyo and the commander of the Primrose police station, officers were sent into the settlement. They found Moyo addressing a crowd and, under instructions from their commander, arrested him and two others for failing to have 'a letter that authorised them to march'. This is not an offence under the Gatherings Act. The arresting officer added that the arrest was peaceful because 'only stun grenades were used to effect the arrest'.[53] They were then detained overnight in the Primrose police station's holding cells, until bail was agreed. Between October 2012 and June 2013, the case was postponed seven times – as the accused's lawyers sought to force the state to clarify their charges and the police claimed that they needed more time to gather evidence. Eventually, the charges against the two other activists were dropped, and Moyo was accused of intimidating the station commander. References to the original arrest have been dropped from the case, no doubt because it was improperly made. Regardless, two years after the event, Moyo is still wrapped up in litigation.

In Marikana, in the days after the massacre, this use of the criminal justice system to enforce a social and political order reached an absurd apogee. Approximately 250 of the striking miners were arrested by the police, and charged by the National Prosecuting Agency with the murder of their colleagues.[54] According to statements issued by the National Prosecuting Agency in the press: 'In a situation where there are suspects that confront members of the South African Police and a shooting takes place resulting in the fatalities of either SAPS or the suspects . . . those who got arrested, irrespective of whether they shot police members or the police shot them, are charged with murder'.[55] This is an entirely novel claim, and seems to have no basis in South African law.[56] Regardless, although the charges have not been aggressively pursued since the start of the Farlam Commission, they remained in abeyance for more than two years – and were only abandoned in August 2014.

In a recent article, Jane Duncan has argued that the politicisation of the criminal justice system represented by these practices is creating a parallel 'criminal injustice system' – a system in which the law is exposed as 'the repressive apparatus of the ruling political class'.[57] The term carries a powerful charge. It captures the visceral sense that there is something deeply inappropriate about the actions of the police and the state's prosecutorial services in these cases – that they are acting beyond their proper remit, and in so doing are distorting the functioning of the legitimate order.

There is some truth to this idea, although it should not be overstated.

The framework established by the Regulation of Gatherings Act is founded on a disciplinary assumption – that citizens should be encouraged to control and constrain their own acts of political expression. This framework is one in which it is understood that 'the permitted crowd is not an irrational and violent beast, the ultimate folk devil which must be eliminated' and nor is it 'dictated by a primitive unconscious . . . driven by irrational urges.'[58] It is founded on a belief in the rationality and reasonableness of South African citizens – even if it also encodes a suspicion of disruption.

The 'criminal injustice system', by contrast, abandons this faith in the reasoning capacity of South African citizens, and abandons any formal attempt to encourage the development of disciplined restraint in political expression. Instead, it recapitulates archaic notions of the irrationality and violence of crowds – and is founded on a rejection of the legitimacy of disruptive political actions.

The initial impulse behind the regulatory framework, as proposed by the expert committee of the Goldstone Commission, was to recognise an intrinsic relationship between acts of protest and acts of political expression. As such, the committee's recommendations sought to entrench processes which would enable these acts while minimising the possibilities of violence occurring in them – while also recognising that the police, as well as protestors, could easily be the source of such potential violence. These efforts, though, were abandoned in the final version of the Regulation of Gatherings Act, which entrenched an official suspicion of protest – and a scepticism about its usefulness as a form of political expression. It also entrenched a distrust of protestors, and their motives. As a consequence of this, the Act adopted a restrictive approach to protest – seeking to discipline protestors into appropriate behaviour, and to empower the police to support this. Such powers are more than sufficient to contain the disruptive potential of insurgent political expression; but in the years since the adoption of the Act, even this regime has been repeatedly disregarded by the police and the prosecutorial system. They have abused and exceeded their powers, as defined by the Act. In doing so, they have adopted a practice of political repression.

In South Africa, the disciplinary system is the state's ideal – but the repressive system too often its reality.

FIVE

Political Ambiguities

No law, judge or police protected us. Instead of being protected by the South African Police Services they chose to protect the municipality and support the African National Congress . . . When I was arrested . . . it was a way to silence me and others who were protesting against the murder of Nqobile Nzuza. No one has been arrested for the murder . . . When I was in Cato Crest police station I was isolated from other women prisoners because it was said I will corrupt their minds. Basically they feared that I would open their minds into reality. I was kept in a cell with no water. It was smelling and had dirty blankets. They kept bringing in food which I did not eat because I suspected that it might be poisoned to finish me off. . . .[1]

Bandile Mdalose was arrested in Cato Crest on Monday 30 September. She was held in detention, awaiting a bail hearing, in Durban's Westville prison for a week – until her release, on bail, the next Monday. That Wednesday, she published this account of her detention.

In her experience, the police had no interest in ensuring that the spontaneous gathering in Cato Crest was peaceful; they were only interested in ending it, and in ending any political disruption that it might cause – and thus securing established political power brokers in the area. The Magistrates' Court was not willing to look beneath the police's statements, and adopted them at face value, remanding her to prison for a week on their flimsy assurances. In the light of this experience, the state's adoption of an ideal of discipline – of engaging with citizens to encourage responsible and peaceful forms of public political expression, whether through providing alternative venues for participation to encouraging self-discipline in large crowds – seemed to be nothing other than a mask, adopted to hide the true reality of state repression.

She is not alone in this belief.

The experiences of Abahlali baseMjondolo, the Makause Community Development Forum, the Thembelihle Crisis Committee (TCC), and the miners at Marikana all testify to the undeniable significance of repressive action in recent years – and suggest that in the dynamic between expression and repression, it is repression that is currently dominant. In South Africa, acts of political expression are fraught with risk. But this does not mean that they are abandoned.

Instead, in the face of these repressive tactics, activists and communities are forced into finding new ways to exert their rights to protest and political expression. In the short term, this often means that they must find ways to defend themselves against criminal charges in the aftermath of a suppressed protest. In the medium term, they may forge alliances and create structures that entrench their activities either within a community or in broader civil society. They may also find themselves in uncomfortable alliances with structures that seek to discipline them. And in the longer term – for those groups or organisations that survive and grow – they may begin to think about intervening in the arena of formal politics – in the arena of elections and elected representatives. In each of these phases of political action, activists and community groups may have to make compromises – and, indeed, may also run the risk of having their energies and experiences co-opted by other interests. And yet: if they refrain from making any compromises they are liable to face the repressive forces of the state without external support or protection.

An ambiguous politics of ensuring political expression thus comes to the fore. This chapter traces the development of these ambiguities through three potential moments of action – securing legal support in the aftermath of police repression, experimenting with alternative forms of expression, and attempts to intervene in the formal political arena. In each of these moments, proponents of disruptive forms of politics are forced to engage with potentially disciplinary institutions and structures. In doing so, they run the risk that cooperation and compromise might slide into co-option – as well as the risk that, in attempting to resist repression, they might embrace alternative forms of discipline and, in so doing, sap the disruptive potential of their political actions to date.

Securing legal support

The first of these moments occurs in the immediate aftermath of protest – as activists, participants, and sometimes random bystanders are arrested, detained, and hauled into a Magistrates' Court.

In these circumstances, an immediate priority for any arrested person is to secure some form of defensive legal support. This is not always straightforward. Although the South African constitution guarantees a right to legal representation, accessing this right can be a complex matter. In a document outlining events in Thembelihle in the aftermath of the 2007 protests, Silumko Radebe, an Anti-Privatisation Forum (APF) activist, described the 'appearance of the Thembelihle 17 at the Protea magistrate court' in August. The accused activists did not have legal representation because 'the community members are poor and they can't afford to acquire the services of a private lawyer'. Private legal support was considered because 'the pro-bono lawyers who have worked for the APF communities in the past failed to fully defend the accused in previous cases especially the Legal Aid lawyers'. Radebe was able to identify a reason for these failures: 'The matter is that these are political cases and the justice system in the country views them as criminal cases.'[2]

These comments sketch out the range of options available to arrested activists. In South Africa, as elsewhere, private legal representation is expensive and thus often practically inaccessible to members of poor communities, or their representatives. Indeed, in the words of one of South Africa's senior appellate judges, 'There can be no doubt that legal services are expensive and out of the reach of most people in South Africa.'[3] Although some communities have been able to raise the funds to secure private representation – or to convince independent practitioners or small firms to support them pro bono – most are forced to look for alternative forms of support.

A number of different institutions offer non-profit legal services, in part to redress the inequities that can result from the inaccessibility of legal representation and in part to fulfil the constitutional right to representation.[4] However, each of these institutions comes with potential complications. The largest of them – Legal Aid South Africa (LASA) – is funded by the state.[5] LASA imposes a means test on potential clients, and exercises a discretion on whether or not to represent any given client of community – leading, in some cases, to popular suspicion of the organisation's motives.[6] A wider range of legal support services are provided by university-linked law clinics (such as that at the University of the Witwatersrand) and non-governmental organisations (NGOs) such as Lawyers for Human Rights (LHR), the Centre for Applied Legal Studies (CALS), the Legal Resources Centre (LRC), Section 27, and the Socio-Economic Rights Institute of South Africa (SERI). All of these NGOs have a primary focus on developing strategic 'impact' litigation, but most aim to offer some support in response to immediate crises – depending on the NGO's own focus. None, however, can respond to all crises – and so triage is an unavoidable element in their engagement with communities.

Whether they turn to state-funded legal aid (LASA) or to the various donor-funded NGOs, protesting communities are then required to engage with the expectations of the institution.

These are not always clear. In the case of LASA, for example, the details of their means test are clearly explained on their website; their discretion to take or refuse cases, however, is only mentioned in a handful of phrases – 'if you qualify for legal aid, and *we have agreed to represent you*'; 'Legal Aid South Africa tries to help *as many people as possible*';

and, 'if you are refused legal aid but still feel you deserve it'.[7] In their lengthy Legal Aid Guide, the normal operation of LASA's discretion is revealed: if a practitioner decides that 'there is little or no prospect of success and enforcement on a balance of probabilities [then] legal aid will be refused'. In addition, LASA is entitled to withdraw previously tendered representation 'on the grounds the NOE [National Operations Executive] deems appropriate'.[8] These discretionary powers are exactly that, discretionary, and need not be used; but because they exist, they shape the expectations held by those who can exercise them. In the context of defending members of a community against charges of public violence – incurred in the course of protests that, inarguably, involved violence, such as those in Thembelihle in 2007 and 2011 – what would count as reasonable 'prospects of success'? It is disturbingly easy to imagine an overworked junior practitioner recommending that an amorphous group of defendants plead guilty, and avoid a complex, long-winded, and expensive trial – as it appears happened in Thembelihle, in at least one case prior to the 2007 protest and arrests, during which legal aid lawyers 'requested the accused to admit to guilt even if they were not part of the protests that are viewed by the community as justifiable'.[9]

In the case of litigating NGOs, the expectations differ from organisation to organisation. Some organisations may be focussed on litigating particular kinds of cases – such as the Aids Law Project's emphasis on cases involving HIV and the rights to health, and its successor organisation's, Section 27's, focus on a cluster of similar socio-economic rights. Others have explicitly adopted broader remits – LHR and the LRC have multiple offices across the country, and litigate many different kinds of cases. Although there are exceptions, it is also notable that relatively few of these litigating NGOs take on criminal cases with any regularity. (Indeed, the vast majority of criminal cases are in fact taken on by LASA – and constitute approximately 93% of the organisation's work.[10]) Most of the cases mentioned in the preceding chapters have been litigated by a small number of NGOs – including SERI, which takes cases that engage with issues of access to 'political space' and represents communities and activists in the most recent cases in Makause, Cato

Crest, and Thembelihle, CALS (which is based at the University of the Witwatersrand) and LHR's Strategic Litigation Unit – which represented the seventeen accused in Thembelihle in 2007.

However, the LHR unit's name indicates one further set of expectations held by these litigation NGOS – all of these organisations also focus their efforts on strategic litigation, that is, on cases that are likely to establish significant precedents and have a sweeping impact on many different communities. Although most provide some emergency services, communities that seek to muster support from NGOs do face the expectations that their cases should raise generalisable legal issues. In general terms, this means that arrested men and women facing criminal charges must be able to argue that these charges are related to explicitly political events – and even that a challenge to the charges they face could have an impact on other communities facing similar charges. In some of the cases already considered, this has happened: the arrest of General Moyo, in Makause, has led to a challenge to the constitutionality of the relevant provisions of the Intimidation Act, while the debates arising out of Bhaiza Miya's arrest, in Thembelihle in 2012, concerned the standards of evidence required to refuse bail to activists arrested during protests.

Communities may also face the expectation that they will be suitable litigants – in other words, that nothing in their conduct will distract the court from the legal substance of their case, and their representatives will be sufficiently empowered to interact with the legal representatives. This is not unusual, and is often invoked in discussions of strategic and impact litigation across the globe – more often than not, in the context of somewhat bemused comments on the inevitable imperfections of the litigants at the centre of ground-breaking legal cases.[11] Nonetheless, at least some legal commentators continue to emphasise the image of an ideal (and, no doubt, unrealistically idealised) client community as a necessary part of the strategic litigation process.[12]

This needs to be explored a little, as the idea that NGOs seek a particular model of litigant has also been at the root of many activist critiques of the relationships that might develop between public-interest litigators and their clients. Some critiques focus on the potential influence of international funding agencies – and suggest that their global political and ideological priorities distort the activities of the recipients of their funding on the ground. Support is thus only offered to communities and causes that fit certain ideological criteria.[13] Other critiques suggest that the opaque structures, alien rules, and the jargon-ridden language of the courtroom can serve as a screen behind which legal practitioners act in their own interests. For proponents of this perspective, the egos and interests of legal practitioners may trump the needs of a core community.[14] Litigation may be extended beyond its usefulness, so as to burnish the reputation of the litigators and the litigating NGO. This may come at the cost of alternative forms of redress for the community – such as, in these cases, the abandonment of the charges by the state, or the proffering of some other form of negotiated settlement; it may also lead to a growing sense of disempowerment within the community itself, as its struggles are co-opted by outside actors.[15]

It should be noted that critiques of the legal system do not only come from within an activist community, but are also made by legal practitioners. Stuart Wilson warns that a lawyer should guard against 'the over confidence of the intellectually able, but socially dislocated, elite practitioner who equates social change with "good jurisprudence".' He suggests that, instead, 'the law, rights and the institutions that enforce them . . . should be evaluated as partially developed and rather half-hearted gestures at regulating behaviour in more or less predictable ways in line with dimly perceived conceptions of the good'. Because of this, practitioners and litigants should be 'keenly aware of [litigation's] limitations and the social conditions necessary for its effective deployment'.[16] These practitioners may not accept the full range of critiques offered by outsiders, but are keenly aware of the limits of the law and its potential disciplinary effects on communities.

And yet, whatever the influence exerted upon communities may be, litigious strategies are often the only way of providing immediate and effective support in the face of the abuse of the criminal justice system by the police and some state prosecutors. Given this reality, the choice for many insurgent citizens and their communities is between arrest and detention, on the one hand, and accepting the potential disciplinary effects of litigation, on the other. For most, there is no choice.

The ambiguities of engagement

In all of the cases surveyed so far, the deployment of legal support has ensured the eventual release of arrested activists and other citizens; it has provided some small space for the politics exposed in moments of disruptive protest to develop, and to confront the world outside of those moments. Some communities may continue to work with litigating NGOs to pursue their claims through the courts – whether these claims are for the immediate relief of a pressing crisis, or a challenge to the particular logic of local governance, or an assertion of a fundamental equality.

Others may seek to deploy different tools to protect their rights to express themselves and – sometimes – to extend their practices of expression into more formal and more regulated arenas. Notably, these tools can include ambiguous engagements with formal processes of participation – and, sometimes, a deployment of factional strife within the ruling party – to advance local issues. The struggles of a community in Rooigrond, an informal settlement outside Mahikeng in the North West province, about 220 kilometres to the west of Marikana, provide a crisp example of these ambiguous engagements. In this community, political struggles over the past decade have involved both disruptive protests and engagement with formal institutions of participation.

Disruptive protests came relatively late to Rooigrond, though. In July 2012, a protest on the R503 – a regional road that runs alongside the Rooigrond informal settlement – attracted the attention of the police. According to the community, the protest was met with police violence.[17] Almost two years later – in April 2014 – the same process repeated itself. Residents gathered on the same road, and barricaded it; the police arrived, fired rubber bullets into the crowd, and arrested fifty people. Their actions were identical to those taken elsewhere, as they appear to have rounded up a random selection of residents. In the words of one resident, told to the press: 'The police came to my home and I was not part of the protests, as I was doing my household chores, I saw them coming and I immediately ran away. One of them caught me and hit me with her gun on the forehead.'[18]

These events took place against the backdrop of a history of political engagement in Rooigrond. It is a semi-rural location primarily characterised by small farm holdings, on the outskirts of today's Mahikeng municipality. Other than farming, and some small-scale tourism, the economy appears to be dominated by the Rooigrond prison – once the property of the Bophuthatswana homeland government, and now administered by the post-apartheid state. Nowhere in South Africa, no matter how remote, seems to have been spared a turbulent political history. In the past, Rooigrond lay on the border between Bophuthatswana and apartheid South Africa. As such, the region was the base for a dissident Bophuthatswanan group, the Mafikeng Anti-Repression Forum, and the prison was the site of a significant strike by political prisoners in the early transition era.[19] This history of politics simmered in the background when, in 1993, a group of farmworkers were dismissed from their farms and founded an informal settlement on otherwise unworked land.

In the late 1990s, the status of the settlement was the subject of debates between the provincial departments of Agriculture and 'Developmental Local Government and Housing' and the local municipal council. Agriculture sought to convince the municipality to expropriate the land, and to formalise the settlement, while Developmental Local Government objected to its exclusion from the initial discussions, and registered its concern over the 'invasion of and squatting on' this land. In the early 2000s, the community began to pursue its cause through formal structures, including participating in the ward committee elections, and in IDP meetings – both of which are part of the state's broader efforts to entrench a discipline of participatory democracy. This participation had immediate effects, as a third of the community was connected to the national electrical grid in 2003, as part of the IDP process. In 2005, the community signed agreements with the provincial departments and the municipality in which the community was promised an in situ upgrade of the settlement and security of tenure in their current location.[20]

And then the participatory system stopped working.

In 2006, the municipality changed its approach. The agreement was withdrawn, and a new plan was announced – to remove and then resettle the community on neighbouring land. The land they were living on was apparently demarcated for a housing development and shopping centre. The settlement would no longer be serviced – no new electrical connections would be made, and other services were withdrawn. Even in the face of this, the Rooigrond community continued to attempt to use participatory mechanisms, petitioning the Premier of the province, officials in the national Presidency, and the provincial secretary of the African National Congress (ANC).[21]

Rather than abandon these institutions, activists within the community formed 'Operation Rooigrond' – a movement organised around mobilising social media attention to their complaints.[22] It also supported the candidacy of a local woman – Monametsi Moeti, the mother of the movement's key organiser – in the upcoming 2011 local government election. Moeti has been a member of the ANC since 1993, and ran for office as part of the governing party – and thus not, as some might have expected, as part of an opposition. It is possible to discern, in a brief comment given by Moeti to the media, the importance of ANC factionalism – in particular the ascendance of President Zuma, and his 'recognition of the rights of the rural poor' – in creating political space.[23] Moeti's candidacy was embraced by the local community, and she won the largest share of votes in the branch meeting. She was not unopposed, however – and her name was repeatedly removed from the ANC's party list, despite her inconvenient habit of winning elections. Eventually, the Independent Electoral Commission – the institution that oversees South Africa's elections – insisted that Moeti's nomination be respected, and she was allowed to stand as the party's candidate for the local ward. She won the election, gaining about 70% of the vote.[24]

It is important to recognise that these efforts to engage with the participatory systems of the state were at least intermittently successful: at first, involvement in the IDP brought electrification to the settlement; engagement with the provincial government brought a promise of tenure security; and in 2011, the community's candidate for ward councillor was elected – despite opposition within the governing party. But throughout this process, the rules on the ground kept changing: external interests appear to have trumped participatory processes in 2006, and led to the collapse of the earlier agreements. Another challenge emerged immediately following Moeti's election: according to local activists, she was sidelined from council decision-making processes.

It was at this point that the community resorted to disruptive protest – gathering on the road to protest their exclusion from these processes. But this use of disruption did not lead to the abandonment of participatory and formal methods of engagement: in the weeks and months immediately following the protest, the community continued to engage with the local municipality and the provincial government. Operation Rooigrond, Moeti, and the community's activists were able to both mobilise support from outside the local political system – including SERI's legal support, and the support of other NGOs such as the Local Government Action network – and, at the same time, to activate the internal structures of the state, through their embedded supporters.

And at first, this mixed approach bore results. Representatives of the municipality and the province met with the community; the planned relocation of the community was publicly rescinded; contractors were appointed to install water pumps in the settlement, and thus to enable the resumption of the provision of services to Rooigrond. And then – once again – the system ground to a halt; nothing happened in 2013 – and in 2014, violence erupted again. The protests of March – and the arrests of community residents – were followed by increased conflict. According to a brief note compiled by SERI, Moeti was 'forced to flee the settlement after a mob from outside Rooigrond burnt down her house under the guise of a service delivery protest'. This targeted violence – SERI suggests – appears to stem 'from political battles for positions in the municipality ahead of the upcoming local government election in 2016'.[25]

The story of political expression, contestation, and engagement in Rooigrond over the past decade and a half is an ambiguous one:

despite the several gains made by the community over the years, more often than not, their political claims have been expressed through the prism of existing institutional engagements. This has limited the effect of those gains won through participation. The provision of services – notably, the electrification of part of the settlement – was achieved through the IDP process, and was constrained by these processes. When community engagement stopped, so too did the services. When it resumed, services were once again promised. All victories were thus provisional – and retractable. Likewise, the disruptions of protest and contestation were rapidly abandoned in favour of resuming engagement, which again brought with it temporary relief before, shortly afterwards, falling back into disrepair.

And yet, this should not obscure the fact that fifteen years after the first engagements, and almost ten years since the municipality took a decision to evict and relocate the community, the Rooigrond informal settlement remains in place. The processes of engagement have staved off attacks. The use of social media has presented an image of the community to a wider public. Even though it does not follow that these efforts actually created or entrenched a shared identity, the representation allowed activists within Rooigrond to mobilise networks of support. These have embedded the local struggles of the settlement within a national politics.

All of this suggests that a decision to engage in formal structures of politics – whether these be those of participatory governance, or of elected representation – is one of several strategies available to communities. As Miraftab and others have argued, strategies of formal engagement can coexist with strategies of confrontation and protest – of informal political action, outside of invited spaces. Nonetheless, that coexistence does not come easily. Nor does it come without a price. For activists in Rooigrond, the victories won through protest have not been built upon by victories won through participation; rather, protest has been used to try to claw back victories initially won through the system, and then withdrawn – sometimes mysteriously – without consultation. Each is an ambiguous and incomplete victory, contingent on external factors.

Contesting elections

Meanwhile, the activists of Operation Rooigrond are not unique in their attempts to engage with formal electoral politics. At several points in the past decade, community organisations and social movements have mobilised around elections – sometimes by organising boycotts, sometimes by supporting particular parties, and sometimes by forming their own alliances, and contesting the election as an independent opposition force. In each case, different consequences followed attempts to conform to the norms of the electoral politics.

In Johannesburg, the Operation Khanyisa Movement (OKM) has provided some activists and dissenting communities with an example of the latter – a new electoral alliance. The initial 'Operation Khanyisa' began as a challenge to electricity disconnections in Johannesburg in the early 2000s; activists associated with the initial campaign assisted communities to reconnect their electricity – sometimes legally, sometimes not – and launched campaigns in collaboration with the Soweto Electricity Crisis Committee and the Anti-Privatisation Forum, amongst others, to challenge the politics around the commodification of electricity. In 2006, a core of activists associated with original campaigns launched the OKM as a means of intervening in the electoral arena.[26] In that year, the OKM contested the local government elections. It did not achieve a significant showing: in ten contested wards, the OKM candidate received no more than 4% of the vote. Across all 109 wards in Johannesburg, the OKM received 0.45% of the votes directed towards proportional representation candidates (a category that, in South Africa's local government elections, sits alongside the constituency-linked ward candidates).[27] This was enough for one proportional representation candidate to be elected to office – thus saving the OKM from electoral failure.

Despite this unimpressive showing, the OKM once again contested the next local government elections, held in 2011. In Thembelihle, Baiza Miya stood for election as ward councillor against the local ANC candidate – as he had done, five years earlier, in the previous local government election. His showing, this time, was no more impressive than before: as a ward candidate, Miya received 6.46% of the local vote

(450 votes out of 7155) – enough to make him the third most popular candidate, after the representatives of the ANC and the Democratic Alliance.[28] His candidacy, however, did raise the profile of the TCC within the broader community, as posters with his photograph and the words 'Vote for our Miya' were distributed in Thembelihle. Miya was thus also able to stand for – and be elected to – the ward committee, early in 2012.[29] A similar number of votes went to support the OKM in the proportional representation section of the ballot, contributing to the re-election of the sitting OKM councillor in Johannesburg city.

In a press statement, explaining its decision to contest the 2011 elections within the OKM, the TCC set out what it considered to have been achieved by the election. The first achievement was one of access to information: 'the experience . . . quickly exposed the TCC members to where and how exactly decisions were made about our lives and basic services'. The second was the disruption of the sensible: 'we used our only seat . . . to bring a socialist voice into the bourgeois chamber and this obviously frequently resulted in business being "unusual" to the bourgeois councillors'. And the third was control: 'mere trust in an individual is not enough in politics, we certainly need some degree of control mechanism on those we give the responsibility to lead'.[30]

The last of these points highlighted the difficulties that emerge when community movements elect representatives, and send them to the city council chambers on their behalf. There is an obvious risk that these representatives may become disconnected from their community base, and become part of the system that they have been elected to challenge. From the perspective of the OKM, this risk became a reality very early in the aftermath of the 2006 election. A year later, the movement's one elected councillor was suspected of planning to cross the floor – to leave the OKM and join the Democratic Alliance, eliminating the OKM's presence in the council chamber. The movement recalled this councillor, and replaced her with another – more loyal – candidate.[31]

The compromised position of its sole elected representative was the most dramatic example of the dissension caused by the foray into electoral politics within the OKM, but it was not the only such sign. In the five years between the two elections – that is, between 2006 and 2011 – the original coalition of social movements and community organisations dissolved. At the heart of this dissolution was the suspension of the APF – which ceased to operate in 2010. The end of the APF came for a variety of reasons, including, in the words of one of its most prominent activists, the 'egoism of leadership, often lax individual and organisational accountability and a failure to confront unequal gender relations as well as the link between macro-nationalist discourse and xenophobic attitudes/practices'.[32] It coincided with a lengthy debate within the movement over the legitimacy of electoral politics, and over the relationship between the various community organisations across Johannesburg, the movement itself, and the practices of representation and representative politics.[33] Although there is no reason to draw a direct connection between these debates and the shuttering of the movement, the consequence for the OKM was a visible decline in membership. Of the nine APF-affiliated community organisations that participated in the 2006 campaign, only two remained in 2011: the Soweto Electricity Crisis Committee and the TCC. Without the support of the APF – limited and contingent as it was, even at its height – the organised membership of the OKM soon fell away.

These experiences point to the difficulties faced by communities attempting to launch themselves into the electoral arena: political parties require coordination and discipline. Elected representatives need to be held accountable – and structures need to be created to ensure this. Communication between representatives and communities can no longer be ensured through personal contact, but must also be institutionalised and regularised. All of this may serve to strain or even sever the links between representatives and communities, and to unsettle political loyalties.

In this context, many movements have either considered removing themselves from the electoral arena, or considered endorsing an existing party in the hope that it will represent their interests. Operation Rooigrond's use of the existing ANC structures provides an example of the latter. And some movements have done both, at different times. One example is Abahlali baseMjondolo – the national shack-dwellers' movement, founded in Durban in the mid-2000s. For most of its existence,

Abahlali boycotted elections. Starting during the 2006 local government elections – those contested in Johannesburg by the OKM – Abahlali
organised a boycott under the slogan 'No land! No house! No vote!'
The campaign was controversial in Durban, giving rise to police harassment of the movement, the prohibition of planned protest marches, and
violence.[34] In the months afterwards, Abahlali continued to attract the
repressive attention of the local state: in September, for example, three
activists, including its president, S'bu Zikode, were arrested on their way
to a radio interview. In response to the gathering convened to protest this
arrest, the police opened fire on the protestors with tear gas, rubber bullets, and then live ammunition.[35]

Despite this harassment, Abahlali decided to continue this campaign
three years later, in the national and provincial elections of 2009.[36]
Once again, Abahlali challenged the representativity of the system,
the effectiveness of electoral politics, and the perceived disconnection
between an elected political elite and the struggles of communities on
the ground. In a documentary filmed during 2009, activists allowed
themselves to be shown writing the campaign slogan 'No land! No
house! No vote!' across the length of the national ballot paper.[37] Once
again, the public attention that accompanied this campaign attracted
baleful political attention. In September 2009, the Kennedy Road
informal settlement – the base of Abahlali's leadership in Durban –
was attacked, members of the community assaulted, and Abahlali
activists driven out of their homes. The police were present during
this attack, and stood by without intervening.[38] Afterwards, the police
arrested twelve members of Abahlali and charged them with murder
and assault. Three years later, their case finally came to trial – and was
dismissed before the defence could lead witnesses, as the police could
offer no evidence linking any of the accused to the charges.[39]

In the period surrounding the assault on Kennedy Road, Abahlali
scrambled to survive and to regroup. There have been debates over
possible shifts in internal structures and democratic accountability
during this time. Among these shifts was the formation of a second
organisational centre in the Western Cape in 2008. Both centres – in

Durban and in the Cape – continued to support the electoral boycott campaign in 2011, arguing in the run-up to the election that:

> We are not fooled by party politics. We are very well aware that party politics is a battle between different factions of the elite. We know very well that the ANC engages in unlawful and criminal evictions . . . [and] has backed violent attacks on our comrades in Durban and the blatant demolition of their homes by party thugs. We remain determined to reject party politics and to build the power of the poor from the ground up.[40]

And then, on 1 May 2014 – a week before the national and provincial elections – Abahlali in Durban announced that they would lend their support to the opposition Democratic Alliance in the KwaZulu-Natal provincial contest. Given Abahlali's long-standing commitment to an extended boycott of the electoral system, the announcement came as a surprise to many of the movement's sympathisers and supporters.[41] And although it came as less of a surprise to activists within the movement, it was an immediate source of tension and conflict between them, shaking Abahlali.

The decision was not, however, taken suddenly or lightly. A year before these elections, at a public meeting held on 20 July 2013, S'bu Zikode asked the membership of Abahlali to discuss whether their electoral boycott should be continued, or abandoned. In a brief account of this meeting, Abahlali noted that 'diverse politically charged views' were expressed without resolution. On the one hand, one member is recorded as having said that 'we vote for people who then come back and kill us. We have a preference of withholding our votes rather than wasting them'; on the other, 'some were obstinate that Abahlali should vote but only by forming an alliance'. The account concludes by emphasising that the boycott had encouraged 'support by many other organisations such as the Western Cape Anti-Eviction Campaign, some in the Landless People's Movement, Mandela Park Backyarders' while 'conversely, this battle has received a lot of disapproval from many government bodies including President Jacob Zuma himself'.[42]

In the first months of the election year, these discussions continued, and on 23 April 2014 Abahlali sent out an invitation to 'all political parties except the ANC', asking them to engage on a series of political questions of urgent interest to the movement and its members. If a party could engage with these questions, then the movement would 'be willing to make a tactical vote against the ANC' and for another party. The first of these questions explains why the movement felt that this new departure was justified: 'Can you guarantee that you will actively and seriously oppose all forms of state repression and that you will support our right to organise independently. . . . ?'[43]

Apparently, only the Democratic Alliance in KwaZulu-Natal responded with any enthusiasm to this invitation, and – despite a great deal of uncertainty about supporting the Democratic Alliance, occasioned in part by its governance of the Western Cape province – Abahlali's leadership decided to lend the party its support. At a meeting of branch representatives, a vote was taken to support this decision – by a majority, if not all, of the delegates present. In an interview given after the decision, Zikode explained that this decision was made in a context of relentless state repression. He emphasised that it was a tactical decision, tied to specific promises, and that it involved 'suspend[ing] ideology for a clear goal: weaken the ANC, guarantee the security and protection of the shack dwellers'.[44]

In the immediate aftermath of the decision, though, Abahlali's message was lost. On the day of the announcement, the movement's website went down – stripping it of its broader presence on social media. The Democratic Alliance issued a press release, which arguably over-stated the extent of Abahlali's commitment. This was on a Friday. The weekend brought with it a hiatus in communications, and the website did not come back online until after the election. These contingent factors contributed to an atmosphere of confusion and mistrust, in which distorted accounts of the agreement circulated at high speed through South Africa's social media. Disbelief soured into a sense of betrayal – and many activists outside of the movement withdrew their support from it, suggesting that Abahlali had either been fooled into accepting a disadvantageous compromise, or that they had chosen to be co-opted by the party in return for vague and unspecified advantages. In the absence of denials or clarification, rumours spread.

Then, in the weeks after the election, the decision became part of a dispute between several of Abahlali's leaders. Bandile Mdalose left the movement, or was expelled, in a cloud of dissension. She accused Zikode and other leaders of excluding her from decision-making processes; she suggested that the reorganisations of the movement in the past years had centralised power – and that although she had come up from the ranks of Abahlali in those years, she was treated as an outsider. She claimed that dissent was being smothered. She hinted, too, that outsider intellectuals, lawyers, and gatekeepers were influencing the movement's decisions.[45] Similar allegations have plagued Abahlali since its beginnings. Often, these have slipped into a discourse in which one set of activists accuses another set of activists of either having or seeking to have an inappropriate influence over the movement. The veracity of these allegations has been asserted by some scholars and activists, and challenged by others.[46] Few of these allegations have had any traction: most have faded with time, and Abahlali has continued to operate regardless. It may very well be that Bandile Mdalose's accusations will follow the same path. Her claims are contestable, and the truth of her description of Abahlali's internal politics undoubtedly partial. And yet, there is something significant about her claims. First, they come from within the movement. Regardless of the truth or falsity of any individual allegation, they gain plausibility from Bandile's past position. Second, they resonate with an idea that community-based movements may be tainted through interactions with more established institutions, and their energies co-opted to serve alien ends. Taken together, they serve to destabilise Abahlali, both internally and in the public gaze.

It is too early to say what the end result of Abahlali's decision to intervene in electoral politics will be. Likewise, it is hard to discern the effect of the OKM's limited success in local government elections on its constituent communities and organisations such as the TCC. But in both cases, the decision to contest elections – directly or indirectly, through supporting an established political party – has exposed tensions both within the movements, and between them and their allies. Any claims to ideological purity have been compromised, and pragmatism has taken their place: for the OKM, the ideal of direct communication and trust had to be discarded in favour of the institution of clear lines of command and control, and thus of internal disciplining processes. For Abahlali, the movement's ability to stand outside of the system and wield a moral authority has been compromised, while some of its civil society support has been withdrawn. Abahlali, too, faces the possibility that its message might be lost in the noise created by this act.

In each of these moments, movements and communities have entered into a relationship with other established interests in the hope of preserving and extending their ability to express their political opinions and beliefs. In the face of immediate state repression, many movements have allowed lawyers and legal NGOs to guide them through the courts. In the face of bureaucratic recalcitrance, activists have sought to both embark upon protests and engage with participatory structures – restricting their ability to fully commit to either strategy. And in the face of political exclusion and continuing repression, some community organisations and movements have attempted to enter into the hotly contested arena of formal politics, through directly contesting local elections or through supporting established parties in national and provincial elections.

These relationships have brought with them fresh complexities and ambiguities. In the first two cases, engagement with legal NGOs and with various branches of the state had provided communities with spaces within which political organisation can take place. They have also provided these communities with political victories – whether these be legal victories over attempts by local police forces to criminalise their political activities, or material concessions wrung from the state through its bureaucratic institutions. By contrast, electoral politics have yet to provide any significant victories: after two elections, the OKM has not grown its share of the vote and Abahlali's support made little or no discernible difference to the Democratic

Alliance's share of the provincial vote in KwaZulu-Natal in 2014. At the same time, regardless of victories won, the energies of each of these communities have been harnessed and potentially disciplined through their engagement with established entities. Lawyers exercise a strong influence over courtroom strategy, and litigant communities are encouraged to present their most respectable selves in court – with respectability being defined according to social norms often external to the community. Citizens who participate in state institutions must trim their claims to fit their expectations: claims for political recognition, for example, may be expressed through demands for electrification, tenure security, or informal settlement upgrading. And movements who seek electoral authority become bound by the rules of the game, restricted to official engagements.

This suggests that if communities and movements choose to intercede in a formal arena – whether of the law, of participation, or of elections – they are also implicitly choosing to harness the disruptive energies created by protest to one or another institution, or institutional framework. These institutions may be controlled by the community itself, lending structures of discipline and respectability to their previously unlicensed politics. They may also be controlled by other groups in civil society, such as legal NGOs, that lend their models of discipline to the community – harnessing their energies for an immediate end. And they may even be controlled by groups in 'political society' – such as parliamentary parties, external to the community – that can harness these communities and their politics to lend authenticity and authority to their claims to represent disadvantaged sectors of society. Whether communities harness their energies for the own purposes – or allow those energies to be harnessed towards other ends – to intercede in these arenas is to accept some model of discipline, and some model of respectability, for themselves.

When considering this, the context of the violent repression of disruptive forms of political expression cannot be overlooked. It is in the face of this repression that each of these communities and movements have chosen to adopt more or less restrictive forms of public discipline. This context has made these decisions urgent – and often necessary. Movements that might have chosen to remain independent, or to grow slowly, have been constrained to adopt defensive strategies and accept political compromises so as to preserve their ability to act.

Given this, it appears that one of the most effective ways for dissenting communities and movements to resist state repression is for them to turn their backs on the full disruptive potential of their political claims and to adopt one or another form of discipline. In doing so, they stake a claim to being part of a system of political respectability, and thus become defensible within it.

SIX

Making Politics from and
in the Courtroom

In the loosely Rancièrean account outlined earlier in this book, 'politics' occur when an action or a claim based on a presumption of equality disrupts a distribution of the sensible – that is, when an act exposes the contingency of a social and political order. In so doing, the limits of that order are exposed and new possibilities for action are revealed. There is no privileged site of politics: a disruption of the sensible can occur in the context of a public protest, during interactions in 'invited spaces of participation', or even within the imposing halls of a country's highest courts. Likewise, no site or form of action is inherently political – inherently disruptive – not even protest.

Of course, certain kinds of disruption are more visible in some sites than in others. The interruption of ordinary social routines in the course of a public protest by a poor community in South Africa disturbs that order in a particularly tangible way: blockades along highways make visible the physical displacement of the poor from bourgeois social space. A mass march into the centre of a city may highlight the private appropriation of public space. Confrontations between protestors and police show the limits of political legitimacy, and the consequences of exceeding them. And – in each of these cases – it is possible (although not inevitable) that the exposure of these exclusions would reveal their contingency, and thus undermine their claims to permanence. In the face of this, new possibilities may emerge – whether they be linked to the inclusion of the poor within the category of citizens who count, or whether they develop new ways of counting.

Similar political disruptions are perhaps less visible in other sites – and, indeed, other sites may appear to be less conducive to fostering political acts. One of these sites is that of the courtroom. This chapter considers the efforts of community organisations, social movements, and their legal interlocutors to forge a politics of equality – and thus of disruption – in South Africa's courts.

This is important because, as the past chapters have shown, the state's efforts to restrict and suppress acts of protest in public spaces have driven communities into different spaces of action, with a concomitant effect on their politics. As public spaces have become dangerous sites of political expression, communities and movements have placed themselves in ambiguous relations with formal institutions – not only with courts, but also with participatory structures and electoral contests. Many of these institutions seem designed to impose a particular public discipline on agents who seek to act through them: a discipline of social and political respectability, of deference to recognised and established authority, and of acquiescence to existing rules and procedures. In the context of these disciplinary pressures, dissenting communities have often had to adapt their politics to the institutions that have protected them from the most severe effects of violent repression; but in doing so, they also risk abandoning the disruptive heart of their politics.

This movement into ambiguously disciplined spaces does not, however, strip these communities of all agency – and nor can it entirely prevent their acts from disrupting the established order. These spaces constrain and discipline, but do not repress. Because politics can still occur in them, we need to understand how assertions of a presumed equality made in these spaces may still act to disrupt and unsettle a broader distribution of the sensible.

The courts provide an example of how politics premised on equality might develop in these spaces. In the previous chapter, dissenting communities were seen to enter the courtroom defensively – when targeted by the police and state prosecutors, and facing criminal charges. In these circumstances, the disciplinary pressures of the courts are obvious – and, often, imposed upon communities as a condition of appearance. Presumptions of inequality are also pervasive: the language of the courts is specialised and technical, jargon-ridden and exclusive. It is not unusual for litigants – whether individuals, or communities – to complain that their experiences in the courtroom have been disempowering and alienating: that lawyers took on their cases, and then took over, or that both lawyers and judges did not hear them, and spoke over their heads.

This is often, unsurprisingly, the primary response of defendants hauled before the courts in the aftermath of a protest. But this is not the only way in which dissenting communities might enter the legal system: it is also possible for them to enter as agents, litigating their own interests, suing the state and other institutions. In these situations, the courts may be used as a tool of disruption – as a way of disturbing the existing relationship between state and citizens, and thus exposing this relationship as constructed, rather than natural, and contingent, rather than inevitable.

An assertion of equality made in this context thus illuminates the possibilities of politics occurring in these and other similar sites – and suggests that the entry into these ambiguously disciplinary spaces by dissenting communities need not foreclose these possibilities. The rules of the court may be used to disrupt the ordinary relationship between citizens and the state and – for a brief moment, at least – create a privileged space in which disruption is legitimised. This might be described as asserting equality from the courtroom. And even when communities are forced into the straitjacketed position of supplicant litigants, they may refuse this position and reshape the pronouncements of the court into a dialogue. This is an assertion of equality in the courtroom.

In the remainder of this chapter, I want to explore both forms of disruption – first, those that use the court as a staging post for a challenge to the established order, and second, those that treat the court as a stage, on which a claim to equality can be staged. Taken together, they present something of the multivalent possibilities of a politics of equality in post-apartheid South Africa.

'Public interest' litigation

The first of these approaches – the use of the courts as a staging post for broad political claims – bears a close relation to models of 'public interest litigation' developed in the USA, and elsewhere, in the second half of the twentieth century.[1] These derive from the possibilities created by the acceptance of a rights-based model of the law in most democratic societies after the Second World War.[2] The concept of inalienable human rights quietly reshaped the legal order, providing for the development of a wide set of interconnected legal and political claims founded on rights – including, for example, the claims made by African Americans in the USA to the exercise of their civil rights, including the right to participate freely in elections, and the more recent claims by gay and lesbian individuals to exercise a right to marriage.

Before continuing, it is important to recognise that different jurisdictions entrench different rights. Almost all democratic states entrench rights to citizenship, political participation, freedom of assembly, and freedom of speech. These are generally referred to as 'civil and political' rights. Others, including South Africa, also entrench a further set of socio-economic rights – to health, to education, to land and to housing, to water and food, and to social security. In South Africa, these rights are entrenched in the post-apartheid Constitution, and form the core of the new political order. In other jurisdictions, the status of these rights within the legal order may take more ambiguous forms – in the UK, for example, in the absence of a written Constitution, rights are litigated through international instruments, through statutes, or through a development of existing principles of common law; in the USA, some rights are entrenched in the Constitution and others developed through judicial decisions. Any generalisation about the kinds of politics that can be developed in these legal contexts must therefore be tempered by an awareness of local histories and experiences.

In South Africa, there is a clear distinction between public interest litigation in the apartheid era, and in the two decades since. Under apartheid, litigants and lawyers sought to use procedural protections to articulate political claims against the interests of the state; at the same time, of course, the state continued to use the courts as an instrument of social hegemony, and political repression. In Richard Abel's phrase, the law was 'politics by other means' – and litigation was a way of contesting politics by using a relatively privileged space to protect its participants. This was never entirely successful, and although battles were won and victories claimed, the apartheid state continued to dominate both politics and the law.[3] At the start of the post-apartheid period, however, the introduction of a new Constitution reshaped the possibilities of politics in the courts.[4] The entrenchment of a wide range of rights in the Bill of Rights has given individuals, communities, and activists a concomitantly wide range of tools with which to pursue rights claims.

In the past fifteen years, in particular, these claims have been the basis of many civil society efforts. In the early 2000s, for example, the Treatment Action Campaign (TAC) launched a series of cases, the most prominent of which aimed to compel the state to extend the provision of effective anti-retroviral medication to HIV-positive pregnant women.[5] The TAC case has been treated as a paradigmatic example of how post-apartheid politics can be pursued through the courts.[6] It is also a clear example of 'public interest litigation' – resonating closely with a set of international experiences. In this case, an organised social movement, the TAC, embarked upon a wide-ranging public campaign, aimed at altering public and official perceptions of, and responses to, HIV and AIDS in South Africa.[7] In the context of this campaign, the TAC focussed its attention on a challenge to the state's decision to restrict the provision of nevirapine – an anti-retroviral drug – to a small number of test sites, despite overwhelming scientific proof of its efficacy at preventing the transmission of HIV from pregnant mothers to their children. This decision was contested in the media and on the streets, and – simultaneously – in the courts, deploying the legal right to health.[8]

The court case was planned in conjunction with a specialist legal non-governmental organisation (NGO), the AIDS Law Project, based at the time at the Centre for Applied Legal Studies (CALS) at the University of the Witwatersrand. The case was narrowly framed, and sought simply to challenge an aspect of the government's policy rather than its entirety. The decision to focus on this particular aspect of the policy underpinning provision of anti-retroviral treatment was taken for strategic reasons, with key activists arguing that a victory on this relatively narrow issue would both provide immediate relief to a severely affected class of persons and, at the same time, widen the possibilities for future political action.[9] In court, this approach was rapidly vindicated. Both in the High Court and the Constitutional Court, the TAC's lawyers were able to persuade the bench of the validity of their argument – and in both arenas, the state's restrictive policy was ruled unconstitutional, irrational, and a violation of South Africans' right to health. The judgments were immediately hailed as political victories, as well as legal ones, and were used to press home the movement's broad campaigns. In the aftermath of the case, the TAC was able to effectively reshape the state's health care policy. It was thus able to use a strategy of focussed litigation to significantly extend its political reach.[10]

Of course, the TAC has not been alone in this strategic use of the courts.

In July 2006, activists affiliated with the Anti-Privatisation Forum (APF) launched a case, also in collaboration with CALS, challenging the implementation of the City of Johannesburg's Free Basic Water (FBW) policy. At the time, the APF was participating in a wide range of public activities – including supporting the electoral efforts of the Operation Khanyisa Movement – aimed at raising awareness of economic and social inequality in the state's semi-privatised provision of basic services. In this particular case, the court was asked to consider whether this FBW policy 'which limited FBW provision to six kilolitres of water per household per month regardless of household size . . .

was reasonable in terms of Section 27(1)(b) of the Constitution, which guarantees everyone's right of access to sufficient water'. In addition, and as a second leg of the legal argument, the court was also asked to consider 'whether the installation of pre-payment water meters as a means of delivering a residential water supply was legal'.[11] This case was thus more broadly framed than the TAC's case, four years earlier, but – like the TAC case – it also sought to develop (and, perhaps, leverage support for) an existing political struggle through the strategic deployment of a legal challenge to a representative element of the state's contested approach.

At first, it followed a similar trajectory. In 2008, the High Court ruled in favour of the applicants, as did the Supreme Court of Appeal, a year later. Both courts found that the City's limitation on the provision of free basic water was unreasonable, and that the figures it used to determine this limitation were inadequate – although each court weighed up the expert evidence differently, and proposed different replacement figures. They also supported the applicants' contentions that the decision to install pre-payment water meters had been taken without consultation, and was thus improper, as was the power to automatically cut off water supplied to a household without a hearing, or without any oversight.[12] Buoyed by these successes, both lawyers and activists anticipated success in the Constitutional Court, and the final confirmation of their legal victories.[13]

However, that hearing did not go as expected. The Constitutional Court reversed the decisions of the two lower courts, and held that the state's policy was sufficiently reasonable. In doing so, the Court essentially applied a different test of reasonableness – one that was weighted in favour of executive autonomy, and which discouraged courts from making specific policy injunctions on the basis of competing expert reports. The Court thus permitted the state to determine the appropriate provision of FBW, unaided by the courts; it said little about the installation of pre-payment water meters, but allowed the existing policy to remain in place.[14] Overall, the Constitutional Court's judgment was a significant defeat for the litigating community and the APF.

In each of these examples, a court case was launched by a social movement as part of a broad campaign of political expression. In both, this campaign sought to simultaneously raise public awareness and alter state policy through mass action, media campaigns, and strategic litigation. The ends of the two cases, however, were different: for the TAC, a victory, and for the APF, a defeat. For the TAC, the success of their court case catapulted their campaign into a new level: suddenly, their long struggles seemed to pay off. The state was ordered to expand its provision of anti-retroviral treatment from its test sites to the whole country – and, in doing so, was forced to reconsider and reconceptualise its approach to providing basic health services to HIV-positive South Africans. The success of the court case made their earlier struggles seem suddenly obsolete: public awareness had increased dramatically, and the state policy had been changed.

After the TAC case, legal activism founded on rights provided a new model of political action. The adoption of such a method by the APF, four years later, was only one of a wave of cases brought by movements and communities, including cases about evictions and electricity provision, brought by Abahlali baseMjondolo and other community movements.[15] Abahlali also brought a more explicitly political case to the court, in 2008 and 2009. In this case (*Abahlali baseMjondolo v. Premier of the Province of KwaZulu-Natal*), the movement challenged a piece of provincial legislation that purported to give the relevant Member of the Executive Council (MEC) the power to order mass evictions without court oversight.[16] This challenge was unusual in many ways, but most notably because it preceded the actual implementation of the Act: the movement anticipated the uses to which it might be put, and sought to have the courts declare that the Act could not possibly be interpreted or applied in a manner consistent with the Constitution and its Bill of Rights. Despite an early defeat in the High Court, Abahlali carried the argument in the Constitutional Court and assured the collapse of the Province's planned actions. These victories followed on from, and then developed, the success of the TAC's case, and seemed to confirm the viability of legal struggle.

However, the collapse of the APF's court case, after several years of struggle and success, soured these possibilities. The unexpected defeat seems likely to have contributed to the APF's malaise in the years immediately following, and to its demise shortly thereafter. More definitely, the cautious and deferential approach of the Constitutional Court undoubtedly acted to discourage many activists from pursuing legal strategies. According to Daria Roithmayr, in a response that captures much of this disillusionment with legal activism, the Court's decision in the water meters case demonstrated that it 'has now embraced cost recovery from the poor as consistent with the Constitution, and has adopted a neo-liberal baseline from which to measure the reasonableness of government action that infringes on socio-economic rights. As a result, rights-based litigation will likely be of limited use in dismantling persistent race and class inequality'. She suggests that, instead, activists should focus their attention on 'the commons' – which appears to be a new way of conceptualising a return to community activism. In sum, the failure of the APF's case 'might well have signalled the beginning of the end of whatever promise legal rights might have held'.[17]

Both these responses – the enthusiasm for legal activism in the early 2000s, and the disillusionment of the beginning of the next decade – are formulaic. The ardour with which legal activism was touted as a solution to the disconnection between citizens and state was excessive; so too is the current rejection of these tactics by many of the same activists and scholars. They are also naive. Both responses reflexively return to established traditions, and thus avoid engaging with either actual or potential legal politics. These politics are inevitably ambiguous and limited. And they offer neither a panacea nor a distraction. Indeed, as Scheingold argued, many decades ago:

> rights are no more than a political resource which can be deployed, primarily through litigation, to spark hopes and indignation. Rights can contribute to political activation and organization, thus planting and nurturing the seeds of mobilization . . . Mobilization thus emerges from this perspective as the strategy, litigation as a contributory tactic, and rights as a source of leverage.[18]

This insight has since been developed, most notably by Michael McCann, into a supple and powerful account of how communities and activists can engage with both the state and the broader public through the use of litigation. Law, according to McCann, is a 'social practice' – which means that law is not 'simply a set of abstract concepts informing our attitudes and practices' but is, instead, 'fundamentally . . . *constitutive* of practical interactions between citizens'. In other words, 'legal knowledge to some degree prefigures social activity; inherited legal conventions shape the very terms of citizen understanding, aspiration, and interaction with others'.[19] In this, McCann explicitly builds upon the work of E.P. Thompson, in *Whigs and Hunters*, on the role of law in shaping the ways in which class relations have been expressed, defended, and challenged.[20] The implication of these arguments is that law is not neatly separable from social or political mobilisation or action, but that it inevitably shapes them. (An example: the 'commons' suggested by Roithmayr as an alternative site for political action has been constituted historically through legal discourses of communal usufruct, and was limited and threatened in more recent times through the imposition of private property rights.[21] It is not a concept beyond the law, but rather one which is fundamentally shaped by the histories of legal discourse.)

This suggests that claims made in the language of the law – in terms of rights, on the one hand, and procedural rationality, on the other – can have a broader political effect. These claims use particular discourses to engage with the structures of an existing social and political order – and can, at times if not inevitably, expose these structures as the contingent product of a specific history. In the TAC's court case, the state's discourse of technical rationality was exposed by the court as the product of political decisions – and, in legal terms, irrational and unreasonable. In the APF's case, the fundamental logic of Johannesburg's FBW policy was examined and considered – and although the Constitutional Court eventually decided that the City was empowered and entitled to act in the way it had, nonetheless the discussions and debates in court revealed the processes through which this final policy had come to be developed and adopted. In neither case could the state present its policy as a simple *fait accompli*, incontestable and inevitable. In both, the policies were shown, inescapably, to be contingent on political will.

Contingency, equality and the law

The recognition of contingency returns us to Rancière's notion of 'politics' as a force of social disruption. For Rancière, a 'police order' is an unquestioned and unchallenged distribution of social identities, which then grounds a political system – thus, for example, a contemporary democracy in which citizens are assigned classes and identities within the social order, and then act in accordance with them. 'Politics' then only occurs when that distribution is disturbed: when a group of citizens cannot be assigned to an existing social identity, or when citizens of one class refuse to accept their position and act out of character, and out of place. (The example that Rancière gives is of workers, in nineteenth-century France, who refused to write as workers and insisted, in their publications, of acting as intellectuals, roaming over a wide social terrain and refusing to confine their interests to the world of their daily work.[22]) In extreme situations, groups of people who have not been recognised as citizens within a given distribution – women, people of colour, the poor – begin to act as if they were already citizens, capable of public action. In doing so, these different groups reveal the constructed and contingent nature of the social distribution: that the 'natural order' has been constructed, and need not remain unchanged.

One of the most exciting aspects of Rancière's account is that it does not presume one or another practice of politics: the contingent nature of an order can be made visible through rejectionist violence, or through more modest claims to social recognition, or through some other intervention. The conjectural nature of his approach – considering the possibility of political change by asking what might happen if a particular series of events developed, rather than prescribing a process that ought to be followed – encourages a flexibility of thought and analysis.

With this in mind, it seems possible to align this approach to politics with the approach adopted by McCann and others in their accounts of the value of legal discourses for political action. As these discourses help constitute social structures and practices, these accounts argue that courtroom-based challenges to those structures and practices resonate beyond the judicial realm. Even negative judgments can excite political change, by making sites of social stress newly visible. Using Rancière's concepts, we might then expand this to suggest that the processes of making these sites visible, through the use of the law, may also be capable of making their contingency apprehensible. Although it is unlikely that every legal challenge would disturb the ordinary operation of the social system, it is still possible to imagine that exerting pressure on key structures will destabilise them, and reveal both their fragility and their potential to change.

This is what has happened in the aftermath of many – although, again, not all – of the cases above. The TAC's victory exposed the political logic behind the avowedly technical decision taken to restrict anti-retroviral provision; in doing so, the judgment opened up the black box of the state, allowing a wide public to consider that all seemingly technical decisions might be equally contingent on specific political interests and pressures. Certainly, this consideration underpinned the APF's further challenge to the City of Johannesburg's FBW policy. At least part of this challenge presumed that the City's apparently unassailable technical decision-making processes were in fact either driven or distorted by partisan political pressures. As this challenge developed, the courts delved into the reasoning behind the specific decisions taken by the City – decisions to determine how much FBW should be provided per person; to determine how many people, on average, lived in a metered household; and to decide to install pre-payment water meters, with automated cut-offs, rather than standard-type meters in these specific households.

It is important to remember that both the High Court and the Supreme Court of Appeal ruled against the City of Johannesburg in this case – and that they did so for different reasons and in different ways. This may have resulted in a 'muddying [of] the waters' in terms of the law[23] – thus creating a confusion that may have enabled the Constitutional Court to step away from the particularities of the dispute – but it also served to emphasise the potential flexibility of these policies. The court case demonstrated that each of the components of the City's FBW policy rested on its own series of decisions, taken by the City. The willingness of the lower courts to interfere in these decisions – to review their reasoning, and to impose different conclusions – showed that the City's original decisions could each have been made differently. If each part of the policy could have been differently decided, or differently formulated, then the overall policy cannot be described as inevitable, or unquestionable. It is, instead, obviously changeable.

This insight animated the politics of the APF and other groups in this period. The examples offered by the TAC case, and then the water meters case, inspired other organisations to challenge the reasoning behind the adoption of policy, and then to pick these reasons apart. For example, a recent string of cases in Johannesburg has focussed on inconsistencies in the City's temporary emergency shelter programme, in which the City was first required to provide shelter to communities that were evicted from land it owned (and who would otherwise become homeless), then required to provide similar shelter to similar communities evicted from privately owned land, and then required to ensure that this shelter conformed to constitutional standards.[24] The awareness of the contingency of policy meant that any interested party – any citizen, any community, or any social movement – could engage critically not just with a policy's effects, but also with the reasoning behind it. This kind of engagement can only proceed on the assumption of an equality of understanding: that is, of the ability of the critic to comprehend and challenge the decision-making process itself in terms that make sense to both the critic and the original drafter. This assumption of equality is – for Rancière, and in our account – the basis of politics.

In this way, then, actions taken in the courts may resonate more broadly: the centrality of legal discourses to contemporary social orders provides the courts – and their processes – with a privileged vantage point from which to interrogate state practices and policies. Within the courtroom, litigating parties are treated as equals – and granted the right to engage with state (and private) policies and practices. Courtroom debates reveal the contingency of these policies and practices, exposing the reasoning behind them. Although a court victory might have more immediate results, even a defeat can bring about further mobilisation: the processes themselves imply a recognition of the rights of litigating communities to act as equals in understanding, and so may encourage others to take up their own struggles. In this sense, the courtroom acts as a staging post for other public interventions premised on the potential for political disruption of the ordinary operations of the state – and more broadly, in Rancière's terms, of the 'police order' itself.

Everyday knowledge in the courtroom

As powerful as these actions might be, this approach only accounts for one potential form of equality. In it, the temporary equality provided by the court's formally level playing field may be used to leverage public perceptions, and allow a litigating entity to assert its otherwise-unrecognised capabilities. But for it to do so, that entity – whether an individual, a community, or an organisation – must demonstrate that it can engage with its opponent on their own terms. In other words, the litigants in the water meters case had to demonstrate that they could engage with the state's technical arguments in similarly technical terms: they had to muster budgetary arguments – or at least, disprove the state's own budgetary arguments – as well as arguments of principle. In this context, equality means little more than the right and the ability to empower an interlocutor to argue your position on someone else's terrain, and in someone else's language.

This is, therefore, a constrained version of equality, dependent on the observance of institutional norms of the courts by the litigants, their representatives, and the officers of the court. It is evanescent, a version that may not last beyond the hearing of a case. And while it is an equality that may be sufficient to unsettle the operations of power, it is unlikely to force greater disruption.

It is not, however, the only form of equality that can be asserted in the courts. It is also possible – admittedly, under unusual circumstances – for litigants to refuse to accept the discursive terrain of the state, or private capital, and to insist that their forms of knowledge be recognised both by their opponents and the bench. This is an assertion of equality as mutual recognition and understanding: not as the ability to convert one party's complaints into another's language, but rather as the capacity for both parties to understand and converse across each other's languages.

Something very much like this happens in a small number of cases, in which one form of knowledge – such as a community's everyday understanding of local events, needs, and norms – is counterposed to another form of knowledge – such as the state's technical and bureaucratic expertise. One example of this is a case that took place in the Free State High Court, litigated and argued intermittently between 2002 and 2013. This case involved a clash between the Governing Body of BopaSetjhaba primary school, located in Tumahole, a township of the small town of Parys, and the Northern Free State Department of Education. In brief, the school was seeking to resist two decisions taken by the Department – first to withdraw funding for a planned new building, and then – after they had complained about this decision – to close the school down entirely.[25]

At first, neither of these decisions was explained. After a lengthy process of consultations and planning, the school and its Governing Body had signed off on a set of architect's plans for a new school building – which would be built on a new site, nearer to the expanding informal settlements on Tumahole's formal boundaries. The provincial Department of Education supported this project: they had commissioned the architect, run consultations with the school, and had allocated a budget for the construction of the new buildings. In a progress report prepared by the Department, it stated that R600,000 had been allocated; that it had approved the drafting of the plans; and that it would advertise a building tender in 2002, for building to commence in 2003. This document was so supportive that it added that 'if more funds than the preliminary allocation indicates are made available, construction will commence earlier'. These early phases of the project suggest a remarkable degree of coordination between the bureaucratic institutions of the state and the local community: participatory planning and consultative decision making had seemingly succeeded in creating a consensus between the community and the state's experts.

Then, a delay was announced. The Department declared that construction would only begin in 2004, a year after the initial agreement; some months later, the school's Principal discovered that no monies had been allocated to the project for the financial period lasting from 2002 until 2005. When he attempted to query this with the Department, he received no response – and so the school took their concerns to the provincial MEC for Education, the media, and other institutions (including the Office of the Public Protector, the Office of the State President, and the Human Rights Commission). Neither their appeals to participatory mechanisms nor their petitions to political entities and institutions succeeded: the construction was delayed, with no reasons given.

Instead, their efforts appeared to have perverse consequences. In this period, the Department decided – according to an internal memo, later disclosed in the court hearing – not only to halt the processes that might lead to the construction of the new building, 'with immediate effect', but also to close BopaSetjhaba altogether. It was to be 'merged' with a second primary school in the area, and the pupils of the one school would formally become pupils of the other.[26] The news was conveyed to the school in a letter bluntly headed 're: Meeting for closing down of school'. A month later – in April 2003 – the school received a faxed message, informing the Principal that he was to be disciplined, and instructing the school's Governing Body to dissolve.

At this point, the school's staff and parents approached CALS for aid, and instituted a court case. As part of their legal strategy, they demanded that the Department provide reasons for its decisions. After some resistance, the Department set out an explanation. Essentially, it argued that there was no need for BopaSetjhaba either to move or, in fact, to exist. This, it argued, was demonstrated by statistical evidence. The overall number of pupils enrolled across the province had declined in the previous five years, from 807,718 in 1998 to 682,150 in 2003. In Tumahole itself, this trend was replicated: 6,717 pupils were enrolled in schools in 1999, while only 5,822 were similarly enrolled in 2003. The number of students at BopaSetjhaba itself had declined by about 50% between 1995 and 2003, while, at the same time, the 'learner to educator ratio in the school' had declined from 40:1 to 32:1. There was a sufficient number of classrooms available, across all schools, to accommodate all currently enrolled students. Insofar as there were not, the Department suggested that the schools in Tumahole were in fact in the same catchment area as the schools in the centre of the town itself, and students from the township might choose to attend the HF Verwoerd Primary School in the centre of the old 'white' town.[27]

The school and its Governing Body could not contest these figures. Self-evidently, they did not have the ability to collect data on school-enrolment figures across the province. They could not contest the ratios of pupils to school rooms proposed by the Department; nor could they deny the decline in their own enrolment figures over the preceding years. Any attempt to engage with the Department on its own terms – to put up different or contrasting figures – would not succeed.

Instead, the school insisted on challenging the technical knowledge deployed by the Department with a different source of knowledge: they argued that, regardless of their accuracy or authenticity, the figures did not capture the complexities of the local situation. First, and perhaps most importantly, the school insisted that the Department had not considered counting the large number of children resident in the expanding informal settlements along Tumahole. The school's staff and parents asserted that – in their experience, unconfirmed by any statistical data – there were many children of school-going age in these informal settlements, few of whom were likely to be enrolled. They would not have been counted by the Department, at least in part because their families were new arrivals to the urban area – and, if they had been counted, they had been nominally assigned to different districts. Second, the abstract geographical terrain seemingly envisaged by the Department in its statements about classroom availability in and around Parys and Tumahole was simply unrecognisable on the ground. In practice, the spatial relationship between the informal settlements, the township, and the town was such that young children would have to walk more than five kilometres from their homes to reach their 'closely located' schools. They would have to cross a bridge over the railway track to reach the town – which had been designed, in the apartheid period, to be as separate from the township as possible. Although this was theoretically possible, its effect was to exhaust young pupils of between six and eight years old, reducing their ability to perform in schools – and thus lowering enrolment.

In other words, the school did not claim that the statistical and technical data offered by the Department to justify its decision was inaccurate or insufficient to, in fact, justify its reasoning. Instead, they argued that this data was incapable of reflecting realities on the ground – that it could not describe the experiences of school-going children, their parents, or their teachers. The Department's knowledge was based on abstractions, and thus irrelevant to actual experience.

The school rested its own arguments in favour of both its continuing existence and its relocation to a new building on a new site on a claim to local, or everyday, knowledge. This form of knowledge, as described by Henri Lefebvre, and others, is grounded in personal and social experience. It is not discernible through a purely 'scientific' investigation (although Lefebvre, at least, would have been unwilling to entirely surrender claims to its potential scientificity).[28] The school and its Governing Body argued that this form of knowledge – gained by parents and teachers through everyday experiences of the spatial dynamics of the area, and of the social interactions between newly arrived and more-established families – allowed them to discern a need that was invisible to the Department. The school could tell that there was likely to be a significant demand for places, if it was relocated as planned; it would come to serve a new, unrecognised community – one that could not yet be described in the Department's terms.

In court, BopaSetjhaba and its Governing Body were asking the judge to recognise their particular form of knowledge as equal in status to the technical knowledge presented by the Department. The judge was required not only to decide whether the state had acted reasonably on its own terms – a standard approach in administrative law – but whether the knowledge upon which the state chose to act was sufficient, in the light of knowledge it could not have accessed. In the end, the judge found that the Department had not consulted with the school in taking its decision – and that, therefore, the decision could be reviewed. He ordered the Department to reverse its decision and to embark upon a new process of consultation, with the aim of reassessing the school's practical needs.

Although the example provided by this case is particularly clear, it is not the only possible one. Arguably, the case brought by Abahlali baseMjondolo against the KwaZulu-Natal provincial government's evictions legislation included a similar claim based on alternative knowledge. The state sought to defend the legislation in terms of its internal rationality, and the need for a centrally planned, bureaucratically coordinated approach to 'slum elimination' to improve living conditions in informal settlements. Abahlali, however, argued that these considerations were ultimately irrelevant. Their experience of policing practice in the province suggested that the results of this legislation would be perverse: widespread uncontrolled evictions, and the abandonment of carefully structured community-based processes necessary to ensure that informal settlement upgrading preserved the livelihood and locational advantages 'slums' currently afforded their inhabitants. These processes could not be legislated into existence: they had to develop on the ground, and be based in everyday and local forms of knowledge.

This is a claim to the equality of apparently incommensurable forms of knowledge, experience, and understanding. It is also, simultaneously, a claim to social equality: to the equal status of the experience gathered living on the margins of the formal social order to that gathered by bureaucratic elites in the course of technical (and technocratic) governance. Implicitly, thus, to make this claim is also to assert a radical understanding of intellectual and political equality: it was not enough for the court – and the state – to recognise the ability of the school and its Governing Body to articulate their claims and their arguments in the language and terms of the state. To do so would only reward the ability of these litigants to go outside of their own experiences, and speak on the state's terms. It would result in a politics of assimilation, in which the equality of persons is reducible to their equal potential to participate in 'invited spaces' on the terms and in the language of the already-established order. Instead, BopaSetjhaba's claims to knowledge presumed and asserted that the courts and the representatives of the state bureaucracy should be equally capable of engaging the school's arguments on its own terrain of experiential knowledge.

The school's claim speaks to Rancière's idea that equality is best understood as the mutual recognition of speaking beings. In place of the mutual incomprehension of citizens and barbarians as the basis of political difference, as in the classic Greek model, Rancière suggests that equality is achieved when two beings recognise each other's sounds as constituting speech and work to understand each other. This understanding can only occur after a moment of mutual recognition – and that recognition is most likely to take place when the standard operating procedures of the existing order are disturbed. In this case, these procedures were disturbed by the staff and parents at BopaSetjhaba – by their insistence that their form of knowledge had an equal status.

That insistence is the basis of politics.

Politics and the law

At first glance, the courts are an unlikely site of disruption and the law an unlikely tool of equality. Even in South Africa – where much of the colonial theatre of the courts has been reduced in the past two decades – the courtroom more often than not is a space of disempowerment. It is still unusual for a community organisation, or a social movement, or a loose set of activists to sue on their own behalf or in the public interest; when they do, their opponents are either typically the state – more often than not – or private capital.[29] These opponents have significantly greater resources available to them, and are likely to assemble larger and more experienced teams of lawyers, delay the hearing of the case, and appeal any inconvenient judgment for years. This 'inequality of arms' – in the pungent phrase of Dali Mpofu, the lawyer for the arrested and injured miners at the Marikana Commission – can easily distort the formal freedoms of the legal order.[30]

That said, the courts have nonetheless provided a site from which and within which assertions of equality have been made. These have been enabled, to an extent, by the existence of a public interest litigation sector – by legal NGOs and associated law clinics, often based at universities, which can litigate selected cases and, in so doing, erode at least some of the inequality of arms faced by poorer communities. As the previous chapter emphasised, this sector is not immune from criticism, and litigants may find themselves struggling to resist legal discipline. Nonetheless, these struggles are not inevitable. After all, there have been times when litigators have been capable of representing a politicised community's interests without distorting them.

Once admitted to this space, and enabled to navigate it, litigating communities and movements have been able to use it to create moments of political contest. In cases that fit a model of public interest litigation, such as those brought by the TAC and the APF, the law has been used as a staging post for a challenge to the state, fought as much in the public sphere as it is in the courts. In cases that fit the model offered by BopaSetjhaba's challenge to the state, the opportunities provided by the court allow communities to express themselves in their own words, and on their own terms. These cases might be won, or they might be lost – and much, of course, hangs on that distinction – but, regardless of the court's decision, they open up new possibilities for politics.

CONCLUSION

The Possibilities of Politics

In South Africa, today, our existing society has inequality at its core. The formal political order seems separate from the social and political worlds of ordinary citizens, and the poor. The state and economic institutions are tools of a governing elite. This elite is fractured – and electoral politics are characterised by contests between fractions of this elite for control over the resources and capabilities of the state. At worst, this control might be used to enrich a few at the expense of the majority; at best, it might be used to ameliorate the conditions in which most citizens currently live. Even at best, these actions presume the continuing inequality – not simply economic, but social and political – between those who can control the state, and its largesse, and those who cannot. Despite this apparent disconnection between elites and other citizens, the existing society is also said to be democratic. This claim rests on the regularity of 'free and fair' elections, and – perhaps more importantly – on the presence of a set of institutions that seek to discipline ordinary men and women's political expression into forms of responsible citizenship, and thus to give these citizens an appropriate voice in governance. This process, however, often amounts to little more than encouraging citizens to petition the state, and governing elites, for consideration, or patronage. These actions again presume an existing inequality between those inside the state and its bureaucracies, and those outside – ordinary citizens, who must petition those who can hold power.

And yet, moments of insurgent political action – sometimes expressed through public protests, sometimes through other strategies of dissent – can provide a lightning flash of illumination that makes these assumptions of inequality obvious. In South Africa, these small insurgencies may be instigated by a recognition of the gap between the lived realities of inequality and the messianic expectations of the immediate past – by the gap between contemporary reality, and the utopian vision of social and economic redress that thrived in an earlier moment. They may also develop in the disjuncture between the state's rhetoric of inclusion and participation and the experiences of many dissenting communities of repression, violence, and exclusion from the social order. Regardless of the specific motivation, each of these acts of insurgency shares a core presumption: that ordinary citizens can act politically, even outside of the state's institutions of participation.

This presumption is not merely a presumption of capability – it is also a presumption of equality.

If this presumption is accepted by all men and women, then it might lead to the creation of a society of equals. But it is not, as a matter of fact, a shared presumption – rather, it is at odds with the fundamental structures of our social order, which presume a set of social roles that align with economic positions, and which define the potential agency of citizens. This is true for South Africa. It is also true for many other countries, and many other avowedly democratic orders.

And if the account that I've presented in this book is true – and I am certain that it is – then it is the assertion of this presumed equality that exposes cracks and shortcomings in the social order, and makes politics happen. It is not enough, though, to simply reveal inequality: that newly visible inequality must also be revealed as contingent, as the product of a series of particular decisions, practices, and habits. It is not, in other words, natural – nor is it inevitable. And it can be changed.

But no order changes easily.

In South Africa, the state responds to the claims of insurgent citizens either with attempts to channel and co-opt their energies into the maintenance of the order itself, or with attempts to forcibly suppress the challenge to that order constituted by their claims and their acts. In practice, the first set of responses – the attempts to discipline, channel, and co-opt insurgent claims – are often institutionalised through 'participatory governance mechanisms' set up to facilitate communication between governing elites and petitioning citizens. These mechanisms can achieve their purposes, and result in the more effective distribution of state resources at a local level – but remain structured in such a way as to presume inequality, and to frustrate unexpected political claims. The existence of these mechanisms has also been used to justify the state's resort to violence, when one or another of its branches has set out to forcibly suppress a potential politics.

The shadow of state violence lies heavy over contemporary South African politics, and society. Although the murderousness apparent at Marikana is rare, the state's police forces are habitually brutal in their attempts to suppress unlicensed politics. The formal structures governing public political expression – although themselves insufficient to guarantee the equal ability of all citizens to act politically – are regularly misused, or circumvented; and in the absence of legislated restraint, police actions are often unsupervised, reactive, and reactionary. A fear of popular violence – and a mistrust of popular organisation, outside of the institutions of participation and co-option – supports the relatively untrammelled use of police force to maintain the social order.

In this context, South African politics are best characterised by the dynamic tension between acts of political expression – often, although not universally, acts of protest and insurgency – and practices of political repression. This produces shifting realities, to which politicised communities and insurgent citizens must adapt. As the political terrain shifts, so too do possibilities for political change emerge and sink back into the general swamp of time. And inside this uncertain moment, it is impossible to say with any certainty what its end will be – what political arrangement will emerge. It may be that the current order survives this moment of insurgency unscathed; or it may be that the order will be significantly altered, and forced to adapt to the demands of equality currently being made. In this case, new classes of citizens may constitute themselves in the future, and eventually return the order to a state of flux. Or events might not resolve themselves so benignly: the 'police order' might embrace an actively repressive and authoritarian practice and, in so doing, radically restrict the spaces available for public action, and the possibilities of politics.

In this moment, these possibilities are all still open – and the story of contemporary South Africa's insurgent citizens and their claims to political agency on the basis of their presumed equality is unfinished. The trajectory of this story – the establishment of a new order, or the reinvigoration of the existing order, or the betrayal of liberalism and the adoption of authoritarianism – is unclear.

Resisting the end of politics

At the end of most political stories are utopian visions. They provide potential resting points for our narratives. They articulate the ideals on which an old order can be transcended, and a new one based. This is not to suggest that all utopias provide realistic or concretely imaginable visions.

At their least convincing – in what Lefebvre calls the 'classic sense of the term' – utopian visions suggest a wish 'to create a new society and an entirely new life, with new men'. This suggests that the new society will be based on 'a pure ideal outside the real' and is 'something to be created *ex nihilo.*'[1] This is the kind of utopianism that is condemned as unrealistic and quixotic mystification; it is the kind of utopianism that Engels famously rejected: 'the more completely they were worked out in detail, the more they could not avoid drifting off into pure phantasies'.[2]

More realistic utopias can also be imagined, and proposed. Erik Olin Wright has called for utopian visions that are grounded in existing practices and politics, which he calls 'Real Utopias'. For Wright, utopian visions are both necessary 'to motivate people to leave on the journey from the status quo in the first place' and also dangerous – fantastical visions likely to be either reductively facile, or unachievable and thus disempowering. Instead, he calls for 'utopian ideals that are grounded in the real potentials of humanity, utopian destinations that have accessible waystations, utopian designs of institutions that can inform our practical task of navigating a world of imperfect conditions for social change'. As such, Wright argues for a practice of engagement with, and critique of, existing institutions so as to develop the possibilities of an emancipated society.[3] Such a realistic utopianism imagines a political process of contest and challenge, working both inside and outside the social order, leading to the development of an ever more perfect consensus. It avoids planning a perfect end to politics, and chooses instead to use the imperfections of the present to build a better, more equal, and realisable society in the present, and for the future.

It is a seductive argument.

But insofar as either version of utopian thinking – fantastic or real – asserts that the creation of consensus is the basis for this future society, then they remain attempts to reduce dissension, disagreement, and dispute in the social order. As such, in Rancière's terms, they are anti-political. It does not matter whether they seek to do so by fiat – as in classic utopianism – or through the progressive realisation of a realistic utopia. They seek to establish an undisputed social order, an order that is perceived by all who belong to it as legitimate, natural, and inevitable. Whether this undisputed order is located in the present, or in the future, it represents the cessation of politics.[4]

The approach adopted in this book – based on Rancière's description of a disruptive politics founded on a presumption of equality – is thus antithetical to these versions of utopian thinking: where they envisage a society founded on the consent of all who live in it, I see groups and individuals unaccounted for, possibilities overlooked, and politics quietly suppressed.

Instead of the end of politics, or even the end of a political story, Rancière's work proposes a continuing politics – a future of endless contest. Instead of a vision of utopia, this is a vision of heterotopia – a

term that both Rancière and Michel Foucault use to describe related
(but not identical) visions of society and social space defined by the
continuing emergence of new possibilities. Foucault's heterotopic
visions are more fully defined than Rancière's, and more commonly
referenced by scholars. It is worth taking a moment to outline his
ideas, before turning to Rancière's and mine, so that the differences
are clear. For Foucault, heterotopias already occur within the existing
social order. These heterotopias emerge either in sites of crisis or in
sites of deviance. The first are those 'privileged or sacred or forbidden
places reserved for individuals who are in a state of crisis with respect
to society and the human milieu in which they live. Adolescents,
menstruating women, women in labour, old people, and so on'.
These sites, he suggests, were more common in pre-modern societies, although some continue to exist today. Modernity, though, has
brought with it new sites: 'those in which individuals are put whose
behaviour is deviant with respect to the mean or the required norms.
These are the rest homes, the psychiatric hospitals; they are also, of
course, the prison, to which we would probably add old people's
homes'.[5] These are sites within which the ordinary operations of the
social order are suspended, and upended. They bear a certain family
resemblance to sites of carnival, as described by Bakhtin, in which the
regular order is reversed for a period of disorder and misrule.[6] In these
heterotopic sites, the order is suspended and new possibilities emerge.

For Foucault, these sites serve as sources of imaginative possibility
within the constraints of a disciplinary society. It is difficult to con-
ceive of a heterotopia independent of a disciplinary order, because
their freedoms are contingent on the existence of external restrictions. Heterotopias either provide a respite from the world, or create
'a different space, a different real space as perfect, as meticulous, as
well-arranged as ours is disorganised, badly arranged, and muddled.
This would be the heterotopia not of illusion, but of compensation'.
The ideal image of a heterotopia might thus be a ship,

> a piece of floating space, a placeless place, that lives by its own
> devices, that is self-enclosed and, at the same time, delivered over

to the boundless expanse of the ocean, and that goes from port to
port, from watch to watch . . . In civilisations without ships, the
dreams dry up, espionage takes the place of adventure, and the
police that of the corsairs.

Rancière uses the term 'independently of the use that Foucault made
of it'. For him, heterotopia 'means a certain way of thinking the
"*heteron*" or the "other": the other as the effect of a reconfiguration
of the distribution of places, identities, and capacities'. This notion
of heterotopia is – according to Rancière – fundamentally aesthetic,
concerned with the ways in which difference and contest may be
perceived and depicted. As such, as heterotopia is not so much the
particular site in which a new and unstable distribution can take
place – as it may be in Foucault's use of the term – but rather the
way of thinking that enables the destabilisation of existing distri-
butions. 'It does not add another *topos* to all the *topoi* [that already
exist] . . . Instead, it creates a point where all those locations and the
oppositions they define are neutralised.' In other words, 'what is
common to all those forms of aesthetic heterotopia is the determina-
tion of a place of the indeterminate, a place anybody can occupy'.
In a political context, this means that 'we may think of the action of
political subjects as the reconfiguration of the field of the common,
enacting, against a given distribution of the parts, places and com-
petences, the power of the demos, which means . . . the power of
those who are not countable as qualified parts of the community . . .
those who have no specific "aptitude" to rule or to be ruled'.[7] It is an
approach to society and politics that is fundamentally challenging,
disturbing, and disruptive: politics as an unending contest.

   This does not mean conflict, or violence. In *The Ignorant Schoolmaster*,
Rancière suggests a vision of what a heterotopic society might look
like. It would be a 'society of the emancipated', a society that is also
'a society of artists'. It 'would repudiate the division between those
who know and those who don't, between those who possess or
don't possess the property of intelligence'. Instead of this fundamental inequality, 'it would only know minds in action: people who do,

who speak about what they are doing, and who thus transform all
their works into ways of demonstrating the humanity that is born in
them as in everyone'. In such a society, everyone would recognise
that 'man's dignity is independent of his position'. Decisions would
be based on a shared reason – and it would be understood that this

> reason begins when discourses organised with the goal of being
> right cease . . . where equality is recognised: not an equality decreed
> by law or force, not a passively received equality, but an equality in
> act, verified, at each step by those marchers who, in their constant
> attention to themselves and in their endless revolving around the truth,
> find the right sentences to make themselves understood by others.

Understanding is not based on external knowledge: 'it is the power to
make oneself understood through another's verification. And only an
equal understands an equal.' Thus: '*equality* and *intelligence* are synonymous
terms, exactly like *reason* and *will*. This synonymy on which each man's
intellectual capacity is based is also what makes society, in general, possible.' Given this, it is clear that 'the equality of intelligence is the common
bond of humankind, the necessary and sufficient condition for a society
of men to exist'. Rancière then concludes by acknowledging:

> It is true that we don't know that men are equal. We are saying
> that they might be. This is our opinion, and we are trying, along
> with those who think as we do, to verify it. But we know that this
> might is the very thing that makes a society of humans possible.[8]

A society of equals is a society of men and women who recognise each
other's capacities and capabilities, who each act as agents, and who
each act to ensure mutual understanding. This is a society in which
political decisions are made through shared reasoning; where daily
life is enriched by enthusiasm and attention; and where social interactions are predicated on an already-accepted equality – of intelligence,
of understanding, of potential and of power. It is a society in which
order does not need to be defended, because it is not institutionalised:
order is an emergent property of social interactions between equals,

and not the structures that guarantee them. (Order is not, in other words, the structures that seek to reduce inequality in social interactions – as the best account of the democratic order in South Africa today might suggest – because that inequality cannot be presumed.) It is, in sum, a vision of a world in which politics is everywhere – in which argument is normal and natural, contest fervent but not fevered, and consensus temporary.

The society of equals is a vision of heterotopia that rejects the possibility of an end to political stories: that resists narrative closure and that insists on the continuing possibilities of politics.

South African politics today

In South Africa, today, relinquishing totalizing stories of utopia and embracing the ambiguities and uncertainties of a heterotopic mode of thinking means – among other things – accepting the limits on any quest to find or create a unifying movement to resist the state's sometimes-violent excesses, challenging the dogmas currently animating government policy, and even contesting elections.

At present, at least two groups are offering – explicitly or implicitly – to provide South Africa with exactly this kind of unifying story: the Economic Freedom Fighters (EFF), formally a political party that articulates a radically redistributive social and political agenda, and the newly launched United Front (UF) – an as-yet undefined amalgam of social movements, union leaders, and high-profile activists loosely aligned with a socialist critique of the current government's economic policy.

Few statements date themselves as fast as political predictions do. The future is uncertain, and these movements might radically alter their approaches in the coming months and years. But – on the basis of what they have achieved so far – we can draw some conclusions about their likely approaches. The two movements have followed different trajectories in 2014, but, nonetheless, both seem – at this early stage in their respective developments – to have committed themselves to a model that seeks to coordinate and organise South Africa's insurgent citizens.

In the months leading up to the 2014 elections, the EFF presented itself as a movement representing the voices of South Africa's insurgent poor. This gave rise to popular speculations that the party would capture a significant percentage of the country's vote – and possibly even attract previously disenchanted voters back into the electoral system. As it turned out, the EFF did do well in the elections: they won over a million votes and became the third-largest party in parliament. They did not, however, bring a new generation of voters into the electoral system; nor did they appear to capture the votes of most insurgent communities – as the electoral choices of Abahlali suggest.[9]

In the months since, the EFF have staked out a highly visible position in parliament. Even before they were sworn in, the party announced that their male representatives would wear overalls to the formal opening of parliament, while their female representatives would wear the uniforms of domestic workers. All uniforms would be red – and would be worn to signify that the EFF remained one with its constituency. This theatrical gesture established the EFF in the public imagination as a confrontational force in parliament. In the months since, this impression has only been confirmed, both by the party's aggressive tactics, haranguing the President and insisting on raising questions out of turn, and also by the government's absurdly defensive reactions, including the president refusing to appear in the National Assembly, the Speaker using the police to expel EFF representatives from parliament, and the suspension of several members of the party's caucus.[10]

However, in showcasing the spectacular theatrics of opposition, media reporting on the EFF has tended to overlook the processes through which the party is continuing to build itself – and its constituency – using established methods. This is perhaps unsurprising, given the histories of many of the party's leaders within the African National Congress's (ANC's) own structures. The EFF's first conference (or 'National People's Assembly', as it was officially termed) provided one of the few moments in which these processes have come to light. In particular, the conference highlighted the importance of both political education and central coordination to the party: new members needed

to have the 'cardinal pillars' of its ideology explained, and the leaders
of the party needed to be confirmed in their existing roles. As por-
trayed in the media accounts of this gathering, the party is seeking to
establish centralised authority – and to emphasise the role of the party
in directing its members.[11] In essence, it appears that the EFF is being
constituted as an institution that seeks to discipline the insurgent energies of South Africa's citizens, and to direct their acts into 'effective'
forms of action.

At the time of writing, the EFF has been in existence for just
over a year. The UF is even younger. It was officially formed in the
month during which I am writing these pages – although it has
been anticipated, discussed, and debated since the National Union
of Metalworkers of South Africa (NUMSA) announced that it would
no longer campaign for the ANC in the 2014 elections. NUMSA has
played the central role in the Front's formation: for over a year it has
publicly flirted with the possibility of entering politics – understood, of
course, as entering the electoral arena. At the start of 2014, commentators speculated on the likelihood of the union somehow contesting that
year's elections as a political party. Even though that speculation was
dismissed by the union, its spokespeople have spent the rest of the
year emphasising their independence from the ANC, the state, and
its supporters in the country's main union federation. This ruffled
feathers. In November, the as-yet-unformed UF was the subject of an
anonymous pamphlet which accused a strange selection of activists
and academics of fomenting a 'secret regime change plot to distabilize
[sic] South Africa'. The language of this pamphlet was unquestionably inflammatory – and the presence of photographs of each of the
accused activists next to their names was, equally, sinister.[12]

In December, the movement held a large-scale 'preparatory assembly'. The events of this assembly give some indications of the ways
in which the UF may come to imagine its own role in contemporary
South African politics. According to the declaration made at the end
of this meeting, the UF called upon 'the workers, the unemployed,
women and youths, shack-dwellers, back yarders, farm workers, landless and dispossessed, to organise, mobilise and build the united front

in every corner of the country'. This call was immediately followed by the assertion that: 'the core social base, engine and locomotive of the UF should be exploited, oppressed and marginalized people – primarily employed workers, informal/atypical workers and the unemployed in both urban and rural areas, as well as women and youth'.[13] The tension in these assertions between unionist modes of thinking – which define categories of citizens by their relationships to work – and the modes of thinking associated with new social movements – which speak of social position, and self-definition – is obvious, and left unresolved. There is, however, an indication in the declaration of how the UF expects to resolve it: by engaging with the organisations rather than communities.

The assembly was constituted by representatives from 'a diverse range of trade unions, social movements, popular organizations, faith-based organizations, NGOs [non-govermental organisations] and anti-capitalist formations'. The National Working Committee, set up to prepare for the official launch of the Front in 2015, is constituted of prominent activists from within these movements: trade unionists, full-time civil society organisers, and retired members of parliament. Many of these activists have familiar names: Zackie Achmat, symbol of the Treatment Action Campaign in the early 2000s; Bandile Mdalose, former Abahlali activist; Ronnie Kasrils, former member of the South African Communist Party and Minister in the Mandela and Mbeki governments. These are highly accomplished men and women, but their familiarity is striking: if this list is to be taken as representative of the UF's self-conception, then it suggests that the movement is likely to emphasise the coordination of existing organisations, and build upon the attempts made in past years to build a concerted civil society opposition.

Both the EFF and the UF thus appear to be offering the possibility of coordination and unification to South Africa's insurgent citizens. They offer grand and general ideological visions, as both use the language of socialism to challenge the economic liberalism underpinning contemporary government policy. Their claims are based on the assumption that power is best contested between similarly constituted groups: that South

Africa's dominant party must face a united opposition movement. The terrain of that contest might be the electoral realm – where the EFF seeks to provide such a coordinated alternative – or it might be the broader terrain of civil society – where the UF seems to be locating itself. In either case, the contest is imagined as between two large powers.

There may be a great deal of truth to these assertions: certainly, it is unlikely that the electoral dominance of the ANC is going to be disturbed by anything other than the emergence of a second plausible governing party, capable of mobilising a wide range of votes from diverse social groups.

But there are also a number of dangers inherent in adopting this model as the default form of political organisation and political practice. It presumes the powerlessness of insurgent citizens as presently constituted: in localised community groups, loose collectives, and temporary movements. It presumes that a diversity of voices produces a kind of cacophony, an incoherent assault of sound without persuasive force. It suggests that it is only by learning to speak together, in the same language, and to the same purpose, that citizens can challenge domination – and it is only by speaking together that they can articulate a counter-hegemonic vision that can resist existing power.

In doing so, this model replicates the presumption of inequality that has shaped the official politics of democracies since their inception: the inequality between those who can speak meaningfully and those who cannot. As Rancière has argued, this distinction marked the limits of classical Greek democracy – and continues to underpin the distinctions between those who have a part in democratic consensus and those who have no such part. If South Africa's political opposition continues to use this model unquestioningly, then it will replicate the inequalities that mark the country and entrench another system of inclusion and exclusion, control, discipline, and repression.

These movements need not do so: if they can succeed in listening to the voices of South Africa's insurgent citizens, rather than speaking over them; if they support the efforts of citizens to articulate their own ideas and their own goals, rather than attempt to correct their apparent ideological misapprehensions; and if they can act to amplify these voices, rather than direct them – then there is hope for a hetero-topic politics, a politics founded on the proliferation of unpredictable possibilities. These actions are open to the EFF, the UF, and even to the current dominant party, the ANC. Each could choose to listen to citizens, support them, and amplify their claims: as it stands, it seems unlikely that either the ANC or the EFF will do so in the near future, as they focus their energies upon each other. The UF's willingness to consider the possibilities of a more open politics appears promising – but although it is too early to draw any conclusions about their future practices, it is not too early to begin to register preliminary concerns, as I and others have now begun to do.[14]

In place of a model of politics founded on ideas of inequality, of the need to educate ordinary citizens, and visions of empowerment, a heterotopic politics suggests an ongoing conversation of equals. The members of the UF, or the EFF, should not assume that local activ-ists and citizen groups are waiting to be coordinated, or educated, or empowered: these men and women are already equally capable of explaining their own situations, articulating their own claims to knowledge, and engaging with other opinions, perspectives, and explanations. This is a more difficult approach – one that does not, as I've said above, have any obvious end-point or conclusion.

But it is the only approach that does not assume that equality is something to be constructed in the future, on behalf of those who are currently disadvantaged. It is the only path that presumes that a soci-ety of equals can be forged in the present moment, by South Africa's already-insurgent citizens.

Imagining a politics of possibility

Contemporary South Africa is not a society of equals. Instead, it is a society in which an established and entrenched order is repeatedly disrupted by the eruption of multiple acts of insurgent politics.

In this moment, the tension between expression and repression is shaping the limits of the social order. Insurgent forms of expres-sion test those limits: they challenge existing norms and practices, undermine established authority, and they threaten our comfort in the social roles which we have accepted. They leave us uncertain of our society's stability, and uncertain of the stability of our lives in it. This is true whether we occupy a privileged position in this order, or not; whether we accept our places in it, or not: disruptions bring uncertainties, doubts, and fears to the surface.

And sometimes, these fears are justified. Certain moments of disruption may be, in effect, destructive: they raze fields to the ground, without providing the seeds from which new flowers can bloom. The men and women who assert their agency may do so at the expense of others – refusing to presume the equality of each to all, but instead asserting a new inequality, a superiority of those who were once excluded. The illiberal politics of xenophobia, sexism, and exclusion may emerge in and amongst insurgent communities: their practices may turn towards authoritarianism, and their actions may result in the attenuation of the field of political possibility.

But disruptions can also bring hope.

They can bring the hope that the current distribution of society – the distribution of roles, responsibilities, and powers – will not last, that we have not reached the end of politics, and that change is possible. At their best, the disruptions created by insurgent politics – by men and women acting as if they were already equals – expand the possibilities of politics, and broaden our horizons. At their best, they bring the hope of creating a society of equals in the real world.

In each event of disruption – each act, each protest, each insurgency – there is no guarantee that the immediate outcome will be either liberal or authoritarian, hopeful or despairing, inclusive or exclusive. Most likely, it will be some mixture of all of these elements. Likewise, there is no way of knowing what the outcome of this current moment in South Africa's political history will be: no way of knowing how the tension between political expression and repression, or the tension between order and disruption, will resolve itself. It is unlikely to do so in any certain way, in the near future.

The vision that best fits this indeterminacy is that of heterotopia – of a resolution to the contests of this moment that is not an ending to all contest. Heterotopic thinking presents an expansive vision of the possibilities of politics – whether those may be ambiguously licensed, occurring on the edges of contemporary social orders, as Foucault suggests, or whether these represent an emancipatory way of conceptualising the relations between equals, as in Rancière's account. Adopting this mode of thinking means rejecting the stasis of utopian futures – whether these utopias be wholly fantastic, or realistic. It means recognising disagreements and disputes as defining politics, and regarding consensus as – at best – a temporary phenomenon, arising in specific contexts and then fading outside them. It means refusing to accept that one kind of citizen is better equipped to hold political opinions than another kind of citizen; refusing to believe that inequality is natural; and refusing to accept that any order is somehow unchangeable.

It means accepting the indeterminacy of politics, and our lack of ultimate control over the future.

If the story everyone knows about South Africa's transition from apartheid presumed a utopian ending – the creation of a new order – today, such a story seems not merely unlikely, but almost impossible. In place of this story, we need a new narrative: one that does not assume that dissension should be replaced by consensus, or even that storytelling should reach an end. Instead, we need a story that is open-ended – a way of imagining our future not as a path towards one or another goal – utopia or dystopia, order and stasis – but as a field of unbounded possibility.

In South Africa, today, the possibilities of heterotopic reasoning emerge when insurgent citizens act as if they are already equal to all other citizens; when they refuse to accept that their positions within the social order are natural, or inevitable; and when they refuse to believe that one group of citizens is better equipped to make decisions on their behalf than they are. These possibilities emerge during protests, on the streets, and in challenges to the institutional reasoning of the state, sometimes within the structures of the state itself. These challenges are themselves open-ended: each gives rise to new possibilities, and new potentials. All citizens are implicated in these possibilities – for if they are founded on a presumption of equality, then it is the equality of each to all. If something like a society of equals is to come into being – as I fervently hope that it will – then the practices of equality must exceed and spill over from these moments of insurgency and come to be part of an everyday politics, and an everyday practice. These practices must reckon with the possibilities of coordination and organisation, but not collapse into them. We must therefore continue to imagine and reimagine what the possibilities of politics might be – and we must fight for those practices and politics that seek to expand, rather than contract, those uncertain possibilities.

Notes

Introduction

1. I am thinking of memoirs such as Nelson Mandela's *Long Walk to Freedom* (Randburg, Macdonald Purnell: 1994); and a short list of high-profile movies, including *Mandela: Long Walk to Freedom* (2013) and *Invictus* (2009).
2. Among a handful of prominent examples, see: R.W. Johnson, *South Africa's Brave New World: The Beloved Country Since the End of Apartheid* (London, Penguin: 2009) and Rian Malan, *The Lion Sleeps Tonight: And Other Stories of Africa* (New York, Grove Press: 2013).
3. See, for example, the range of approaches in William Beinart and Marcelle C. Dawson (eds), *Popular Protest and Resistance Movements in South Africa* (Johannesburg, Wits University Press: 2010). I return to these questions in Chapter Two, where I consider the ways in which South African politics has been written about more generally.
4. There are a multitude of classic works that could be cited here. Let me simply indicate one – Anthony Giddens, *The Constitution of Society: Outline of a Theory of Structuration* (Oxford, Polity Press: 1984) – as representative of its class.
5. Ernesto Laclau and Chantal Mouffe, *Hegemony and Socialist Strategy: Towards a Radical Democratic Politics* (London, Verso: 2nd edn, 2001). See also Mouffe's more recent work on 'agonistic' politics, e.g.: *Agonistics: Thinking the World Politically* (London, Verso: 2013).
6. This summary draws upon a range of Rancière's works – which are more fully canvassed in Chapter One of this book. A starting point, most explicitly

addressing questions of political theory, is Jacques Rancière's *Disagreement: Politics and Philosophy*, trans. Julie Rose (Minneapolis, University of Minnesota Press: 1999).

7. I have also benefitted from the commentaries and interpretations offered by Samuel Chambers, *The Lessons of Rancière* (New York, Oxford University Press: 2012), Todd May, *The Political Thought of Jacques Rancière: Creating Equality* (Edinburgh, Edinburgh University Press: 2008), and Kristin Ross, *May '68 and its Afterlives* (Chicago, University of Chicago Press: 2002) – although my version of Rancière diverges from theirs at significant moments.

Chapter 1

1. These include, for example: Thapelo Lekgowa, Botsang Mmope, and Peter Alexander, 'How Police Planned and Carried Out the Massacre at Marikana,' *Socialist Worker* (21 August 2012), http://socialistworker.co.uk/art. php?id=29403/ and Mandy de Waal, 'Marikana: What Really Happened? We may Never Know,' *Daily Maverick* (23 August 2012), http://www.dailymaverick. co.za/article/2012-08-23-marikana-what-really-happened-we-may-never-know/.

2. Greg Marinovich, 'The Murder Fields of Marikana. The Cold Murder Fields of Marikana,' *Daily Maverick* (30 August 2012, updated 8 September 2012), http://www.dailymaverick.co.za/article/2012-08-30-the-murder-fields-of-marikana-the-cold-murder-fields-of-marikana/.

3. See, for example: Peter Alexander, 'A massive rebellion of the poor,' *Mail and Guardian* (13 April 2012), http://mg.co.za/article/2012-04-13-a-massive-rebellion-of-the-poor/.

4. SAPS, 'An Analysis of the National Crime Statistics 2012/2013 – Addendum to the Annual Report,' published 31 August 2013, http://www.issafrica.org/crimehub/uploads/SAPS-crime-analysis-2013.pdf, pp. 43–44/.

5. Municipal IQ, '2012 Tally: A Violent and Diverse Year for Service Delivery Protests,' press release, published 17 January 2013, http://www.municipaliq. co.za/publications/press/201301170823583255.doc/; J. de Visser and D. Powell, 'Service Delivery Protest Barometer, 2007–2012,' (Cape Town, Multi-Level Government Initiative, Community Law Centre: 2012), http://mlgi.org. za/barometers/service-delivery-protest-barometer/.

6. http://www.afrobarometer.org/.

7. For the specific questions and responses, see: http://www.afrobarometer-online-analysis.com/ and the analysis of these figures published as: Jerry Lavery, 'Protest and Political Participation in South Africa: Time Trends and Characteristics of Protestors,' *Afrobarometer Briefing Paper*, no. 102 (May 2012).

8. To be more precise: in round five of the survey, 29% of South Africans said they would participate in a protest if they had the chance; another 11% said that they had participated in a protest during the previous year; and a further

2% did not know. This was the lowest level of participation recorded by the survey.

9. Lavery, 'Protest and Political Participation', p. 2.

10. Jane Duncan, 'The Politics of Counting Protest,' *Mail and Guardian* (17 April 2014), http://mg.co.za/article/2014-04-16-the-politics-of-counting-protests/.

11. Jane Duncan and Andrea Royeppen, 'Inside Rustenburg's Banned Protests,' *Daily Maverick* (7 March 2013), http://www.dailymaverick.co.za/article/2013-03-07-inside-rustenbergs-banned-protests/.

12. Mzi Memeza, *A Critical Review of the Implementation of the Regulation of Gatherings Act 205 of 1993*, (Johannesburg, Freedom of Expression Institute: 2006). See also: Dale T. McKinley and Ahmed Veriava, *Arresting Dissent: State Repression and Post-apartheid Social Movements* (Braamfontein, Centre for the Study of Violence and Reconciliation: 2005).

13. Robert Mattes, 'Forging Democrats: A Partial Success Story?' in Ian Shapiro and Kahreen Tebeau (eds), *After Apartheid: Reinventing South Africa* (Charlottesville, University of Virginia Press: 2011), p. 76.

14. Doreen Atkinson, 'Taking to the Street: Has Developmental Local Governance Failed?' in Sakhela Buhlungu, John Daniel, Roger Southall, and Jessica Lutchman (eds), *State of the Nation: South Africa 2007* (Pretoria, HSRC Press: 2007), pp. 53–77.

15. SA Government News Agency, 'High Level Task Team to Address Violent Protest' (10 February 2014), http://www.sanews.gov.za/south-africa/high-level-task-team-address-violent-protests/.

16. Faranak Miraftab, 'Invited and Invented Spaces of Participation: Neoliberal Citizenship and Feminists' Expanded Notion of Politics,' *Wagadu* 1 (2004); Andrea Cornwall, 'Locating Citizen Participation,' *IDS Bulletin*, 33.2 (2002).

17. See, for two prominent examples, Charles Tilly, *The Politics of Collective Violence* (Cambridge, Cambridge University Press: 2003) and Sidney Tarrow, *Power in Movement: Social Movements and Contentious Politics* (Cambridge, Cambridge University Press: 3rd edn, 2011).

18. Lavery, 'Protest and Political Participation', p. 6.

19. See: Frances Fox Piven and Richard A. Cloward, *Poor People's Movements: Why they Succeed, How they Fail* (New York, Pantheon Books: 1979); these particular quotes come from: Frances Fox Piven, *Challenging Authority: How Ordinary People Change America* (New York, Rowman & Littlefield: 2006), pp. 23–37.

20. Piven, *Challenging Authority*, p. 104.

21. The wage demands of rock drill operators (the key figures in the strike) have been widely considered. See: Paul Stewart, '"Kings of the Mine": Rock Drill Operators and the 2012 Strike Wave on South African Mines,' *South African Review of Sociology*, 44.3 (2013), 42–63.

22. The rejection of both unions was expressed in the opening statements at the Farlam Commission of Inquiry into the events at Marikana; the origin of the strike in shaft committees has been noted by Peter Alexander,

Thapelo Lekgowa, Botsang Mmope, Luke Sinwell, and Bongani Xezwi, *Marikana: A View from the Mountain and a Case to Answer* (Johannesburg, Jacana Press: 2012).

23. Jacques Rancière, *Disagreement: Politics and Philosophy*, trans. Julie Rose (Minneapolis, University of Minnesota Press: 1999), p. 30.

24. Jacques Rancière, *Hatred of Democracy*, trans. Steve Corcoran (London, Verso: 2006).

25. Jacques Rancière, *The Ignorant Schoolmaster: Five Lessons in Intellectual Emancipation*, trans. Kristin Ross (Stanford, Stanford University Press: 1991), p. 71.

26. Rancière, *Disagreement*, pp. 36–37. In the original text, the translator refers to the 'partition' of the sensible – I have standardised the translation in this text to the more common 'distribution'.

27. Rancière, *Disagreement*, p. 32.

28. Peter Hallward, 'Staging Equality: Rancière's Theatrocracy and the Limits of Anarchic Equality,' in Gabriel Rockhill and Philip Watts (eds), *Jacques Rancière: History, Politics, Aesthetics* (Durham, Duke University Press: 2009), pp. 140–157.

29. See: Slavoj Zizek, 'The Lesson of Rancière,' in Jacques Rancière, *The Politics of Aesthetics*, trans. and ed. Gabriel Rockhill (London, Continuum: 2004); Alain Badiou, 'The Lessons of Jacques Rancière: Knowledge and Power after the Storm,' in: Gabriel Rockhill and Philip Watts (eds) *Jacques Rancière*; Hallward, 'Staging Equality.'

30. This correspondence was widely reported. See, for example: Graeme Hosken, 'Ramaphosa Exposed,' *The Times* (24 October 2012), http://www.timeslive. co.za/thetimes/2012/10/24/ramaphosa-exposed/.

31. See, for example, the conclusions drawn in the documentary, *Miners Shot Down*, dir. Rehad Desai (2014).

32. The text of these emails was read into the record of the Commission's hearing on 5 February 2013, day 43 of the record.

33. This is the conclusion drawn by Alexander et al. in *Marikana: A View from the Mountain*.

34. e.g. Raphaël Botiveau, 'Briefing: The Politics of Marikana and South Africa's Changing Labour Relations,' *African Affairs*, 113.450 (2014), 128–137.

35. Proclamation: Establishment of a Commission of Inquiry in the Tragic Incident at or Near the Area Commonly Known as Marikana Mine in Rustenburg, North West Province, South Africa (no. 50, 2012).

36. See: Ian Macun, 'Workers Bypassing Unions: How to Respond?' submission to the Marikana Commission of Inquiry, Phase 2: Panel on Bargaining Arrangements in Platinum (31 March 2014), http://www.marikanacomm. org.za/docs/20140331-SeminarPhase02-platinum.pdf/.

37. Lisa Steyn, 'Amcu Declared Majority Union at Lonmin,' *Mail and Guardian* (14 August 2013), http://mg.co.za/article/2013-08-14-amcu-declared-official-majority-union-at-lonmin/.

38. *Association of Mineworkers and Construction Union v Lonmin Platinum (Comprising Eastern Platinum Ltd and Western Platinum Ltd) and Others* (J1134/14) [2014] ZALCJHB 196 (2 June 2014).
39. Jacques Rancière, 'A Few Remarks on the Method of Jacques Rancière,' *Parallax*, 15.3 (2009), 114–123.

Chapter 2

1. Julian Brown, 'Public Protest and Violence in South Africa, 1948–1976,' DPhil thesis (University of Oxford, Faculty of Modern History: 2009); Clive Glaser, *Bo-Tsotsi: The Young Gangs of Soweto* (Oxford, James Currey: 2000); Colin Bundy, 'Street Sociology and Pavement Politics: Aspects of Youth and Student Resistance in Cape Town, 1985' *Journal of Southern African Studies*, 13.3 (1987), 303–330; William Beinart, 'Politics and Collective Violence in Southern African Historiography'. *Journal of Southern African Studies*, 18.3 (1992), 455–486.
2. An early analysis of the first democratic election can be found in: Roger Southall, 'The South African Elections of 1994: The Remaking of a Dominant-Party State,' *Journal of Modern African Studies*, 32.4 (1994), 629–655.
3. Andrew Reynolds, *Electoral Systems and Democratization in Southern Africa* (New York, Oxford University Press: 1999); Lia Nijink and Jessica Piombo, 'Parliament and the Electoral System: How are South Africans Being Represented?' in *Electoral Politics in South Africa: Assessing the First Democratic Decade* (Pretoria, HSRC: 2005), pp. 64–86.
4. Roger Southall provides a useful overview of this argument in the mid-2000s: 'The 'Dominant Party' Debate in South Africa,' *Africa Spectrum*, 40.1 (2005), 61–82.
5. For an analysis of shifts in electoral participation, and the disputes around these figures, see Colette Shulz-Herzenberg, 'Voter Participation in the South African Elections of 2014,' Institute for Security Studies Policy Brief 61 (August 2014), http://www.issafrica.org/uploads/PolBrief61_Aug14.pdf/.
6. Here, I am referring to a series of incidents that took place towards the end of 2014 in which the South African Police Services entered into parliament and removed representatives of the EFF from the Chamber. This was allegedly at the request of the Speaker's Office – although the details are contested.
7. Anthony Giddens, *The Constitution of Society: Outline of A Theory of Structuration* (Oxford, Polity Press: 1984).
8. A crisp and early summary of this is provided by: Gary Baines, 'The Rainbow Nation? Identity and Nation Building in Post-apartheid South Africa,' *Mots Pluriels*, 7 (1998), 1–10.
9. Preamble to the *Promotion of National Unity and Reconciliation Act* (Act 34 of 1995). See also: Desmond Tutu, *No Future Without Forgiveness* (London, Random House: 1999).

10. *Constitution of the Republic of South Africa Act* (Act 200 of 1993). This interim constitution was repealed in 1996 by the final *Constitution of the Republic of South Africa Act* (Act 108 of 1996).

11. A powerful critique of this discourse was offered by Pumla Gqola, 'Defining People: Analysing Power, Language and Representation in Metaphors of the New South Africa,' *Transformation*, 47 (2001), 94–106.

12. e.g. Tom Lodge, *Politics in South Africa: From Mandela to Mbeki* (Oxford, James Currey: 2002).

13. For a balanced take on Mbeki's personality, see: Mark Gevisser, *Thabo Mbeki: The Dream Deferred* (Cape Town, Jonathan Ball: 2007); for a series of academic analyses premised on the tone that this personality gave to the state, see: Daryl Glaser (ed.), *Mbeki and After: Reflections on the Legacy of Thabo Mbeki* (Johannesburg, Wits University Press: 2010).

14. It has also given rise to the political biography as one of the principal sites of political analysis. In addition to Gevisser's biography of Mbeki, see Jeremy Gordin, *Zuma: A Biography* (Cape Town, Jonathan Ball: 2010); Anthony Butler, *Cyril Ramaphosa* (Johannesburg, Jacana: rev. edn, 2011); Fiona Forde, *An Inconvenient Youth: Julius Malema and the 'New' ANC* (Johannesburg, Picador Africa: 2011); Ebrahim Harvey, *Kgalema Motlanthe: A Political Biography* (Johannesburg, Jacana: 2012).

15. e.g. Adam Habib, *South Africa's Suspended Revolution* (Johannesburg, Wits University Press: 2013).

16. e.g. Stephen Gelb, 'The RDP, GEAR, and all that: reflections 10 years later,' *Transformation*, 62 (2006), 1–8; Hein Marais, *South Africa: Limits to Change: The Political Economy of Transition* (London, Zed Books: 2nd edn, 2001).

17. e.g. John S. Saul, 'Cry for the Beloved Country: The Post-apartheid Denouement,' *Review of African Political Economy*, 28.89 (2001), 429–460.

18. e.g. Patrick Bond, *Elite Transition: From Apartheid to Neoliberalism in South Africa* (London, Pluto Press: 2002) and Bond, *Talk Left, Walk Right: South Africa's Frustrated Global Reforms* (Pietermaritzburg, UKZN Press: 2004).

19. Simon Kimani Ndung'u (ed.), *The Right to Dissent: Freedom of Expression, Assembly and Demonstration in South Africa* (Johannesburg, Freedom of Expression Institute: 2003); Carl Death, 'Troubles at the Top: South African Protests and the 2002 Johannesburg Summit,' *African Affairs*, 109.437 (2010), 555–574.

20. Nathan Geffen, *Debunking Delusions: The Inside Story of the Treatment Action Campaign* (Johannesburg, Jacana: 2010); Mandisa Mbali, *South African AIDS Activism and Global Health Politics* (New York, Palgrave Macmillan: 2013).

21. Alex Wafer, 'Scale and Identity in Post-apartheid Soweto,' *Transformation*, 66/67 (2008), 98–115; Prishani Naidoo and Ahmed Veriava, 'From Local to Global (and Back Again?): Anti-commodification Struggles of the Soweto Electricity Crisis Committee,' in David A. McDonald (ed.), *Electric Capitalism: Recolonising Africa on the Power Grid* (Pretoria, HSRC Press: 2009), pp. 321–337.

22. Marcelle Dawson, 'Phasi Privatisations! Phansi! The Anti-privatisation Forum and Ideology in Social Movements,' in W. Beinart and M. Dawson (eds), *Popular Politics and Resistance Movements in South Africa* (Johannesburg, Wits University Press: 2010), pp. 266–285.

23. Ashwin Desai, *'We Are the Poors'*: *Community Struggles in Post-Apartheid South Africa* (New York, Monthly Review Press: 2002).

24. See, in particular, the work associated with the Centre for Civil Society (CCS) at the University of KwaZulu-Natal: http://ccs.ukzn.ac.za/.

25. Richard Ballard, Adam Habib, and Imraan Valodia (eds), *Voices of Protest: Social Movements in Post-apartheid South Africa* (Pietermaritzburg, UKZNPress: 2006).

26. e.g. Richard Pithouse, 'That the Tool Never Possess the Man: Taking Fanon's Humanism Seriously,' *Politikon*, 30.1 (2003), 107–131; Pithouse, 'A Politics of the Poor: Shack Dweller's Struggles in Durban,' *Journal of Asian and African Studies*, 43.1 (2008), 63–94; Pithouse, 'Conjunctural Notes on the Politics of the Local in South Africa,' *Thesis* 11, 115.1 (2013), 95–111; and Nigel Gibson, *Fanonian Practices in South Africa: From Steve Biko to Abahlali baseMjondolo* (New York, Palgrave Macmillan: 2011).

27. e.g. William Beinart and Marcelle C. Dawson (eds), *Popular Protest and Resistance Movements in South Africa* (Johannesburg, Wits University Press: 2010).

28. The eviction at Bredell has been written about by several scholars. I draw upon two in particular: Marie Huchzermeyer, 'Housing Rights in South Africa: Invasions, Evictions, the Media, and the Courts in the Cases of Grootboom, Alexandra, and Bredell,' *Urban Forum*, 14.1 (2003), 80–107; Gillian Hart, *Rethinking the South African Crisis: Nationalism, Populism, Hegemony* (Pietermaritzburg, UKZN Press: 2013).

29. As quoted in Huchzermeyer, 'Housing Rights,' pp. 98 and 96.

30. Hart, *Rethinking the South African Crisis.*

31. On housing, see: Marie Huchzermeyer, *Cities With 'Slums': From Informal Settlement Eradication to a Right to the City in Africa* (Cape Town, UCT Press: 2011). On trading, see: Caroline Skinner, 'The Struggle for the Streets: Processes of Exclusion and Inclusion of Street Traders in Durban, South Africa,' *Development Southern Africa* 25.2 (2008), 227–242.

32. Stuart Wilson, 'Breaking the Tie: Evictions from Private Land, Homelessness and a New Normality,' *South African Law Journal*, 126 (2009), 270–290.

33. Karl von Holdt, 'Nationalism, Bureaucracy, and the Developmental State: the South African case,' *South African Review of Sociology*, 41.1 (2010), 4–27; Ivor Chipkin, 'Transcending Bureaucracy: State Transformation in the Age of the Manager,' *Transformation*, 77 (2011), 31–51.

34. Julian Brown and Stuart Wilson, 'A Presumed Equality: The Relationship Between State and Citizens in Post-apartheid South Africa,' *African Studies*, 72.1 (2013).

35. Government of South Africa (SA), Ministry for Provincial Affairs and Constitutional Development, *The White Paper on Local Government* (Pretoria: 1998), Foreword.

36. SA, Department for Provincial and Local Government, *Draft National Policy Framework for Public Participation* (Pretoria, Department for Provincial and Local Government: 2005).
37. Steven Friedman, *Participatory Governance and Citizen Action in Post-apartheid South Africa*, International Labour Organisations Discussion Paper (Geneva, International Institute for Labour Studies: 2006).
38. Friedman, *Participatory Governance*; Doreen Atkinson, 'Taking to the Streets: Has Developmental Local Governance Failed in South Africa?' in Sakhela Buhlungu, John Daniel, Roger Southall, and Jessica Lutchman (eds), *State of the Nation: South Africa 2007* (Pretoria, HSRC Press: 2007); Susan Booysen, 'Public Participation in Democratic South Africa: From Popular Mobilisation to Structured Co-optation and Protest,' *Politeia*, 28.1 (2009), 1–27.

Chapter 3

1. Flyer, 'One Makause, One Community Police Brutality Campaign' (October 2012). In author's possession.
2. Socio-Economic Rights Institute (SERI), *Makause: Resisting Relocation on the East Rand*, Community Practice Note, Informal Settlement Series no. 1 (Johannesburg, SERI: 2014).
3. *State v Moyo, Setswana and Sisulu*, Germiston Magistrates' Court, case number 4SH 382/12. Sworn statement of Grant Layton Glenn.
4. Clive Plasket and Richard Spoor, 'The New Offence of Intimidation,' *Industrial Law Journal*, 12 (1991). See also: Shannon Hoctor, 'How far Should the Crime of Intimidation Extend?' *Obiter* (2002).
5. *S v Moyo et al.*, charge sheet.
6. *S v Moyo et al.*, sworn statement of Kgabo Gabriel Kwenaile.
7. A brief history of the Forum can be found in Malcolm Langford, 'Housing Rights Litigation: Grootboom and Beyond,' in Malcolm Langford, Ben Cousins, Jackie Dugard, and Tshepo Madlingozi (eds), *Socio-Economic Rights in South Africa: Symbols or Substance?* (Cambridge, Cambridge University Press: 2014).
8. T.H. Marshall, 'Citizenship and Social Class,' in *Sociology at the Crossroads and Other Essays* (London, Heinemann: 1963), p. 87.
9. J.G.A. Pocock, 'The Ideal of Citizenship since Classical Times,' in Ronald Beiner (ed.), *Theorising Citizenship* (Albany, SUNY Press: 1995), pp. 29–52.
10. Jacques Rancière, *Disagreement*, trans. Julie Rose (Minneapolis, University of Minnesota Press: 1999), especially pp. 1–17.
11. Ruth Lister, *Citizenship: Feminist Perspectives* (New York, NYU Press: 2003); Iris Marion Young, 'Polity and Group Difference: A Critique of the Ideal of Universal Citizenship', *Ethics*, 99.2 (1989), 250–274.
12. Sandra Liebenberg, 'Social Citizenship – A Precondition for Meaningful Democracy,' *Agenda*, 40 (1999), 59–65.

13. Shireen Hassim, 'Nationalism Displaced: Citizenship in the Transition,' in Amanda Gouws (ed.), (Un)Thinking Citizenship: Feminist Debates in South Africa (Cape Town, UCT Press: 2005), pp. 55, 57.

14. e.g. Peter Dwyer, Understand Social Citizenship: Themes and Perspectives for Policy and Practice (Bristol, Policy Press: 2010); see also Patrick Heller, 'Moving the State: The Politics of Democratic Decentralisation in Kerala, South Africa, and Porto Alegre', Politics and Society, 29.1 (2001), 131–163; Michelle Williams, The Roots of Participatory Democracy: Democratic Communists in South Africa and Kerala, India (New York, Palgrave Macmillan: 2008).

15. Engin F. Isin, 'Theorising Acts of Citizenship,' in Engin F. Isin and Greg M. Nielsen (eds), Acts of Citizenship (London, Zed Books: 2008), pp. 15–43. See also: Isin, 'Citizenship in Flux: The Figure of the Activist Citizen,' Subjectivity, 29 (2009), 367–388.

16. This last set of categories is the focus of Peter Nyers, 'No One is Illegal: Between City and Nation,' in Isin and Nielsen (eds), Acts of Citizenship (2008), pp. 160–181.

17. Isin, 'Theorising Acts of Citizenship,' pp. 28–35.

18. Mikhail Bakhtin, Toward a Philosophy of the Act, trans. Vadim Liapunov (Austin, University of Texas Press: 1993). For a useful account of this long (and unfinished) essay, see: Gary Saul Morson and Caryl Emerson, 'Introduction: Rethinking Bakhtin,' in Morson and Emerson (eds), Rethinking Bakhtin: Extensions and Challenges (Evanston, Northwestern University Press: 1989), especially pp. 5–30.

19. Gary Saul Morson and Caryl Emerson, Mikhail Bakhtin: Creation of a Prosaics (Stanford, Stanford University Press: 1990).

20. Isin, 'Theorising Acts of Citizenship,' pp. 37–38.

21. James Holston, Insurgent Citizenship: Disjunctions of Democracy and Modernity in Brazil (Princeton, Princeton University Press: 2008).

22. See, in particular, Carin Runciman's PhD thesis: Runciman, Mobilisation and Insurgent Citizenship of the Anti-Privatisation Forum, South Africa: An Ethnographic Survey (PhD thesis, University of Glasgow: 2012); also, for a more passing use, Karl von Holdt, et al., The Smoke that Calls: Insurgent Citizenship, Collective Violence and the Struggle for a Place in the New South Africa – Eight Case Studies of Community Protest and Xenophobic Violence (Johannesburg, CSVR and SWOP: 2011).

23. Mikhail Bakhtin, Rabelais and His World, trans. Helen Iswolsky (Cambridge, MIT Press: 1968).

24. Faranak Miraftab, 'Feminist Praxis, Citizenship and Informal Politics: Reflections on South Africa's Anti-Eviction Campaign,' International Feminist Journal of Politics, 8.2 (2006), 194–218. See also: Miraftab, 'Invited and Invented Spaces of Participation: Neoliberal Citizenship and Feminists' Expanded Notion of Politics,' Wagadu Volume 1 (Spring 2004), and – for another version of this argument – Luke Sinwell, 'Participatory Spaces and the Alexandra Vukuzenzele Crisis Committee (AVCC): Reshaping Government Plans', Social Dynamics, 35.2 (2009), 436–449.

25. Miraftab, 'Feminist Praxis,' p. 208.

26. Barbara Cruikshank, *The Will to Empower: Democratic Citizens and Other Subjects* (Ithaca, Cornell University Press: 1999), p. 123.

27. For an influential version of this argument in the Africanist context, see: Mahmood Mamdani, *Citizen and Subject: Contemporary Africa and the Legacy of Late Colonialism* (Cape Town, David Philip: 1996).

28. The influence of Foucault is central to Cruikshank's work. See, in particular: Michel Foucault, *Discipline and Punish: The Birth of the Prison*, trans. Alan Sheridan (London, Allen Lane: 1977).

29. Government of South Africa, Department of Provincial and Local Government, *Having Your Say: A Handbook for Ward Committees* (Pretoria, Government of South Africa, Department of Provincial and Local Government: 2005).

30. Pearl Sithole, Alison Todes, and Amanda Williamson, 'Gender and Women's Participation in Municipality-driven Development: IDP and Project-level Participation in Msinga, eThekwini and Hibiscus Coast,' *Critical Dialogue – Participation in Review*, 3.1 (2007) draws attention to how, even when the requirement is formally met, differential levels of participation at stages of participatory processes are not accounted for.

31. Laurence Piper and Nonhlanhla Chanza, 'Too 'Raw' to Represent: The Marginalisation of Youth in Msunduzi Ward Committees,' *Critical Dialogue – Participation in Review*, 2.2 (2006).

32. SA, Department of Provincial and Local Government, *The White Paper* (1998).

33. Government of South Africa, Department of Provincial and Local Government, *National Policy Framework on Participation* (Pretoria, Government of South Africa, Department of Provincial and Local Government: 2007), p. 55.

34. Laurence Piper and Roger Deacon, 'Too Dependent to Participate: Ward Committees and Local Democratisation in South Africa,' *Local Government Studies*, 35.4 (2009), 415–433.

35. Not all of these were foreign nationals. A significant percentage – about a third – were South Africans. This has been used to problematise the discourse of xenophobic violence as it emerged at the time – but, regardless, it is undeniable that the majority of the brutality was aimed at foreign nationals.

36. See, amongst others: Jonathan Crush (ed.), *The Perfect Storm: The Realities of Xenophobia in Contemporary South Africa*, Migration Policy Series, no. 50 (Cape Town, South African Migration Project: 2008); and Shireen Hassim, Tawana Kupe, and Eric Worby (eds), *Go Home or Die Here: Violence, Xenophobia and the Reinvention of Difference in South Africa* (Johannesburg, Wits University Press: 2008).

37. e.g. Tamlyn Jane Monson, 'Sub-National Sovereignties? Territory, Authority and Regulation in Three Sites of "Xenophobic Violence" in South Africa,' MA thesis (University of the Witwatersrand: 2010).

38. Michael Neocosmos, *From 'Foreign Natives' to 'Native Foreigners': Explaining Xenophobia in Post-apartheid South Africa – Citizenship and Nationalism, Identity and Politics* (Dakar, Codesria Monograph Series: 2006), p. vi.

39. Crush (ed.), *The Perfect Storm*.

40. Tamlyn Monson and Jean-Pierre Misago, 'Why History Repeats Itself: The Security Risks of Structural Xenophobia,' *SA Crime Quarterly*, 29.25–34, (2009), p. 27. See also a brief comment in Ndodana Nleya, Lisa Thompson, Chris Tapscott, Laurence Piper, and Michele Esau, 'Reconsidering the Origins of Protest in South Africa: Some Lessons from Cape Town and Pietermaritzburg,' *Africanus*, 50.1 (2011), 14.29 – 'Street committees have been associated with many protests, including those regarding xenophobia', (p. 24).

41. e.g. *Mamba v Minister of Social Development* CCT 65/08 (21 August 2008).

42. e.g. the TAC as captured in Steven Robins, 'Humanitarian Aid Beyond "Bare Survival": Social Movement Response to Xenophobic Violence in South Africa,' *American Ethnologist*, 36.4 (2009), 637–650.

43. e.g. Abahlali baseMjondolo, 'Statement on the Xenophobic Attacks in Johannesburg,' (21 May 2008), http://abahlali.org/node/3582/.

44. See the debates around Jacob Zuma's trial for rape, in the period before he became President: e.g. Shireen Hassim, 'Democracy's Shadows: Sexual Rights and Gender Politics in the Rape Trial of Jacob Zuma,' *African Studies*, 68.1 (2009), 57–77; Mark Hunter, 'Beneath the "Zunami": Jacob Zuma and the Gendered Politics of Social Reproduction in South Africa,' *Antipode*, 43.4 (2011), 1102–1126; Raymond Suttner, 'The Jacob Zuma Rape Trial: Power and African National Congress (ANC) Masculinities,' *NORA – Nordic Journal of Feminist and Gender Research*, 17.3 (2009), 222–236.

45. For traditional authority, see: Aninka Claassens and Sizani Ngubane, 'Women, Land and Power: The Impact of the Communal Land Rights Act,' in Ben Cousins and Aninka Claassens (eds), *Land, Power and Custom: Controversies Generated by South Africa's Communal Land Rights Act* (Cape Town, UCT Press: 2008). For the ambiguous position of feminism in SA's courts, see: Catherine Albertyn, 'Defending and Securing Rights Through Law: Feminism, Law and the Courts in South Africa,' *Politikon*, 32.2 (2005), 217–237; Lisa Vetten and Danielle Motelow, 'Creating State Accountability to Rape Survivors: A Case Study of Boksburg Regional Court,' *Agenda*, 18.62 (2004), 45–52 and Lisa Vetten and Francois van Jaarsveld, 'The (Mis)Measure of Harm: An Analysis of Rape Sentences Handed Down in the Regional and High Courts of Gauteng Province,' Tshwaranang Legal Advocacy Centre Working Paper No. 1 (2008).

46. e.g. Steven Robins, 'Sexual Politics and the Zuma Rape Trial,' *Journal of Southern African Studies*, 34.2 (2008), 411–427; Cathi Albertyn and Shamim Meer, 'Citizens or Mothers? The Marginalisation of Women's Reproductive Rights in the Struggle for Access to Health Care for HIV-positive Pregnant Women in South Africa,' *Gender Rights and Development: A Global Sourcebook* (Amsterdam, Royal Tropical Institute: 2008), pp. 27–55.

47. South African Government News Agency, 'High Level Task Team to Address Violent Protests' (10 February 2014), http://www.sanews.gov.za/south-africa/high-level-task-team-address-violent-protests/.

48. South African Government News Agency, 'GP Residents Urged to Respect the Gatherings Act' (12 February 2014), http://www.sanews.gov.za/south-africa/gp-residents-urged-respect-gatherings-act/.
49. This conference was widely reported, along with these figures and the following quotes. See, for three examples: Alex Eliseev, 'Analysis: Bonfires of Discontent, in Terrifying Numbers,' *Daily Maverick* (5 February 2014), http://www.dailymaverick.co.za/article/2014-02-05-analysis-bonfires-of-discontent-in-horrifying-numbers/; SAPA, 'Police: Public Must not be "Armchair Critics",' *Mail and Guardian* (5 February 2014), http://mg.co.za/article/2014-02-05-police-public-must-not-be-armchair-critics;   Nokuthula Manyathi, 'Senior Cop Admits Deployment Strategy Could be "factor" in Shooting of Protestors,' *City Press* (5 February 2014), http://www.citypress.co.za/news/senior-cop-admits-deployment-strategy-factor-shooting-protesters/.
50. Quoted in Michael Clark, *An Anatomy of Dissent and Repression: The Criminal Justice System and the 2011 Thembelihle Protest*, Socio-Economic Rights Institute of South Africa, Working Paper No. 2 (Johannesburg, SERI: 2014).

Chapter 4

1. *Constitution of the Republic of South Africa Act* (no. 108 of 1996).
2. *South African National Defence Union v Minister of Defence* (CCT27/98) [1999] ZACC 7; 1999 (4) SA 469; 1999 (6) BCLR 615 (26 May 1999), para. 8.
3. Anna Majavu, 'Penalizing Protest Action,' *SACSIS* (19 June 2012), http://sacsis.org.za/site/article/1338/.
4. Dale T. McKinley, 'State Security and Civil-Political Rights in South Africa,' *Strategic Review for Southern Africa*, 35.1 (2013), 118–134.
5. Peter Gastrow, *Bargaining for Peace: South Africa and the National Peace Accord* (Washington, USIP Press: 1995).
6. Janine Rauch, 'A Preliminary Assessment of the Impact of the Peace Accord Code of Conduct on Police Behaviour,' Paper presented at the Centre for Criminal Justice Conference, *Policing in the New South Africa II* (Durban: 1992), http://www.csvr.org.za/old/wits/papers/papeasjr.htm/.
7. *The National Peace Accord*, sections 3.2.5.1 and 3.6 (see: http://www.anc.org.za/show.php?id=3967/).
8. Philip B. Heymann (ed.), *Towards Peaceful Protest in South Africa: Testimony of Multinational Panel Regarding Lawful Control of Demonstrations in the Republic of South Africa* (Pretoria, HSRC: 1991).
9. Heymann, *Towards Peaceful Protest*, p. 13.
10. Kevin Durrheim and Marc Foster, 'Technologies of Social Control: Crowd Management in a Liberal Democracy,' *Economy and Society*, 28.1 (1999), 56–74.
11. Heymann, *Towards Peaceful Protest*, pp. 23–36.
12. Heymann, *Towards Peaceful Protest*, p. 4.

13. Heymann, *Towards Peaceful Protest*, p. 15.
14. 'Interim Agreement between the South African Police, the African National Congress, Cosatu, the South African Communist Party and the Inkatha Freedom Party on the Conduct of Public Demonstrations' (Cape Town, Government Printer: 16 July 1992).
15. 'Press Release by the Honourable Mr Justice R.J. Goldstone, Chairman of the Commission of Inquiry Regarding the Prevention of Public Violence and Intimidation,' (Pretoria: 23 July 1992), in Heymann, *Towards Peaceful Protest*, pp. 194–196.
16. R.J. Goldstone, 'Final Report of the Commission of Inquiry regarding the Prevention of Public Violence and Intimidation by the Committee Established to Inquire into Public Violence and Intimidation at Mass Demonstrations, Marches and Picketing' (Pretoria, Government Printer: 28 April 1993).
17. Government Gazette No. 17623 (15 November 1996).
18. *Regulation of Gatherings Act* (No. 205 of 1993).
19. Durrheim and Foster, 'Technologies of Social Control,' pp. 69–70.
20. Mzi Memeza, *A Critical Review of the Implementation of the Regulation of Gatherings Act 205 of 1993: A Local Government and Civil Society Perspective* (Johannesburg, FXI: 2006). See also: Simon Kimani N'dungu (ed.), *The Right to Dissent: Freedom of Expression, Assembly and Demonstration in South Africa* (Johannesburg, FXI: 2003).
21. Memeza, *Critical Review*, p. 7.
22. 'DA to Appeal JMPD Decision to Ban March for Six Million REAL Jobs' (1 February 2014), http://dajhb.co.za/?p=1398/.
23. SAPA, 'DA Wins March Appeal,' *City Press* (3 February 2014), http://www.city-press.co.za/politics/da-wins-march-appeal/.
24. Marie Huchzermeyer, 'The Struggle for *in Situ* Upgrading of Informal Settlements: A Reflection on Cases in Gauteng,' *Development Southern Africa*, 26.1 (2009), 59–73.
25. J. du Plessis and S. Wilson, *Any Room for the Poor? Forced Evictions in Johannesburg, South Africa* (Geneva, Centre on Housing Rights and Evictions: 2005), pp. 86–90.
26. Interview with Siphiwe Segodi, conducted by Dale McKinley, Johannesburg, 23 August 2010. Transcript held in the South African History Archive (SAHA), AL3290 (Records of the Anti-Privatisation Forum), p. 6.
27. Ann Eveleth, 'Criminalising dissent: experiences of the Landless People's Movement and the National Land Committee during the WSSD,' in Ndung'u (ed.), *The Right to Dissent*, p. 88.
28. *The City of Johannesburg v Occupiers of the Thembelihle Informal Settlement*, South Gauteng High Court, Case No. 03/10106. Unreported case.
29. Thapelo Tselapedi and Jackie Dugard, 'Reclaiming Power: A Case Study of Thembelihle Crisis Committee,' *Active Citizenship Matters: Perspectives from Civil Society on Local Governance in South Africa* (Cape Town, Good Governance Learning Network: 2013), pp. 57–65.
30. Memeza, *A Critical Review*, pp. 14–20.

31. These quotations can be found in Memeza, *A Critical Review*, p. 19.
32. Segodi, transcript, p. 9.
33. Durrheim and Foster, 'Technologies of Social Control,' p. 66.
34. Stuart Hall, quoted in Durrheim and Foster, 'Technologies of Social Control,' p. 66.
35. *South African Transport and Allied Workers Union and Another v Garvas and Others* (CCT 112/11) [2012] ZACC 13; 2012 (8) BCLR 840 (CC); [2012] 10 BLLR 959 (CC); (2012) 33 ILJ 1593 (CC); 2013 (1) SA 83 (CC) (13 June 2012).
36. *South African Transport and Allied Workers Union v Garvis [sic] & Others* (007/11) [2011] ZASCA 152; 2011 (6) SA 382 (SCA); 2011 (12) BCLR 1249 (SCA); [2011] 4 All SA 475 (SCA); [2011] 12 BLLR 1151 (SCA); (2011) 32 ILJ 2426 (SCA) (27 September 2011), paras. 36–38.
37. See: *Abahlali baseMjondolo Movement South Africa and 30 Others v Ethekwini Municipality and the MEC for Human Settlements of the Province of KwaZulu-Natal*, case no. 9189/2013, KwaZulu-Natal High Court, Durban.
38. Abahlali baseMjondolo, 'Marikana Continues: Statement on the Murder of Nqobile Nzuzao' (3 October 2013), http://abahlali.org/node/12292/.
39. *State v Bandile Mdalose*, Durban Regional Court, case no. 23/16747/13 (2013), unreported case. Video exhibit.
40. *State v Mdalose*, Sworn Statement of Valen Govender (30 September 2013).
41. SAHA, APF Papers, *Note: Tembalihle [sic] Struggle, Complied by APF Organiser – Silumko Radebe* (2007).
42. See, for example: APF, 'Charges Against Boiketlong and Thembelihle Activists Dropped,' (16 August 2007), http://apf.org.za/spip.php?article209/.
43. A useful overview of the complexities of electoral politics in Thembelihle can be found in a recent Masters thesis: Nicholette Pingo, 'Institutionalisation of a Social Movement: The Case of Thembelihle, the Thembelihle Crisis Committee, and the Operation Khanyisa Movement, and the Use of the Brick, the Ballot, and the Voice,' MSc thesis (Johannesburg, University of the Witwatersand: 2013).
44. Quoted in Michael Clark, *An Anatomy of Dissent and Repression: The Criminal Justice System and the 2011 Thembelihle Protest*, Socio-Economic Rights Institute of South Africa Working paper no. 2 (Johannesburg, SERI: 2014).
45. See: 'Thembelihle Protests Caused R1.5 Million in Damage,' *City Press* (7 September 2011), http://www.citypress.co.za/news/thembelihle-protests-caused-r15m-in-damage-20110907/; 'Thembelihle protestors' fire causes R1.5m damage,' *Mail and Guardian* (7 September 2011), http://mg.co.za/article/2011-09-07-thembelihle-protesters-fire-causes-r15m-damage/; 'Thembelihle Protest Costs City R1.5bn,' *Eye Witness News* (7 September 2011), http://ewn.co.za/2011/09/07/Thembelihle-protest-costs-City-R15-bn/.
46. *The State v Bhayi Bhayi Miya*, Magistrates' Court for the District of Protea, Gauteng, case no. 69/4121/11 (2011). Unreported case. Sworn statement of Lt-Col L.K. Ndlovu, p. 4.

47. *State* v *Miya*. Sworn statement of Ndlovu, p. 4
48. *State* v *Wonder Nkosi and Thirteen Others*, Magistrates' Court for the District of Protea, Gauteng, case no. 43/01308/2011. Unreported case.
49. *State* v *Miya*, charge sheet.
50. SAHA, APF Papers, 'Note – Tembalihle [sic] Struggle', p. 2.
51. Clark, *An Anatomy of Dissent*, pp. 34–46.
52. Bandile Mdalose, 'Seven Days of Thoughts in Westville Prison,' http://abahlali.org/node/12544/.
53. *State* v *Moyo, Swetsana and Sisulu*, case no. 320/10/2012, Magistrates' Court for the District of Germiston. Sworn statement of Mthota Derick Khanya.
54. The figure is disputed – the Terms of Reference for the Marikana Commission specify 'approximately 250', while news reports have tended to estimate 270 arrested miners: e.g. http://www.bbc.com/news/world-africa-19424484/.
55. As reported by Alex Duval Smith, 'Miners Charged with Murder – of Colleagues Shot Dead by the Police,' *The Independent* (30 August 2012), http://www.independent.co.uk/news/world/africa/miners-charged-with-murder--of-colleagues-shot-dead-by-police-8092835.html/.
56. Pierre de Vos, 'Marikana: No Common Purpose to Commit Suicide,' (30 August 2012), http://constitutionallyspeaking.co.za/marikana-no-common-purpose-to-commit-suicide/.
57. Jane Duncan, 'The Criminal Injustice System,' *SACSIS* (18 February 2013), http://www.sacsis.org.za/site/article/1574/.
58. Durrheim and Foster, 'Technologies of Social Control,' p. 70.

Chapter 5

1. Bandile Mdalose, 'Seven Days of Thoughts in Westville Prison,' http://abahlali.org/node/12544/.
2. SAHA, APF Archives, 'Note – Tembalihle [sic] Struggle, Compiled by APF Organiser, Silumko Radbe' (2007).
3. Malcolm Wallis, 'Some Thoughts on the Commercial Side of Practice,' *Advocate*, 25.1 (2012), p. 35. See also the comments of the Constitutional Court on the disproportionate rise in legal fees in recent years in *Camps Bay Ratepayers and Residents Association and Another* v *Harrison and Another* (CCT 76/12) [2012] ZACC 17; 2012 (11) BCLR 1143 (CC) (20 September 2012).
4. David McQuoid-Mason, 'The Delivery of Civil Legal Aid Services in South Africa,' *Fordham International Law Journal* 24.6 (2000), pp. S111–S142, provides a useful survey of the political and legislative background to the state provision of legal aid in post-apartheid South Africa.
5. A survey of LASA's activities is provided by Hennie van As, 'Legal Aid in South Africa: Making Justice Reality,' *Journal of African Law*, 49.1 (2005), 54–72.

6. See the litigation that followed from LASA's decision to refuse to support legal representation for the approximately 250 miners arrested after the Marikana massacre at the Commission: *Magidiwana and Another v President of the Republic of South Africa and Others* (37904/2013) [2013] ZAGPPHC 292; [2014] 1 All SA 76 (GNP) (14 October 2013).

7. My emphasis. See: http://www.legal-aid.co.za/?p=956/.

8. Legal Aid South Africa, *Legal Aid Guide* 2014 (Johannesburg, Juta: 13th edn, 2014) pp. 94 and 143.

9. SAHA, APF Archives, 'Note – Tembalihle [sic] Struggle.'

10. Van As, 'Legal Aid in South Africa,' p. 54. This figure relates to the 2002/3 reporting period.

11. See, for a recent example of a non-South African case: Dale Carpenter, *Flagrant Conduct: The Story of Lawrence v Texas: How a Bedroom Arrest Decriminalised Gay Americans* (New York, Norton: 2012).

12. e.g. Gilbert Marcus and Steven Budlender, *A Strategic Evaluation of Public Interest Litigation in South Africa* (Atlantic Philanthropies, Johannesburg: 2008), pp. 124–126.

13. Although it does not focus on litigating NGOs, Julie Hearn's 'Aiding Democracy? Donors and Civil Society in South Africa,' *Third World Quarterly*, 21.5 (2000), 815–830, provides a clear and detailed articulation of this argument, suggesting that international influence had shaped the focus of some South African NGOs and CSOs on arguing for 'formal democracy' rather than more substantive forms of redistributive politics.

14. e.g. Heinrich Bohmke, 'The Shackdwellers and the Intellectuals,' (21 October 2010) http://www.politicsweb.co.za/politicsweb/view/politicsweb/en/page71619?oid=206254&sn=Detail/; Shannon Walsh, Patrick Bond, and Ashwin Desai,. '"Uncomfortable Collaborations": Contesting Constructions of the "Poor" in South Africa,' *Review of African Political Economy*, 35.116 (2008), 255–279.

15. See the discussions in Tshepo Madlingozi, 'Post Apartheid Social Movements and Legal Mobilisation,' in M. Langford, B. Cousins, J. Dugard, and T. Madlingozi (eds) *Socio-Economic Rights in South Africa: Symbols or Substance?* (Cambridge, Cambridge University Press: 2013), pp. 92–130, and Michael Neocosmos, 'Civil Society, Citizenship and the Politics of the (Im)Possible: Rethinking Militancy in Africa Today,' *Interface*, 1.2 (2009), 263–334.

16. Stuart Wilson, 'Litigating Housing Rights in Johannesburg's Inner City, 2004–2008,' *South African Journal on Human Rights*, 27 (2011), 127–151; 127 and 151.

17. SERI, *Rooigrond: Community Struggle in the North West*, Community Practice Notes, Informal Settlement Series no. 2 (SERI, Johannesburg: 2014), p. 7.

18. SABC, 'N West Rooigrond Residents Protest' (27 April 2014), http://www.sabc.co.za/news/a/6261b98043cb18f198069afocofe2c4c/N-West-Rooigrond-residents-protest/.

19. Andrew Manson, '"Punching Above its Weight"': The Mafikeng Anti-Repression Forum (Maref) and the Fall of Bophuthatswana,' *African Historical Review*, 43.2 (2011), 55–83.

20. SERI, *Rooigrond*.

21. Linda Stewart, '14 Years in Limbo: Waiting for the Promised Land,' Report prepared for Rooigrond (2011), http://www.academia.edu/1095984/_14_ years_in_limbo_waiting_for_the_Promised_Land_/.

22. http://operationrooigrond.wordpress.com/; http://www.twitter.com/ orooigrond/.

23. 'The People who Hold the Power: Monametsi Moeti,' *City Press* (10 November 2012), http://www.citypress.co.za/news/the-people-who-hold-the-power-monametsi-moeti-20121110/.

24. SERI, *Rooigrond*, p. 6.

25. SERI, *Rooigrond*, p. 12.

26. Boitumelo Matlala and Claire Benit-Gbaffou, 'Against Ourselves – Local Activists and the Management of Contradicting Political Loyalties: The Case of Phiri, Johannesburg,' *Geoforum* 43 (2012), 207–218. See also the detailed account given in Nicollete Pingo, 'Institutionalisation of a Social Movement: The Case of Thembelihle, the Thembelihle Crisis Committee, the Operation Khanyisa Movement and the Use of the Brick, the Ballot, and the Vote,' MSc thesis (Johannesburg, University of the Witwatersrand: 2013).

27. The website of the Independent Electoral Commission (www.elections.org. za/) provides data on all South African elections. These figures come from its report on the party support of the OKM in all wards of Johannesburg in the 2006 local government elections. They differ slightly from the figures published in Mcebisi Ndletyana, 'Municipal Elections 2006: Protests, Independent Candidates and Cross-border Municipalities,' in Sakhela Buhlungu, John Daniel, Roger Southall, and Jessica Lutchman et al., *State of the Nation: South Africa 2007* (Pretoria, HSRC Press: 2007).

28. www.elections.org.za/ – results for Johannesburg's Ward 8 (coded as 79800008 on the website) in 2011.

29. Pingo, 'Institutionalisation of a Social Movement,' pp. 101–106.

30. Siphiwe Segodi, 'Thembelihle Crisis Committee Contesting Elections Through Operation Khanyisa Movement' (30 April 2011), http://www.socialistsouth-africa.co.za/index.php?option=com_content&view=article&id=48/:themb elihle-crisis-committee-contesting-elecstions-through-operation-khanyisa-movement&catid=1:latest-news/.

31. Pingo, 'Institutionalisation of a Social Movement,' p. 59.

32. Dale T. McKinley, 'Lessons of Struggle: The Rise and Fall of the Anti-Privatisation Forum,' *SACSIS* (8 February 2012), http://sacsis.org.za/site/article/1197/.

33. Peter Alexander, 'Barricades, Ballots and Experimentation: Making Sense of the 2011 Local Government Elections with a Social Movement Lens,' in Marcelle C.

Dawson and Luke Sinwell (eds), *Contesting Transformation: Popular Resistance in Twenty-First-Century South Africa* (London, Pluto Press: 2012).

34. Richard Pithouse, 'Elections: A Dangerous Time for Poor People's Movements in South Africa,' *SACSIS* (12 March 2009), http://sacsis.org.za/site/article/245.1/.

35. Niren Tolsi, 'I was Punched, Beaten,' *Mail and Guardian* (16 September 2006), http://mg.co.za/article/2006-09-16-i-was-punched-beaten/.

36. M'du Hlongwa, 'The No Land, No House, No Vote Campaign Still on for 2009,' (18 January 2007), http://abahlali.org/node/510/.

37. *Dear Mandela* (2012), dir. Dara Kell and Christopher Nizza.

38. Kerry Chance, 'The Work of Violence: A Timeline of Armed Attacks at Kennedy Road,' *School of Development Studies Research Report* (Durban, University of KwaZulu Natal: 2010). See also the damages claim instituted as: *Abahlali baseMjondolo and 52 Others v Minister of Police and Others*, KwaZulu-Natal High Court, case no. 9955/2012. (The case has not been heard, at time of writing.)

39. *State v Limpathi and 11 Others*, Durban Magistrates' Court, case no. 41/2174/10. Unreported case.

40. Abahlali baseMjondolo Western Cape, 'Open Letter to DA Leader Helen Zille' (17 February 2011), http://abahlali.org/node/7800/.

41. See my comment at the time: Julian Brown, 'Abahlali's Choice,' *Daily Maverick* (4 May 2014), http://www.dailymaverick.co.za/article/2014-05-03-5365753498943/. See also: Raymond Suttner, 'The Abahlali/DA Pact: Difficult Situations Require Difficult Decisions,' *Polity* (5 May 2014), http://www.polity.org.za/article/the-abahlalida-pact-difficult-situations-require-difficult-decisions-2014-05-05/; and Richard Pithouse, 'On Abahlali baseMjondolo Voting for the DA in Durban,' *SACSIS* (9 May 2014), http://sacsis.org.za/site/article/1999/.

42. Sthembiso Shozi, 'Should No Land! No House! No Vote! Battles Take Place in the 2014's Elections?' (24 July 2014), http://abahlali.org/node/9988/.

43. Abahlali baseMjondolo, 'An Invitation to All Political Parties Except the ANC' (23 April 2014), http://abahlali.org/node/13696/.

44. Sibusiso Tshabalala, 'Why Abahlali Endorsed the DA: S'bu Zikode Speaks to GroundUp' (5 May 2014), http://groundup.org.za/content/why-abahlali-endorsed-da-sbu-zikode-speaks-groundup/.

45. These allegations were made in a letter circulated on email listserves and social media. I have a copy in my possession. A version of this letter has been published in a recent edition of *Politikon* – apparently without any critical engagement on the part of the editors. The letter's personal attacks on individuals have been replaced by vague references to outsiders, but nothing beyond Mdalose's personal account is provided to verify her allegations. Bandile Mdalose, 'The Rise and Fall of Abahlali baseMjondolo, A South African Social Movement,' *Politikon*, 41.3 (2014), 345–353.

46. e.g. Walsh, Bond, and Desai, "Uncomfortable Collaborations"; Anna Selmeczi, 'Abahlali's Vocal Politics of Proximity: Speaking, Suffering and Political Subjectivization,' *Journal of Asian and African Studies*, 47.5 (2012), 498–515.

Chapter 6

1. e.g. Stuart A. Scheingold, *The Politics of Rights: Lawyers, Public Policy, and Political Change* (New Haven, Yale University Press: 1974); John Denvir, 'Towards a Political Theory of Public Interest Litigation,' *North Carolina Law Review*, 54 (1975–1976), 1133–1160.
2. See Lynn Hunt, *Inventing Human Rights: A History* (New York, Norton: 2007).
3. Richard Abel, *Politics by Other Means: Law in the Struggle Against Apartheid* (London, Routledge: 1995).
4. See: Sandra Liebenberg, *Socio-Economic Rights: Adjudication Under a Transformative Constitution* (Cape Town, Juta: 2010); Theunis Roux, *The Politics of Principle: The First South African Constitutional Court, 1995–2005* (Cambridge, Cambridge University Press: 2013).
5. The judgment of the Constitutional Court in this case was reported as: *Minister of Health and Others v Treatment Action Campaign and Others* (No 2) (CCT8/02) [2002] ZACC 15; 2002 (5) SA 721; 2002 (10) BCLR 1033 (5 July 2002).
6. Gilbert Marcus and Steven Budlender, *A Strategic Evaluation of Public Interest Litigation in South Africa* (Johannesburg, Atlantic Philanthropies: 2008).
7. Steven Friedman and Shauna Mottiar, 'A Rewarding Engagement? The Treatment Action Campaign and the Politics of HIV/AIDS,' *Politics & Society*, 33.4 (2005), 511–565.
8. See: Nathan Geffen, *Debunking Delusions: The Inside Story of the Treatment Action Campaign* (Johannesburg, Jacana: 2010); Mandisa Mbali, *South African AIDS Activism and Global Health Politics* (New York, Palgrave Macmillan: 2013).
9. Mark Heywood, 'South Africa's Treatment Action Campaign: Combining Law and Social Mobilization to Realize the Right to Health,' *Journal of Human Rights Practice*, 1.1 (2009), 14–36.
10. Steven Robins, *From Revolution to Rights in South Africa: Social Movements, NGOs and Popular Politics* (Oxford, James Currey Publishers & University of KwaZulu Natal Press: 2008).
11. Stuart Wilson and Jackie Dugard, 'Constitutional Jurisprudence: The First and Second Waves,' in Malcolm Langford, Ben Cousins, Jackie Dugard and Tshepo Madlingozi (eds), *Socio-Economic Rights in South Africa: Symbols or Substance?* (Cambridge, Cambridge University Press: 2014), pp. 54–55.
12. In the High Court: *Mazibuko and Others v City of Johannesburg and Others* (06/13865) [2008] ZAGPHC 491; [2008] 4 All SA 471 (W) (30 April 2008). In the SCA: *City of Johannesburg and Others v Mazibuko and Others* (489/08) [2009] ZASCA 20; 2009 (3) SA 592 (SCA) ; 2009 (8) BCLR 791 (SCA) ; [2009] 3 All SA 202 (SCA) (25 March 2009).

1 3. Something of this excitement is captured in Jackie Dugard, 'Civic Action and Legal Mobilisation: The Phiri Water Meters Case,' in Jeff Handmaker and Remko Berkhout (eds), *Mobilising Social Justice in South Africa: Perspectives from Researchers and Practitioners* (Pretoria, PULP: 2010), pp. 71–99.

1 4. In the Constitutional Court: *Mazibuko and Others v City of Johannesburg and Others* (CCT 39/09) [2009] ZACC 28; 2010 (3) BCLR 239 (CC) ; 2010 (4) SA 1 (CC) (8 October 2009).

1 5. For evictions, see: *Occupiers of 51 Olivia Road, Berea Township and 197 Main Street Johannesburg v City of Johannesburg and Others* (24/07) [2008] ZACC 1; 2008 (3) SA 208 (CC); 2008 (5) BCLR 475 (CC) (19 February 2008). For electricity, see: *Joseph and Others v City of Johannesburg and Others* (CCT 43/09) [2009] ZACC 30; 2010 (3) BCLR 212 (CC); 2010 (4) SA 55 (CC) (9 October 2009). Also: Stuart Wilson, 'Litigating Housing Rights in Johannesburg's Inner City: 2004–2008,' *South African Journal on Human Rights*, 27.1 (2011), 127–151 and, more generally, Liebenberg, *Socio-Economic Rights* (see note 4).

1 6. *Abahlali baseMjondolo Movement SA and Another v Premier of the Province of Kwazulu-Natal and Others* (CCT 12/09) [2009] ZACC 31; 2010 (2) BCLR 99 (CC) (14 October 2009).

1 7. Daria Roithmayr, 'Lessons from *Mazibuko*: persistent inequality and the commons,' in Stuart Woolman, Theunis Roux, and Danie Brand (eds), *Constitutional Court Review* (Pretoria, PULP: 2010), pp. 317–346.

1 8. Scheingold, *The Politics of Rights*, pp. 204–205.

1 9. Michael W. McCann, *Rights at Work: Pay Equity and the Politics of Legal Mobilization* (Chicago, University of Chicago Press: 1994), p. 6. In addition, see: Sally Engle Merry, *Getting Justice and Getting Even: Legal Consciousness among Working Class Americans* (Chicago, University of Chicago Press: 1990) and Patricia Ewick and Susan S. Silbey, *The Common Place of Law: Stories from Everyday Life* (Chicago, University of Chicago Press: 1998) for further developments of a discursive theory of the law as social practice.

20. E.P. Thompson, *Whigs and Hunters: The Origins of the Black Acts* (New York, Pantheon: 1976).

2 1. e.g. Colin Ward, *Cotters and Squatters: Housing's Hidden History* (Nottingham, Five Leaves: 2005).

2 2. Jacques Rancière, *Proletarian Nights: The Workers' Dream in Nineteenth Century France*, trans. John Drury (London, Verso: 2012).

2 3. Jackie Dugard and Sandra Liebenberg, 'Muddying the Waters? The Supreme Court of Appeal's Judgement in the *Mazibuko* Case: Case Review,' *ESR Review: Economic and Social Rights in South Africa*, 10.2 (2009), 11–17.

24. *Occupiers of 51 Olivia Road v City of Johannesburg* (see note 15); *City of Johannesburg Metropolitan Municipality v Blue Moonlight Properties 39 (Pty) Ltd and Another* (2012 (2) BCLR 150 (CC); 2012 (2) SA 104 (CC)) [2011] ZACC 40; [2011] ZACC 33 (1 December 2011); *Dladla v City of Johannesburg Metropolitan Municipality and Another* (39502/12) [2014] ZAGPJHC 184 (22 August 2014).

25. Some of the following comes from: Julian Brown and Stuart Wilson, 'A Presumed Equality: The Relationship Between Citizens and the State in Post-apartheid South Africa,' *African Studies* 72.1 (2013), which draws upon the case file and judgment: *Governing Body of BopaSetjhaba and Others v Premier of the Free State Province and Others* (2238/2003) [2005] ZAFSHC 5 (17 March 2005) (unreported case).

26. *BopaSetjhaba v Premier of the Free State*, case file. Correspondence. Head: Education to Head: Public Works, 7 February 2003; Superintendent General: Education to Director: NFS, 18 February 2003.

27. These figures were disclosed in the founding affidavit in the case, in paragraphs 7.1–7.8.

28. See: Henri Lefebvre, *Critique of Everyday Life: The One Volume Edition* (London, Verso: 2014); Lefebvre, *Rhythmanalysis: Space, Time, and Everyday Life* (London, Continuum: 2004). These books incorporate material written in French between the 1940s and the 1980s.

29. For supporting the human rights abuses of the apartheid state, the most notable attempt to hold private capital liable is the set of cases launched by the Khulumani Support Group, in South Africa and internationally, in an attempt to hold companies liable. For an overview, see: Tshepo Madlingozi, 'How the Law Shapes and Structures Post-Apartheid Social Movements: Case Study of the Khulumani Support Group,' in Marcelle C. Dawson and Luke Sinwell (eds), *Contesting Transformation: Popular Resistance in Twenty-First-Century South Africa* (London, Pluto: 2012), pp. 222–239.

30. This 'inequality of arms' is at the core of the case compelling Legal Aid SA to provide public funding for the miners' representation at the Commission: *Magidiwana and Another v President of the Republic of South Africa and Others* (37904/2013) [2013] ZAGPPHC 292; [2014] 1 All SA 76 (GNP) (14 October 2013).

Conclusion

1. Henri Lefebvre, *Critique of Everyday Life: The One Volume Edition* (London, Verso: 2014), pp. 560–561.

2. Frederick Engels, 'Socialism: Utopian and Scientific (1860),' in R.C. Tucker (ed.), *The Marx-Engels Reader* (New York, Norton: 1978), p. 609.

3. Erik Olin Wright, *Envisioning Real Utopias* (London, Verso: 2010), p. 6.

4. See Jacques Rancière, 'The End of Politics, or the Realist Utopia' in *On the Shores of Politics*, trans. Liz Heron (London, Verso: 1995).

5. Michel Foucault, 'Different Spaces,' in *Aesthetics: Essential Works of Foucault, 1954–1984. Volume 2.* (Harmondsworth, Penguin: 1998), pp. 175–186.

6. Mikhail Bakhtin, *Rabelais and His World*, trans. Helen Iswolsky (Cambridge, MIT Press: 1968).

7. Jacques Rancière, 'The Aesthetic Heterotopia,' *Philosophy Today*, 54. Supplement (2010), pp. 15–25.

8. Jacques Rancière, *The Ignorant Schoolmaster: Five Lessons in Intellectual Emancipation*, trans. Kristin Ross (Stanford, Stanford University Press: 1991), pp. 71–73.

9. The EFF won about 6.4% of the vote in the 2014, claiming 25 seats in the National Assembly – a fraction of the ANC's 62%, and 249 seats.

10. These actions have been widely reported on. Some indicative examples include: SAPA and Staff Reporter, 'Interjections and Frustrations as EFF Disciplinary Hearing Gets Underway,' *Mail and Guardian* (7 October 2014), http://mg.co.za/article/2014-10-07-interjections-and-frustration-as-eff-disciplinary-hearing-gets-underway/; Rebecca Davis, 'Parliament Diary: Scenes of Shame,' *Daily Maverick* (14 November 2014), http://www.dailymaverick.co.za/article/2014-11-14-parliament-diary-scenes-of-shame/; and SAPA, 'EFF MPs Suspended for Disrupting Parliament,' *Mail and Guardian* (28 November 2014), http://mg.co.za/article/2014-11-28-eff-mps-suspended-for-disrupting-parliament/.

11. The most interesting accounts of this conference are by Richard Poplak, in the *Daily Maverick*: 'Painting South Africa Red: Notes from the EFF's National Assembly' (15 December 2014), http://www.dailymaverick.co.za/article/2014-12-15-painting-south-africa-red-notes-from-the-effs-national-assembly and 'Burning Berets: the EFF People's Assembly Takes a Turn/' (15 December 2014), http://www.dailymaverick.co.za/article/2014-12-15-burning-berets-the-eff-peoples-assembly-takes-a-turn/.

12. This document was widely circulated. I have a copy in my possession. It was also reported on in the media, e.g. Sarah Evans, 'Mystery Document Alleges Numsa is Bent on Regime Change,' *Mail and Guardian* (1 December 2014), http://mg.co.za/article/2014-12-01-mystery-document-alleges-numsa-is-bent-on-regime-change/.

13. 'Declaration of the Preparatory Assembly of the United Front' (15 December 2014), http://www.numsa.org.za/article/declaration-preparatory-assembly-united-front/.

14. Steven Friedman, 'Poor Need to be Heard Rather Than Spoken for,' *Business Day* (7 January 2015), http://www.bdlive.co.za/opinion/columnists/2015/01/07/poor-need-to-be-heard-rather-than-spoken-for/.

Bibliography

Archival Sources

South African History Archives. Records of the Anti-Privatisation Forum. AL3290.

Note: Tembalihle [sic] Struggle, Complied by APF Organiser - Silumko Radebe (2007)
Interview with Siphiwe Segodi, conducted by Dale McKinley. Johannesburg, 23 August 2010

Films and Documentaries

Dear Mandela. 2012. Dir. Dara Kell and Christopher Nizza
Invictus. 2009. Dir. Clint Eastwood
Mandela: Long Walk to Freedom. 2013. Dir. Justin Chadwick
Miners Shot Down. 2014. Dir. Rehad Desai

Legislation

Constitution of the Republic of South Africa Act (Act 200 of 1993)
Constitution of the Republic of South Africa Act (Act 108 of 1996)
Promotion of National Unity and Reconciliation Act (Act 34 of 1995)
Regulation of Gatherings Act (No. 205 of 1993).

Official Documents and Statements

— 1991. 'The National Peace Accord.'

Goldstone, R.J. 1993. 'Final Report of the Commission of Inquiry regarding the Prevention of Public Violence and Intimidation by the Committee Established to Inquire into Public Violence and Intimidation at Mass Demonstrations, Marches and Picketing'

Government Gazette. 2012. *Proclamation: Establishment of a Commission of Inquiry in the Tragic Incident at or near the Area Commonly Known as Marikana Mine in Rustenburg, North West Province, South Africa.*

Government of South Africa, Ministry for Provincial Affairs and Constitutional Development. 1998. *The White Paper on Local Government.*

Government of South Africa, Department for Provincial and Local Government. 2005. *Draft National Policy Framework for Public Participation.*

Government of South Africa, Department of Provincial and Local Government. 2005. *Having Your Say: A Handbook for Ward Committees.*

Government of South Africa, Department of Provincial and Local Government. 2007. *National Policy Framework on Participation.*

Legal Aid South Africa. 2014. *Legal Aid Guide 2014.* Juta: 13th Edition.

South African Police Services. 2013. 'An Analysis of the National Crime Statistics 2012/2013 - Addendum to the Annual Report,' published 31 August. http://www.saps.gov.za/statistics/reports/crimestats/2013/downloads/crime_stats_analysis.pdf/

Court Cases

Reported Cases

Abahlali baseMjondolo Movement SA and Another v Premier of the Province of Kwazulu-Natal and Others (CCT12/09) [2009] ZACC 31; 2010 (2) BCLR 99 (CC) (14 October 2009).

Camps Bay Ratepayers and Residents Association and Another v Harrison and Another (CCT 76/12) [2012] ZACC 17; 2012 (11) BCLR 1143 (CC) (20 September 2012).

City of Johannesburg and Others v Mazibuko and Others (489/08) [2009] ZASCA 20; 2009 (3) SA 592 (SCA); 2009 (8) BCLR 791 (SCA); [2009] 3 All SA 202 (SCA) (25 March 2009).

City of Johannesburg Metropolitan Municipality v Blue Moonlight Properties 39 (Pty) Ltd and Another (2012 (2) BCLR 150 (CC); 2012 (2) SA 104 (CC)) [2011] ZACC 40; [2011] ZACC 33 (1 December 2011).

Dladla and Others v City of Johannesburg Metropolitan Municipality and Another 2014 (6) SA 516 (GJ)

Joseph and Others v City of Johannesburg and Others (CCT 43/09) [2009] ZACC 30; 2010 (3) BCLR 212 (CC); 2010 (4) SA 55 (CC) (9 October 2009).

Magidiwana and Another v President of the Republic of South Africa and Others (37904/2013) [2013] ZAGPPHC 292; [2014] 1 All SA 76 (GNP) (14 October 2013).

Mazibuko and Others v City of Johannesburg and Others (06/13865) [2008] ZAGPHC 491; [2008] 4 All SA 471 (W) (30 April 2008).

Mazibuko and Others v City of Johannesburg and Others (CCT 39/09) [2009] ZACC 28; 2010 (3) BCLR 239 (CC); 2010 (4) SA 1 (CC) (8 October 2009).

Minister of Health and Others v Treatment Action Campaign and Others (No 2) (CCT8/02) [2002] ZACC 15; 2002 (5) SA 721; 2002 (10) BCLR 1033 (5 July 2002).

Occupiers of 51 Olivia Road, Berea Township and 197 Main Street Johannesburg v City of Johannesburg and Others (24/07) [2008] ZACC 1; 2008 (3) SA 208 (CC); 2008 (5) BCLR 475 (CC) (19 February 2008).

South African National Defence Union v Minister of Defence (CCT27/98) [1999] ZACC 7; 1999 (4) SA 469; 1999 (6) BCLR 615 (26 May 1999).

South African Transport and Allied Workers Union and Another v Garvas and Others (CCT 112/11) [2012] ZACC 13; 2012 (8) BCLR 840 (CC); [2012] 10 BLLR 959 (CC); (2012) 33 ILJ 1593 (CC); 2013 (1) SA 83 (CC) (13 June 2012).

South African Transport & Allied Workers Union v Garvis [sic] & Others (007/11) [2011] ZASCA 152; 2011 (6) SA 382 (SCA); 2011 (12) BCLR 1249 (SCA); [2011] 4 All SA 475 (SCA); [2011] 12 BLLR 1151 (SCA); (2011) 32 ILJ 2426 (SCA) (27 September 2011).

Unreported Cases

Abahlali baseMjondolo movement South Africa and 30 Others v Ethekwini Municipality and the MEC for Human Settlements of the Province of KwaZulu-Natal, Case No. 9189/2013, KwaZulu-Natal High Court, Durban.

Abahlali baseMjondolo and 52 Others v Minister of Police and Others, KwaZulu-Natal High Court, Case No. 9955/2012.

Association Of Mineworkers And Construction Union v Lonmin Platinum (Comprising Eastern Platinum Ltd And Western Platinum Ltd) and Others (J1134/14) [2014] ZALCJHB 196 (2 June 2014)

The City of Johannesburg v Occupiers of the Thembelihle Informal Settlement, South Gauteng High Court, Case No. 03/10106.

Governing Body of BopaSetjhaba and Others v Premier of the Free State Province and Others (2238/2003) [2005] ZAFSHC 5 (17 March 2005).

Mamba v Minister of Social Development CCT 65/08 (21 August 2008).

The State v Bandile Mdalose, Durban Regional Court, Case No. 23/16747/13 (2013).

The State v Bhayi Bhayi Miya, Magistrates' Court for the District of Protea, Gauteng, Case No. 69/4121/11 (2011). Unreported Case.

The State v Limpathi and 11 Others, Durban Magistrates' Court, Case no. 41/2174/10.

The State v Moyo, Swetsana and Sisulu, Case No 320/10/2012, Magistrates' Court for the District of Germiston.

The State v Wonder Nkosi and Thirteen Others, Magistrates' Court for the District of Protea, Gauteng, Case No: 43/01308/2011.

News Articles and Press Releases

— 1992. 'Interim Agreement between the South African Police, the African National Congress, Cosatu, the South African Communist Party and the Inkatha Freedom Party on the conduct of public demonstrations.'

— 1992. 'Press release by the honourable Mr Justice R.J. Goldstone, Chairman of the Commission of Inquiry regarding the prevention of public violence and intimidation.'

— 2011. 'Themblihle protestors' fire causes R1.5m damage,' *Mail and Guardian*, 7 Sept. http://mg.co.za/article/2011-09-07-thembelihle-protesters-fire-causes-r15m-damage/

— 2011. 'Thembelihle protest costs City R1.5bn,' *Eye Witness News*, 7 Sept. http://ewn.co.za/2011/09/07/Thembelihle-protest-costs-City-R15-bn/

— 2011. 'Thembelihle protests caused R1.5 million in damage,' *City Press*, 7 Sept. http://www.citypress.co.za/news/thembelihle-protests-caused-r15m-in-damage-20110907/

— 2012. 'The people who hold the power: Monametsi Moeti,' *City Press*, 10 Nov. http://www.citypress.co.za/news/the-people-who-hold-the-power-monametsi-moeti-20121110/

Abahlali baseMjondolo. 2008. 'Statement on the Xenophobic Attacks in Johannesburg,' 21 May. http://abahlali.org/node/3582/

Abahlali baseMjondolo. 2013. 'Marikana Continues: Statement on the Murder of Nqobile Nzuza,' 3 Oct. http://abahlali.org/node/12292/

Abahlali baseMjondolo. 2014. 'An Invitation to All Political Parties Except the ANC,' 23 April. http://abahlali.org/node/13696/

Abahlali baseMjondolo Western Cape. 2011. 'Open Letter to DA Leader Helen Zille,' 17 Feb. http://abahlali.org/node/7800/

Alexander, Peter. 2012. 'A massive rebellion of the poor,' *Mail and Guardian*, 13 April. http://mg.co.za/article/2012-04-13-a-massive-rebellion-of-the-poor/

Anti Privatisation Forum, 2007. 'Charges against Boiketlong and Thembelihle activists dropped,' 16 August, http://apf.org.za/spip.php?article209/

Bohmke, Heinrich. 2010. 'The shackdwellers and the intellectuals,' 21 Oct. http://www.politicsweb.co.za/politicsweb/view/politicsweb/en/page71619?oid=206254&sn=Detail/

Brown, Julian. 2014. 'Abahlali's Choice,' *Daily Maverick*. 4 May. http://www.dailymaverick.co.za/article/2014-05-03-5365753498943/

Davis, Rebecca. 2014. 'Parliament diary: Scenes of shame,' *Daily Maverick*, 14 Nov. http://www.dailymaverick.co.za/article/2014-11-14-parliament-diary-scenes-of-shame/

Democratic Alliance. 2014. 'DA to appeal decision to ban March for Six Million REAL Jobs,' 1 Feb. http://www.dajhb.co.za/2014/02/01/da-to-appeal-jmpd-decision-to-ban-march-for-six-million-real-jobs/

de Waal, Mandy. 2012. 'Marikana: What Really Happened? We May Never Know,' Daily Maverick, 23 August. http://www.dailymaverik.co.za/article/2012-08-23-marikana-what-really-happened-we-may-never-know/

de Vos, Pierre. 2012. 'Marikana: No Common Purpose to Commit Suicide,' Constitutionally Speaking, 30 August. http://constitutionallyspeaking.co.za/marikana-no-common-purpose-to-commit-suicide/

Duncan, Jane. 2013. 'The Criminal Injustice System,' SACSIS, 18 Feb. http://www.sacsis.org.za/site/article/1574/

Duncan, Jane. 2014. 'The Politics Of Counting Protest,' Mail and Guardian, 17 April. http://mg.co.za/article/2014-04-16-the-politics-of-counting-protests/

Duncan, Jane, and Andrea Royeppen. 2013. 'Inside Rustenburg's Banned Protests,' Daily Maverick, 7 March. http://www.dailymaverick.co.za/article/2013-03-07-inside-rustenbergs-banned-protests/

Eliseev, Alex. 2014. 'Analysis: Bonfires of Discontent, In Terrifying Numbers,' Daily Maverick, 5 Feb. http://www.dailymaverick.co.za/article/2014-02-05-analysis-bonfires-of-discontent-in-horrifying-numbers/

Evans, Sarah. 2014. 'Mystery Document Alleges Numsa Is Bent on Regime Change,' Mail and Guardian, 1 Dec. http://mg.co.za/article/2014-12-01-mystery-document-alleges-numsa-is-bent-on-regime-change/

Friedman, Steven. 2015. 'Poor Need To Be Heard Rather Than Spoken for,' Business Day, 7 Jan. http://www.bdlive.co.za/opinion/columnists/2015/01/07/poor-need-to-be-heard-rather-than-spoken-for/

Hlongwa, M'du. 2007. 'The No Land, No House, No Vote Campaign Still on for 2009', Abhahlali website, 18 Jan. http://abahlali.org/node/510/

Hosken, Graeme. 2012. 'Ramaphosa Exposed,' The Times, 24 Oct. http://www.timeslive.co.za/thetimes/2012/10/24/ramaphosa-exposed/

Lekgowa, Thapelo, Botsang Mmope and Peter Alexander. 2012. 'How Police Planned and Carried Out the Massacre at Marikana,' Socialist Worker, 21 August. http://socialistworker.co.uk/art.php?id=29403/

Majavu, Anna. 2012. 'Penalizing Protest Action,' SACSIS, 19 June. http://sacsis.org.za/site/article/1338/

Manyathi, Nokuthula. 2014. 'Senior Cop Admits Deployment Strategy Could Be 'Factor' in Shooting of Protestors,' City Press, 5 Feb. http://www.citypress.co.za/news/senior-cop-admits-deployment-strategy-factor-shooting-protesters/

Marinovich, Greg. 2012. 'The Murder Fields of Marikana, The Cold Murder Fields of Marikana,' Daily Maverick, 30 August, updated 8 Sept. http://www.dailymaverick.co.za/article/2012-08-30-the-murder-fields-of-marikana-the-cold-murder-fields-of-marikana/

McKinley, Dale T. 2012. 'Lessons of Struggle: The Rise and Fall of the Anti-Privatisation Forum,' SACSIS, 8 Feb. http://sacsis.org.za/site/article/1197/

Mdalose, Bandile. 2013. 'Seven Days of Thoughts in Westville Prison,' Daily News, 10 Oct. http://abahlali.org/node/12544/

Municipal IQ. 2013. '2012 Tally: A Violent and Diverse Year for Service Delivery Protests,' Press Release, published 17 Jan. http://www.municipaliq.co.za/publications/press/30120117082358325.doc/

Pithouse, Richard. 2009. 'Elections: A Dangerous Time for Poor People's Movements in South Africa,' *SACSIS*, 2 March. http://sacsis.org.za/site/article/245.1/

Pithouse, Richard. 2014. 'On Abahlali baseMjondolo Voting for the DA in Durban,' *SACSIS*, 9 May. http://sacsis.org.za/site/article/1999/

Poplak, Richard. 2014, 'Painting South Africa Red: Notes from the EFF's National Assembly,' *Daily Maverick*, 15 Dec. http://www.dailymaverick.co.za/article/2014-12-15-painting-south-africa-red-notes-from-the-effs-national-assembly/

Poplak, Richard. 2014. 'Burning Berets: the EFF People's Assembly Takes a Turn,' *Daily Maverick*, 15 Dec., http://www.dailymaverick.co.za/article/2014-12-15-burning-berets-the-eff-peoples-assembly-takes-a-turn/

Segodi, Siphiwe. 2012. 'Thembelihle Crisis Committee Contesting Elections through Operation Khanyisa Movement' Press Release,' 20 April. http://www.socialistsouthafrica.co.za/index.php?option=com_content&view=article&id=48:thembelihle-crisis-committee-contesting-elecstions-through-operation-khanyisa-movement&catid=1:latest-news/

Shozi, Sthembiso. 2013. 'Should No Land! No House! No Vote! Battles Take Place in the 2014's Elections?' Abahlali website, 24 July. http://abahlali.org/node/9988/

Smith, Alex Duval. 2012. 'Miners Charged with Murder - of Colleagues Shot Dead by the Police,' *The Independent*, 30 Aug. http://www.independent.co.uk/news/world/africa/miners-charged-with-murder—of-colleagues-shot-dead-by-police-8092835.html/

South African Broadcasting Company. 2014. 'N West Rooigrond Residents Protest,' 27 April. http://www.sabc.co.za/news/a/6261b98043cb18f19806 9afocofe2c4c/N-West-Rooigrond-residents-protest/

South African Government News Agency. 2014. 'High Level Task Team to Address Violent Protest,' Press Release, 10 Feb. http://www.sanews.gov.za/south-africa/high-level-task-team-address-violent-protests/

South African Government News Agency. 2014. 'GP Residents Urged to Respect the Gatherings Act,' Press Release 12 Feb. http://www.sanews.gov.za/south-africa/gp-residents-urged-respect-gatherings-act/

South African Press Agency (SAPA). 2014. 'Police: Public Must Not Be 'Armchair Critics' *Mail and Guardian*, 5 Feb. http://mg.co.za/article/2014-02-05-police-public-must-not-be-armchair-critics/

South African Press Agency (SAPA). 2014. 'DA Wins March Appeal,' *City Press*, 3 Feb. http://www.citypress.co.za/politics/da-wins-march-appeal/

South African Press Agency (SAPA). 2014. 'EFF MPs Suspended for Disrupting Parliament,' *Mail and Guardian*, 28 Nov. http://mg.co.za/article/2014-11-28-eff-mps-suspended-for-disrupting-parliament/

South African Press Agency (SAPA) and Staff Reporter. 2014. 'Interjections and Frustrations as EFF Disciplinary Hearing Gets Underway,' *Mail and Guardian*. 7 Oct. http://mg.co.za/article/2014-10-07-interjections-and-frustration-as-eff-disciplinary-hearing-gets-underway/

Steyn, Lisa. 2013. 'Amcu Declared Majority Union at Lonmin,' *Mail and Guardian*, 14 August. http://mg.co.za/article/2013-08-14-amcu-declared-official-majority-union-at-lonmin/

Suttner, Raymond. 2014. 'The Abahlali/DA Pact: Difficult Situations Require Difficult Decisions,' *Polity*, 5 May. http://www.polity.org.za/article/the-abahlali-da-pact-difficult-situations-require-difficult-decisions-2014-05-05/

Tolsi, Niren. 2006. 'I Was Punched, Beaten,' *Mail and Guardian*, 16 Sept. http://mg.co.za/article/2006-09-16-i-was-punched-beaten/

Tshabalala, Sibusiso. 2014. 'Why Abahlali Endorsed the DA: S'bu Zikode Speaks to GroundUp', *Ground Up*, 5 May. http://groundup.org.za/content/why-abahlali-endorsed-da-sbu-zikode-speaks-groundup/

United Front, 2-14. 'Declaration of the Preparatory Assembly of the United Front' Press Release, 15 Dec. http://www.numsa.org.za/article/declaration-preparatory-assembly-united-front/

Books, Journal Articles and Research Reports

Abel, Richard. 1995. *Politics by Other Means: Law in the Struggle Against Apartheid*. Routledge.

Albertyn, Catherine. 2005. 'Defending and Securing Rights Through Law: Feminism, Law and the Courts in South Africa,' *Politikon*, 32.2.

Albertyn, Cathi and Shamim Meer. 2008. 'Citizens or Mothers? The Marginalisation of Women's Reproductive Rights in the Struggle for Access to Health Care for HIV-positive Pregnant Women in South Africa,' *Gender Rights and Development: A Global Sourcebook*. Amsterdam, Royal Tropical Institute.

Alexander, Peter. 2012. 'Barricades, Ballots and Experimentation: Making Sense of the 2011 Local Government Elections with a Social Movement Lens,' in Marcelle C. Dawson and Luke Sinwell (eds), *Contesting Transformation: Popular Resistance in Twenty-First-Century South Africa*. Pluto Press.

Alexander, Peter, Thapelo Lekgowa, Botsang Mmope, Luke Sinwell and Bongani Xezwi. 2012. *Marikana: A View from the Mountain and a Case to Answer*. Jacana Press.

Atkinson, Doreen. 2007. 'Taking to the Street: Has Developmental Local Governance Failed?' in Sakhela Buhlungu, John Daniel, Roger Southall and Jessica Lutchman (eds), *State of the Nation: South Africa 2007*. HSRC Press.

Badiou, Alain. 2009. 'The Lessons of Jacques Rancière: Knowledge and Power after the Storm,' in Gabriel Rockhill and Philip Watts (eds), *Jacques Rancière: History, Politics, Aesthetics*. Duke University Press.

Baines, Gary. 1998. 'The Rainbow Nation? Identity and Nation Building in Post-apartheid South Africa,' *Mots Pluriels 7*.

Bakhtin, Mikhail. 1968. *Rabelais and His World*, trans. Helen Iswolsky. MIT Press.
Bakhtin, Mikhail. 1993. *Toward A Philosophy of the Act*, trans. Vadim Liapunov. University of Texas Press.
Ballard, Richard, Adam Habib and Imraan Valodia, eds. 2006. *Voices of Protest: Social Movements in Post-apartheid South Africa*. UKZN Press.
Beinart, William. 1992. 'Politics and Collective Violence in Southern African Historiography,' *Journal of Southern African Studies*, 18.3.
Beinart, William, and Marcelle C. Dawson, eds. 2010. *Popular Protest and Resistance Movements in South Africa*. Wits University Press.
Bond, Patrick. 2002. *Elite Transition: From Apartheid to Neoliberalism in South Africa*. Pluto Press.
Bond, Patrick. 2004. *Talk Left, Walk Right: South Africa's Frustrated Global Reforms*. UKZN Press.
Booysen, Susan. 2009. 'Public Participation in Democratic South Africa: From Popular Mobilisation to Structured Co-optation and Protest,' *Politeia*, 28.1.
Botiveau, Raphaël. 2014. 'Briefing: The Politics of Marikana and South Africa's Changing Labour Relations,' *African Affairs* 113.450.
Brown, Julian. 2009. 'Public Protest and Violence in South Africa, 1948-1976,' DPhil Thesis, University of Oxford, Faculty of Modern History.
Brown, Julian and Stuart Wilson. 2013. 'A Presumed Equality: The Relationship between State and Citizens in Post-apartheid South Africa,' *African Studies*, 72.1.
Bundy, Colin. 1987. 'Street Sociology and Pavement Politics: Aspects of Youth and Student Resistance in Cape Town, 1985,' *Journal of Southern African Studies*, 13.3.
Butler, Anthony. 2011. *Cyril Ramaphosa*. Rev. ed. Jacana.
Carpenter, Dale. 2012. *Flagrant Conduct: The Story of Lawrence v Texas: How a Bedroom Arrest Decriminalised Gay Americans*. Norton.
Chambers, Samuel. 2012. *The Lessons of Rancière*. Oxford University Press.
Chance, Kerry. 2010. 'The Work of Violence: A Timeline of Armed Attacks at Kennedy Road,' School of Development Studies Research Report, University of KwaZulu Natal.
Chipkin, Ivor. 2011. 'Transcending Bureaucracy: State Transformation in the Age of the Manager,' *Transformation* 77.
Claassens, Aninka and Sizani Ngubane. 2008. 'Women, Land and Power: The Impact of the Communal Land Rights Act,' in Ben Cousins and Aninka Claassens (eds.), *Land, Power and Custom: Controversies Generated by South Africa's Communal Land Rights Act*. UCT Press.
Clark, Michael. 2014. *An Anatomy of Dissent and Repression: The Criminal Justice System and the 2011 Thembelihle Protest*, Socio-Economic Rights Institute of South Africa, Working Paper No. 2.
Cornwall, Andrea. 2002. 'Locating Citizen Participation,' *IDS Bulletin* 33.2.
Cruikshank, Barbara. 1999. *The Will to Empower: Democratic Citizens and Other Subjects*. Cornell University Press.

Crush, Jonathan, ed. 2008. *The Perfect Storm: The Realities of Xenophobia in Contemporary South Africa*, Migration Policy Series, No. 50. South African Migration Project.

Dawson, Marcelle C. 2010. 'Phansi Privatisations! Phansi! The Anti-Privatisation Forum and Ideology in Social Movements,' in W. Beinart and M. Dawson (eds), *Popular Politics and Resistance Movements in South Africa*. Wits University Press.

Death, Carl. 2010. 'Troubles at the Top: South African Protests and the 2002 Johannesburg Summit,' *African Affairs*, 109.437.

Denvir, John. 1975-1976. 'Towards a Political Theory of Public Interest Litigation,' *North Carolina Law Review*, 54.

Desai, Ashwin. 2002. *'We Are the Poors': Community Struggles in Post-Apartheid South Africa.* Monthly Review Press.

de Visser, J. and D. Powell. 2012. 'Service Delivery Protest Barometer, 2007-2012,' Multi-Level Government Initiative, Community Law Centre. http://mlgi.org.za/barometers/service-delivery-protest-barometer/.

Dugard, Jackie. 2010. 'Civic Action and Legal Mobilisation: The Phiri Water Meters Case,' in Jeff Handmaker and Remko Berkhout (eds), *Mobilising Social Justice in South Africa: Perspectives from Researchers and Practitioners.* PULP.

Dugard, Jackie and Sandra Liebenberg. 2009. 'Muddying the Waters? The Supreme Court of Appeal's Judgement in the *Mazibuko* Case: Case Review,' *ESR Review: Economic and Social Rights in South Africa*, 10.2.

du Plessis, Jean and Stwart Wilson. 2005. *Any Room for the Poor? Forced Evictions in Johannesburg, South Africa.* Centre on Housing Rights and Evictions.

Durrheim, Kevin and Marc Foster. 1999. 'Technologies of Social Control: Crowd Management in a Liberal Democracy,' *Economy and Society*, 28.1.

Dwyer, Peter. 2010. *Understand Social Citizenship: Themes and Perspectives for Policy and Practice.* Policy Press.

Engels, Frederick. 1978. 'Socialism: Utopian and Scientific (1860),' in *The Marx-Engels Reader*, ed. R.C. Tucker. Norton.

Eveleth, Ann. 2003. 'Criminalising Dissent: Experiences of the Landless People's Movement and the National Land Committee during the WSSD,' in Simon Kimani Ndung'u, ed. *The Right to Dissent: Freedom of Expression, Assembly and Demonstration in South African.* Freedom of Expression Institute

Ewick, Patricia, and Susan S. Silbey. 1998. *The Common Place of Law: Stories from Everyday Life.* University of Chicago Press.

Forde, Fiona. 2011. *An Inconvenient Youth: Julius Malema and the 'New' ANC.* Picador Africa.

Foucault, Michel. 1977. *Discipline and Punish: The Birth of the Prison*, trans. Alan Sheridan. Allen Lane.

Foucault, Michel. 1998. 'Different Spaces,' in *Aesthetics: Essential Works of Foucault, 1954-1984. Volume 2.* Penguin.

Friedman, Steven. 2006. *Participatory Governance and Citizen Action in Post-apartheid South Africa.* International Labour Organisations Discussion Paper, International Institute for Labour Studies.

Friedman, Steven, and Shauna Mottiar. 2005. 'A Rewarding Engagement? The Treatment Action Campaign and the Politics of HIV/AIDS,' Politics & Society, 33.4.

Gastrow, Peter. 1995. Bargaining for Peace: South Africa and the National Peace Accord. USIP Press.

Geffen, Nathan. 2010. Debunking Delusions: The Inside Story of the Treatment Action Campaign. Jacana.

Gelb, Stephen. 2006. 'The RDP, GEAR, and All That: Reflections 10 Years Later,' Transformation 62.

Gevisser, Mark. 2007. Thabo Mbeki: The Dream Deferred. Jonathan Ball.

Gibson, Nigel. 2011. Fanonian Practices in South Africa: From Steve Biko to Abahlali baseMjondolo. Palgrave Macmillan.

Giddens, Anthony. 1984. The Constitution of Society: Outline of a Theory of Structuration. Polity Press.

Glaser, Clive. 2000. Bo-Tsotsi: The Young Gangs of Soweto. James Currey.

Glaser, Daryl, ed. 2010. Mbeki and After: Reflections on the Legacy of Thabo Mbeki. Wits University Press.

Gordin, Jeremy. 2010. Zuma: A Biography. Jonathan Ball.

Gqola, Pumla. 2001. 'Defining people: Analysing Power, Language and Representation in Metaphors of the New South Africa,' Transformation 47.

Habib, Adam. 2013. South Africa's Suspended Revolution. Wits University Press.

Hallward, Peter. 2009. 'Staging Equality: Rancière's Theatrocracy and the Limits of Anarchic Equality,' in Gabriel Rockhill and Philip Watts (eds), Jacques Rancière: History, Politics, Aesthetics. Duke University Press.

Hart, Gillian. 2013. Rethinking the South African Crisis: Nationalism, Populism, Hegemony. UKZN Press.

Harvey, Ebrahim. 2012. Kgalema Motlanthe: A Political Biography. Jacana.

Hassim, Shireen. 2004. 'Nationalism Displaced: Citizenship in the Transition,' in Amanda Gouws (ed.), (Un)Thinking Citizenship: Feminist Debates in South Africa. UCT Press.

Hassim, Shireen. 2009. 'Democracy's Shadows: Sexual Rights and Gender Politics in the Rape Trial of Jacob Zuma,' African Studies, 68.1.

Hassim, Shireen, Tawana Kupe, and Eric Worby. eds. 2008. Go Home or Die Here: Violence, Xenophobia and the Reinvention of Difference in South Africa. Wits University Press.

Hearn, Julie. 2000. 'Aiding democracy? Donors and Civil Society in South Africa,' Third World Quarterly, 21.5.

Heller, Patrick. 2001. 'Moving the State: The Politics of Democratic Decentralisation in Kerala, South Africa, and Porto Alegre,' Politics and Society, 29.1.

Heymann, Philip B. ed. 1991. Towards Peaceful Protest in South Africa: Testimony of Multinational Panel Regarding Lawful Control of Demonstrations in the Republic of South Africa. HSRC Press.

Heywood, Mark. 2009. 'South Africa's Treatment Action Campaign: Combining Law and Social Mobilization to Realize the Right to Health,' Journal of Human Rights Practice, 1.1.

Hoctor, Shannon. 2002. 'How far should the crime of intimidation extend?' *Obiter*.

Holston, James. 2008. *Insurgent Citizenship: Disjunctions of Democracy and Modernity in Brazil*. Princeton University Press.

Huchzermeyer, Marie. 2003. 'Housing Rights in South Africa: Invasions, Evictions, the Media, and the Courts in the Cases of Grootboom, Alexandra, and Bredell,' *Urban Forum*, 14.1.

Huchzermeyer, Marie. 2009. 'The Struggle for *in situ* Upgrading of Informal Settlements: A Reflection on Cases in Gauteng,' *Development Southern Africa*, 26.1.

Huchzermeyer, Marie. 2011. *Cities With 'Slums': From Informal Settlement Eradication to a Right to the City in Africa*. UCT Press.

Hunt, Lynn. 2007. *Inventing Human Rights: A History*. Norton.

Hunter, Mark. 2011. 'Beneath the 'Zunami': Jacob Zuma and the Gendered Politics of Social Reproduction in South Africa,' *Antipode*, 43.4.

Isin, Engin F. 2008. 'Theorising Acts of Citizenship,' in Engin F. Isin and Greg M. Nielsen (eds), *Acts of Citizenship*. Zed Books.

Isin, Engin F. 2009. 'Citizenship in Flux: The Figure of the Activist Citizen,' *Subjectivity* 29.

Johnson, R.W. 2009. *South Africa's Brave New World: The Beloved Country Since the End of Apartheid*. Penguin.

Laclau, Ernesto, and Chantal Mouffe. 2001. *Hegemony and Socialist Strategy: Towards a Radical Democratic Politics*. 2nd Edition. Verso.

Langford, Malcolm. 2014. 'Housing Rights Litigation: *Grootboom* and Beyond,' in Malcolm Langford, Ben Cousins, Jackie Dugard and Tshepo Madlingozi (eds), *Socio-Economic Rights in South Africa: Symbols or Substance?* Cambridge University Press.

Lavery, Jerry. 2012. 'Protest and Political Participation in South Africa: Time Trends and Characteristics of Protestors,' *Afrobarometer Briefing Paper*, No. 102.

Lefebvre, Henri. 2004. *Rhythmanalysis: Space, Time, and Everyday Life*. Continuum.

Lefebvre, Henri. 2014. *Critique of Everyday Life: The One Volume Edition*. Verso.

Liebenberg, Sandra. 1999. 'Social Citizenship: A Precondition for Meaningful Democracy,' *Agenda* 40.

Liebenberg, Sandra. 2010. *Socio-Economic Rights: Adjudication Under a Transformative Constitution*. Juta.

Lister, Ruth. 2003. *Citizenship: Feminist Perspectives*. NYU Press.

Lodge, Tom. 2002. *Politics in South Africa: From Mandela to Mbeki*. James Currey.

Macun, Ian. 2014. 'Workers Bypassing Unions: How to Respond?' submission the Marikana Commission of Inquiry, Phase 2: Panel on Bargaining Arrangements in Platinum (31 March), http://www.marikanacomm.org.za/docs/20140331-SeminarPhase02-platinum.pdf/

Madlingozi, Tshepo. 2012. 'How the Law Shapes and Structures Post-Apartheid Social Movements: Case Study of the Khulumani Support Group,' in Marcelle C. Dawson and Luke Sinwell (eds), *Contesting Transformation: Popular Resistance in Twenty-First-Century South Africa*. Pluto Press.

Madlingozi, Tshepo. 2013. 'Post Apartheid Social Movements and Legal Mobilisation,' in M. Langford, B. Cousins, J. Dugard, and T. Madlingozi, eds. Socio-Economic Rights in South Africa: Symbols or Substance? Cambridge University Press.

Malan, Rian. 2013. The Lion Sleeps Tonight: And Other Stories of Africa. Grove Press.

Mamdani, Mahmood. 1996. Citizen and Subject: Contemporary Africa and the Legacy of Late Colonialism. David Philip.

Mandela, Nelson. 1994. Long Walk to Freedom. Macdonald Purnell.

Manson, Andrew. 2011. 'Punching Above its Weight': The Mafikeng Anti-Repression Forum (Maref) and the Fall of Bophuthatswana,' African Historical Review, 43.2.

Marais, Hein. 2001. South Africa: Limits to Change: The Political Economy of Transition, 2nd ed. Zed Books.

Marcus, Gilbert and Steven Budlender. 2008. A Strategic Evaluation of Public Interest Litigation in South Africa. Atlantic Philanthropies Research Report.

Marshall, T.H. 1963. 'Citizenship and Social Class,' in Marshall, Sociology at the Crossroads and Other Essays. Heinemann.

Matlala, Boitumelo and Claire Benit-Gbaffou. 2012. 'Against ourselves - Local activists and the management of contradicting political loyalties: The case of Phiri, Johannesburg,' Geoforum 43.

Mattes, Robert. 2011. 'Forging Democrats: A Partial Success Story?' in Ian Shapiro and Kahreen Tebeau (eds), After Apartheid: Reinventing South Africa. University of Virginia Press.

May, Todd. 2008. The Political Thought of Jacques Rancière: Creating Equality. Edinburgh University Press.

Mbali, Mandisa. 2013. South African AIDS Activism and Global Health Politics. Palgrave Macmillan.

McCann, Michael W. 1994. Rights at Work: Pay Equity and the Politics of Legal Mobilization. University of Chicago Press.

McKinley, Dale T. 2013. 'State Security and Civil-Political Rights in South Africa,' Strategic Review for Southern Africa, 35.1.

McKinley, Dale T. and Ahmed Veriava. 2005. Arresting Dissent: State Repression and Post-apartheid Social Movements. Centre for the Study of Violence and Reconciliation.

McQuoid-Mason, David. 2000. 'The Delivery of Civil Legal Aid Services in South Africa,' Fordham International Law Journal 24.6.

Mdalose, Bandile. 2014. 'The Rise and Fall of Abahlali baseMjondolo, A South African Social Movement,' Politikon, 41.3.

Merry, Sally Engle. 1990. Getting Justice and Getting Even: Legal Consciousness among Working Class Americans. University of Chicago Press.

Memeza, Mzi. 2006. A Critical Review of the Implementation of the Regulation of Gatherings Act 205 of 1993. Freedom of Expression Institute.

Miraftab, Faranak. 2004. 'Invited and Invented Spaces of Participation: Neoliberal Citizenship and Feminists' Expanded Notion of Politics,' Wagadu 1.

Miraftab, Faranak. 2006. 'Feminist Praxis, Citizenship and Informal Politics: Reflections on South Africa's Anti-Eviction Campaign,' *International Feminist Journal of Politics*, 8.2.

Monson, Tamlyn Jane. 2010. 'Sub-National Sovereignties? Territory, Authority and Regulation in Three Sites of "Xenophobic Violence" in South Africa,' MA Thesis, University of the Witwatersrand.

Monson, Tamlyn and Jean-Pierre Misago. 2009. 'Why History Repeats Itself: The Security Risks of Structural Xenophobia,' *SA Crime Quarterly* 29.

Morson, Gary Saul and Caryl Emerson. 1989. 'Introduction: Rethinking Bakhtin,' in Morson and Emerson (eds), *Rethinking Bakhtin: Extensions and Challenges*. Northwestern University Press.

Morson, Gary Saul, and Caryl Emerson. 1990. *Mikhail Bakhtin: Creation of a Prosaics*. Stanford University Press.

Mouffe, Chantal. 2013. *Agonistics: Thinking the World Politically*. Verso.

Naidoo, Prishani, and Ahmed Veriava. 2009. 'From Local to Global (and Back Again?): Anti-commodification Struggles of the Soweto Electricity Crisis Committee,' in David A. McDonald (ed.), *Electric Capitalism: Recolonising Africa on the Power Grid*. HSRC Press.

Ndletyana, Mcebisi. 2007. 'Municipal Elections 2006: Protests, Independent Candidates and Cross-Border Municipalities,' in Sakhela Buhlungu, John Daniel, Roger Southall and Jessica Lutchman (eds), *State of the Nation: South Africa 2007*. HSRC Press.

Ndung'u, Simon Kimani, ed. 2003. *The Right to Dissent: Freedom of Expression, Assembly and Demonstration in South African*. Freedom of Expression Institute.

Neocosmos, Michael. 2006. *From 'Foreign Natives' to 'Native Foreigners': Explaining Xenophobia in in Post-apartheid South Africa - Citizenship and Nationalism, Identity and Politics*. Codesria Monograph Series.

Neocosmos, Michael. 2009. 'Civil Society, Citizenship and the Politics of the (Im) Possible: Rethinking Militancy in Africa Today,' *Interface*, 1.2.

Nijzink, Lia, and Jessica Piombo. 2005. 'Parliament and the Electoral System: How are South Africans Being Represented?' in *Electoral Politics in South Africa: Assessing the First Democratic Decade*. HSRC Press.

Nleya, Ndodana, Lisa Thompson, Chris Tapscott, Laurence Piper and Michele Esau. 2011. 'Reconsidering the Origins of Protest in South Africa: Some Lessons from Cape Town and Pietermaritzburg,' *Africanus* 50.1.

Nyers, Peter. 2008. 'No One is Illegal: Between City and Nation,' in Engin F. Isin and Greg M. Nielsen (eds), *Acts of Citizenship*. Zed Books.

Piper, Laurence, and Nonhlanhla Chanza. 2006. 'Too "Raw" to Represent: The Marginalisation of Youth in Msunduzi Ward Committees,' *Critical Dialogue - Participation in Review*, 2.2.

Piper, Laurence, and Roger Deacon. 2009. 'Too Dependant to Participate: Ward Committees and Local Democratisation in South Africa,' *Local Government Studies*, 35.4.

Pithouse, Richard. 2003. 'That the Tool Never Possess the Man: Taking Fanon's Humanism Seriously,' Politikon, 30.1.

Pithouse, Richard. 2008. 'A Politics of the Poor: Shack Dweller's Struggles in Durban,' Journal of Asian and African Studies, 43.1.

Pithouse, Richard. 2013. 'Conjunctural Notes on the Politics of the Local in South Africa,' Thesis 11, 115.1.

Pingo, Nicholette. 2013. 'Institutionalisation of a Social Movement: The Case of Thembelihle, the Thembelihle Crisis Committee, and the Operation Khanyisa Movement, and the Use of the Brick, the Ballot, and the Voice,' MSc Thesis, University of the Witwatersand.

Piven, Frances Fox. 2006. Challenging Authority: How Ordinary People Change America. Rowman & Littlefield.

Piven, Frances Fox and Richard A. Cloward. 1979. Poor Peoples' Movements: Why they Succeed, How they Fail. Pantheon Books.

Plasket, Clive, and Richard Spoor. 1991. 'The new offence of intimidation,' Industrial Law Journal 12.

Pocock, J.G.A. 1995. 'The Ideal of Citizenship since Classical Times,' in Ronald Beiner (ed.), Theorising Citizenship. SUNY Press.

Rancière, Jacques. 1991. The Ignorant Schoolmaster: Five Lessons in Intellectual Emancipation, trans. Kristin Ross. Stanford University Press.

Rancière, Jacques. 1995. On the Shores of Politics, trans. Liz Hero. Verso.

Rancière, Jacques. 1999. Disagreement: Politics and Philosophy, trans. Julie Rose. University of Minnesota Press.

Rancière, Jacques. 2006. Hatred of Democracy, trans. Steve Corcoran. Verso.

Jacques Rancière. 2006. The Politics of Aesthetics: The Distribution of the Sensible, trans. and ed. Gabriel Rockhill. Bloomsbury.

Rancière, Jacques. 2009. 'A few remarks on the method Jacques Rancière,' Parallax, 15.3.

Rancière, Jacques. 2010. 'The Aesthetic Heterotopia,' Philosophy Today, 54. Supplement.

Rancière, Jacques. 2012. Proletarian Nights: The Workers' Dream in Nineteenth Century France, trans. John Drury. Verso.

Rauch, Janine. 199. 'A Preliminary Assessment of the Impact of the Peace Accord Code of Conduct on Police Behaviour,' Paper presented at the Centre for Criminal Justice Conference, Policing in the New South Africa II, http://www.csv.org.za/index.php/component/content/article/1475-a-preliminary-assessment-of-the-impact-of-the-peace-accord-code-of-conduct-on-police-behaviour.html/

Reynolds, Andrew. 1999. Electoral Systems and Democratization in Southern Africa. Oxford University Press.

Robins, Steven. 2008. From Revolution to Rights in South Africa: Social Movements, NGOs and Popular Politics. James Currey.

Robins, Steven. 2008. 'Sexual Politics and the Zuma Rape Trial,' Journal of Southern African Studies, 34.2.

Robins, Steven. 2009. 'Humanitarian Aid Beyond "Bare Survival": Social Movement Response to Xenophobic Violence in South Africa,' *American Ethnologist*, 36.4.

Roithmayr, Daria. 2010. 'Lessons from *Mazibuko*: Persistent Inequality and the Commons,' in Stuart Woolman, Theunis Roux, and Danie Brand (eds), *Constitutional Court Review*. PULP.

Ross, Kristin. 2002. *May' 68 and Its Afterlives*. University of Chicago Press.

Roux, Theunis. 2013. *The Politics of Principle: The First South African Constitutional Court, 1995-2005*. Cambridge University Press.

Runciman, Carin. 2012. *Mobilisation and Insurgent Citizenship of the Anti-Privatisation Forum, South Africa: An Ethnographic Survey*. Phd Thesis, University of Glasgow.

Saul, John S. 2001. 'Cry for the Beloved Country: The Post-apartheid Denouement,' *Review of African Political Economy*, 28.89.

Scheingold, Stuart A. 1974. *The Politics of Rights: Lawyers, Public Policy, and Political Change*. Yale University Press.

Selmeczi, Anna. 2012. 'Abahlali's Vocal Politics of Proximity: Speaking, Suffering and Political Subjectivization,' *Journal of Asian and African Studies*, 47.5.

Shulz-Herzenberg, Colette. 2014. 'Voter Participation in the South African Elections of 2014,' Institute for Security Studies Policy Brief 61. http://www.issafrica.org/uploads/PolBrief61_Aug14.pdf

Sinwell, Luke. 2009. 'Participatory Spaces and the Alexandra Vukuzenzele Crisis Committee (AVCC): Reshaping Government Plans,' *Social Dynamics*, 35.2.

Sithole, Pearl, Alison Todes, and Amanda Williamson. 2007. 'Gender and Women's Participation in Municipality-Driven Development: IDP and Project-Level Participation in Msinga, eThekwini and Hibiscus Coast,' *Critical Dialogue - Participation in Review*, 3.1.

Skinner, Caroline. 2008. 'The Struggle for the Streets: Processes of Exclusion and Inclusion of Street Traders in Durban, South Africa,' *Development Southern Africa* 25.2.

Socio-Economic Rights Institute (SERI). 2014. *Makause: Resisting Relocation on the East Rand*, Community Practice Note, Informal Settlement Series no. 1.

Socio-Economic Rights Institute (SERI). 2014. *Rooigrond: Community Struggle in the North West*, Community Practice Notes, Informal Settlement Series no. 2.

Southall, Roger. 1994. 'The South African Elections of 1994: The Remaking of a Dominant-Party State,' *Journal of Modern African Studies* 32.4.

Southall, Roger. 2005. 'The "Dominant Party" Debate in South Africa,' *Africa Spectrum*, Vol. 40, No. 1.

Stewart, Linda. 2011. '14 Years in Limbo: Waiting for the Promised Land,' Report Prepared for Rooigrond, http://www.academia.edu/1095984/_14_years_in_limbo_waiting_for_the_Promised_Land_/

Stewart, Paul. 2013. '"Kings of the Mine": Rock Drill Operators and the 2012 Strike Wave on South African Mines,' *South African Review of Sociology*, 44.3.

Suttner, Raymond. 2009. 'The Jacob Zuma Rape Trial: Power and African National Congress (ANC) Masculinities,' *NORA - Nordic Journal of Feminist and Gender Research*, 17.3 (2009).

Tarrow, Sidney. 2011. *Power in Movement: Social Movements and Contentious Politics*. 3rd edition. Cambridge University Press.

Thompson, E.P. 1976. *Whigs and Hunters: The Origins of the Black Acts*. Pantheon.

Tselapedi, Thapelo, and Jackie Dugard. 2013. 'Reclaiming Power: A Case Study of Thembelihle Crisis Committee,' *Active Citizenship Matters: Perspectives from Civil Society on Local Governance in South Africa*. Good Governance Learning Network.

Tutu, Desmond. 1999. *No Future Without Forgiveness*. Random House.

Tilly, Charles. 2003. *The Politics of Collective Violence*. Cambridge University Press.

van As, Hennie. (2005) 'Legal Aid in South Africa: Making Justice Reality,' *Journal of African Law*, 49.1.

Vetten, Lisa, and Danielle Motelow. 2004. 'Creating State Accountability to Rape Survivors: A Case Study of Boksburg Regional Court,' *Agenda*, 18.62.

Vetten, Lisa, and Francois van Jaarsveld. 2008. 'The (Mis)Measure of Harm: An Analysis of Rape Sentences Handed Down in the Regional and High Courts of Gauteng Province,' Tshwaranang Legal Advocacy Centre Working Paper No 1.

von Holdt, Karl. 2010. 'Nationalism, Bureaucracy, and the Developmental State: the South African case,' *South African Review of Sociology*, 41.1.

von Holdt, Karl, et al. 2011. *The Smoke that Calls: Insurgent Citizenship, Collective Violence and the Struggle for a Place in the New South Africa - Eight Case Studies of Community Protest and Xenophobic Violence*. CSVR and SWOP.

Wafer, Alex. 2008. 'Scale and Identity in Post-apartheid Soweto,' *Transformation* 66/67.

Wallis, Malcolm. 2012. 'Some Thoughts on the Commercial Side of Practice,' *Advocate*, 25.1.

Walsh, Shannon, Patrick Bond, and Ashwin Desai. 2008. '"Uncomfortable Collaborations": Contesting Constructions of the "Poor" in South Africa,' *Review of African Political Economy*, 35, no. 116.

Ward, Colin. 2005. *Cotters and Squatters: Housing's Hidden History*. Five Leaves Press.

Williams, Michelle. 2008. *The Roots of Participatory Democracy: Democratic Communists in South Africa and Kerala, India*. Palgrave Macmillan.

Wilson, Stuart. 2009. 'Breaking the Tie: Evictions from Private Land, Homelessness and a New Normality,' *South African Law Journal* 126.

Wilson, Stuart. 2011. 'Litigating Housing Rights in Johannesburg's Inner City, 2004-2008,' *South African Journal on Human Rights*, 27.

Wilson, Stuart, and Jackie Dugard. 2014. 'Constitutional Jurisprudence: The First and Second Waves,' in Malcolm Langford, Ben Cousins, Jackie Dugard and Tshepo Madlingozi (eds), *Socio-Economic Rights in South Africa: Symbols or Substance?* Cambridge University Press.

Wright, Erik Olin. 2010. *Envisioning Real Utopias*. Verso.

Young, Iris Marion. 1989. 'Polity and Group Difference: A Critique of the Ideal of Universal Citizenship,' *Ethics* 99.2.

Žižek, Slavoj. 2006. 'The Lesson of Rancière,' in Jacques Rancière, *The Politics of Aesthetics: The Distribution of the Sensible*, trans. and ed. Gabriel Rockhill. Bloomsbury.

Index

Abahlali baseMjondolo 46, 70, 95, 96, 106, 119–24, 134, 145
Abahlali baseMjondolo v. Premier of the Province of KwaZulu-Natal 134
Abel, Richard 131
Achmat, Zackie 159
active citizens/citizenship 59, 60, 61, 65
activism 34, 44–5, 134, 135
activists, legal representation of 107–8
acts: of citizenship 60–1; political 61–2
African National Congress (ANC): and Abahlali baseMjondolo 122; adoption of GEAR 42; dominance of 160; emergence of 34; following the first post-apartheid election 37–8; and NUMSA 158; and political expression 17; and protests 35; and Rooigrond 114, 119; and Thembelihle 99
Afrobarometer 13–14, 15, 18

agency: and citizenship 57; complexity of 18; and disruptions 6–7; political 3, 36, 45, 57, 58, 59, 60, 69, 75; of the poor 45, 46; v. structure 40
AIDS 41, 44, 131–2 *see also* anti-retroviral medication; HIV
AIDS Law Project 109, 132
alienation 48, 69
Anti-Eviction Campaign (AEC), Cape Town 63, 64
anti-feminist politics 71
Anti-Privatisation Forum (APF): demise of 135; emergence of 44; and Free Basic Water (FBW) policy 132–3, 133–4, 136, 138–9; and OKM 117, 132–3; suspension of 119; and the TCC 89; and Thembelihle 88, 107; and World Summit on Sustainable Development 88; and xenophobia 70–1